University of Stirling Library, FK9 4LA
Tel: 01786 467220

POPULAR LOAN

This item is likely to be in heavy demand.
Please **RETURN** or **RENEW**
no later than the date on the receipt

LABOUR'S THINKERS

The Intellectual Roots of Labour

from Tawney to Gordon Brown

This book is dedicated to
Sonya, Matthew, Christopher and Sophie
with love.

And to the memory of Alec Beech
(1910 - 2005)

LABOUR'S THINKERS

The Intellectual Roots of Labour
from Tawney to Gordon Brown

MATT BEECH
and
KEVIN HICKSON

Tauris Academic Studies
LONDON • NEW YORK

Published in 2007 by Tauris Academic Studies, an imprint of I.B.Tauris & Co Ltd
6 Salem Road, London W2 4BU
175 Fifth Avenue, New York NY 10010
www.ibtauris.com

In the United States of America and in Canada distributed by
Palgrave Macmillan, a division of St Martins Press
175 Fifth Avenue, New York NY 10010

International Library of Political Studies 13

ISBN: 978 1 84511 208 0

A full CIP record for this book is available from the British Library
A full CIP record for this book is available from the Library of Congress

Library of Congress catalog card: available

Printed and bound in India by Replika Press Pvt. Ltd
camera-ready copy edited and supplied by the authors

3M SelfCheck™ System

Customer ID: 20044498

Title: Best for Britain? : The politics and legacy
Gordon Brown / Simon Lee.
ID: 3607742900
Due: 15-10-12

Title: A new labour nightmare : the return of the
awkward squad / Andrew Murray.
ID: 3560835800
Due: 15-10-12

Title: The contentious alliance : trade unions an
the Labour Party / Lewis Minkin.
ID: 3066186200
Due: 15-10-12

Title: Labour's thinkers : the intellectual roots of
Labour from Tawney to Gordon Brown / Matt
Beech and Ke
ID: 3605357000
Due: 15-10-12

Total items: 4
10/8/2012 2:52 PM

Thank you for using the Library
PLEASE RETAIN YOUR RECEIPT

CONTENTS

Acknowledgements   vii

1. Introduction   1

2. R.H. Tawney   18

3. G.D.H. Cole   38

4. Harold Laski   58

5. Evan Durbin   77

6. John Strachey   100

7. R.H.S. Crossman   121

8. C.A.R. Crosland   144

9. Stuart Holland   172

10. David Owen   195

11. Roy Hattersley   219

12. Anthony Giddens   244

13. Gordon Brown   265

14. Conclusion   284

Bibliography   294

Index   312

ACKNOWLEDGEMENTS

In researching and writing this book we have been indebted to several people. We would like to thank Anthony Giddens and Roy Hattersley for agreeing to be interviewed. Bernard Crick and Stuart Holland also provided useful information.

We are also grateful to a number of people who have read parts of the manuscript, notably Noel Thompson and David Howell and others whose advice improved the book in its initial stages, notably Dilys Hill and Raymond Plant.

A further word of thanks is due to the archivists at the British Library of Political Science, the Labour Party archive at Manchester, the University of Liverpool, the University of Hull and the Modern Records Centre at the University of Warwick for their assistance in using the collected papers on a number of our subjects.

A special mention of thanks goes to Claire Beech for proof-reading and editing the manuscript. Finally, as always we express our love and appreciation to our families.

1

INTRODUCTION

The aim of this book is to offer a fresh examination of the political thought of the Labour Party. In general there has been relatively little academic attention directed to these issues and what there has been has tended adopt a chronological framework.[1] There are several strengths to a chronological approach. It is argued here that the understanding of ideas will be limited if not placed in a wider historical context. However, the approach offered in this book is different since it allows for a more detailed analysis of the individuals who through their engagement in the theoretical examination of political and economic ideas and their association, in different ways, with the Labour Party have done most to develop social democratic ideas in Britain.

The book also differs in its approach from conventional biography since many, though not all, of the individuals discussed in this book have been the subjects of general or specifically intellectual biographies. The book does not seek to retrace these accounts, indeed it could not given that a total of twelve individuals are the subject of primary discussion in this study. Instead, the book seeks to analyse the key aspects of the contributions to social democracy made by these individuals. In so doing, the book allows for a closer examination of specific debates relating to issues of political thought and political economy in the Labour Party than a straight-forward chronological perspective could do.

The authors therefore feel that the book allows for original discussions of key individuals and also through them the broader development of social democracy in Britain since the 1920s. The twelve individuals who the authors feel have made the most significant contribution to British social democracy and therefore discussed in the book are: R.H. Tawney, G.D.H. Cole, Harold Laski, Evan Durbin, John Strachey, R.H.S. Crossman, C.A.R. Crosland, Stuart Holland, David Owen, Roy Hattersley, Anthony Giddens and Gordon Brown. In adopting this approach, it is necessary to explain a number of issues relating to the nature of social democracy and the underlying methodological approach in this study.

The Nature of Social Democracy

Social democracy has often been held to be one of two distinct approaches to socialism, the other being Marxism. This can be traced back to the debate between the followers of Marx and those who sought to reject, or at least radically revise, Marxist theory such as Eduard Bernstein[2]. Marxists regarded power as being derived from the pattern of economic ownership so that democracy provided only a 'superstructure'; the result of this being that there could be little chance of democratic advance towards socialism. In contrast, social democrats regarded electoral and parliamentary processes as a viable mechanism for the advance of socialism. This has led some commentators to argue that social democracy, at least as it has been understood by the Labour Party, constitutes an attempt to manage capitalism in a fairer and more efficient way.[3]

Such an approach to the study of the political thought of the Labour Party is inadequate however since it has been the subject of intense debate in the Labour Party at various stages in its history as to both what is meant by the terms 'capitalism' and 'fairness'. It is therefore necessary to understand the nature of British social democracy in terms of values. The most notable values of British social democracy are liberty, equality and community. However, it is far from clear what these concepts mean. Three issues relate to any particular understanding of these concepts, namely the contestable nature of such concepts, their relationship to one another in terms of relative importance and also the relationship of values to policies, often referred to as the relationship between 'ends' and 'means'. The main aim here is to provide a brief discussion of each and relate them to the substantive issues addressed in this book.

The first problem therefore is the issue of contestability. Each of the essential values of social democracy is open to different meanings. Indeed such meanings are not necessarily true or false since they can all be held to be accurate conceptions of those values: that is to say there is no agreed, single definition of these concepts. This can be best clarified by using a distinction made by John Rawls when he distinguished between concept and conception.[4] A concept such as equality, liberty or community lacks meaning in itself and can only be given meaning once a particular conception of it is formed. This can, in fact, be seen to be the source of considerable debate in British social democracy. Equality can be held to mean a commitment to equality of opportunity, equalisation of outcomes (income and/or wealth) or the pursuit of 'fairer' outcomes. Community may best be conceptualised as a geographic entity, or to collective values or to decentralisation of power. Liberty can be held to be either 'positive' – implying freedom to act and the provision of resources required to act – or negatively as freedom from external constraint. Often debates in the Labour Party reflect such conceptual concerns. For instance, a central issue of contention, traced in this book, is between the conception of equality advocated by Tawney and Crosland and subsequently defended by Hattersley, as fairness of outcome and the Third Way conception of equality of opportunity. Hence, the concepts under debate are frequently the same, but differing conceptions – and therefore values – are maintained. Community is interpreted primarily in terms of the decentralisation of power by Cole and Owen, whereas others such as Tawney have used that particular concept to mean the fostering of shared values.

A second issue relates to how these values should be prioritised, or 'ranked', against one another. This issue was raised in an article written some time ago by the political theorist Anthony Arblaster[5], who argued that the values held to be important in political ideologies are often the same – liberty, equality and community are held in different ways by liberals (both classical[6] and social), socialists and conservatives – but the relative emphasis attached to those values differs. This can also be said to be the same within a particular ideology, in this case social democracy, at different times and between specific individuals. Hence, reading the work of the twelve thinkers studied in this book shows that the ordering of values differs between one social democratic theorist and another. For example, although it is not always clear that Tawney and contemporary social democratic thinkers such as Giddens or Brown hold to a similar conception of community, they both placed emphasis on that particular value whereas Crosland and Hattersley for example did not have such an emphasis in their writing.

One further issue that relates to an understanding of social democracy is the complex relationship between ends and means.[7] This has been taken by some as a straight-forward relationship between values and the policies designed to realise those values. In fact, the ends-means relationship is more complex. There have been at least two occasions when the relationship between ends and means has been the subject of controversy in the period under examination in this book. The first was the attempt by the revisionists in the 1950s to argue that public ownership, previously regarded by many in the Party as essential for the advance of socialism, should no longer be a core socialist commitment. It was a means, not an end, for socialism and in some accounts not an important one at that. This was greeted with derision by the Labour left, who appeared to argue that public ownership was a core socialist commitment. The debate is evaluated in this book through an examination of the arguments made by Crosland, Strachey and Crossman in the 1950s and addressed later by Holland. On closer examination, there are few arguments presented as to why nationalisation should be viewed as a socialist 'end' and instead was viewed by those who were on the Labour left – or who shared the arguments of the Labour left – as an 'essential means' of socialism, a policy position without which socialism could not be realised. The reasons why public ownership should be regarded as an essential means are analysed in this book. The second issue where the complexity of the ends-means relationship is demonstrated is in relation to New Labour, and specifically the Third Way, where values are held to be constant but policies have been said to have been subject to radical revision. This claim is investigated in relation to the contributions of Roy Hattersley and Anthony Giddens where the role of income tax is again seen as an essential means for the pursuit of the socialist value of equality according to Hattersley but not by Giddens

The final issue concerning the nature of social democracy is in relation to the role of ideas in the Labour Party. There are in fact two issues here. First, is the use of the term social democracy itself. In broad terms, the authors believe that the terms social democracy and democratic socialism can be used interchangeably, indeed, many of the individuals featured in the book used these terms interchangeably in their own writings. There was however a period of time when these terms were used to distinguish political positions in the Labour Party. This distinction was used in the 1970s where some who had previously associated with the right of the Labour Party such as Crosland – now described themselves as democratic socialists so as to distinguish themselves in the Party from a more clearly defined social democratic group, many of whom went on to form the Social Democratic Party. This distinction is most clear after the formation of the SDP so that the distinction between David Owen's 'social democratic' position and Roy Hattersley's 'democratic socialist' position held particular resonance. In this sense one of the aims of the chapters on Owen and Hattersley is to ask who has had the most significant impact on the thinking of New Labour. Secondly, the role of ideas in a political party, and the academic analysis of those ideas, raises particular methodological issues, which are the focus of the following section.

Methodological Issues

In broad terms, the methodological approach favoured in this book is best described as hermeneutic.[8] Hermeneutics concerns the uncovering of meaning, in this case of the meaning of the political thought of the twelve individuals analysed in this book. Such an approach requires us to do three things. The first is to unpack the philosophical meanings that can be attached to various concepts, as described in the last section. The second concerns the placing of these thinkers and debates within the broader historical context. For this reason, the chapters proceed in broadly chronological sequence starting, for reasons that will be explained shortly, with Tawney. These individuals did not however write and think in isolation. They considered the broader political developments of their age and debated with their contemporaries, hence the chapters should be read collectively and often the key influences on each individual are considered.

An interesting feature of the development of the political thought of the Labour Party is that much of process of reflection occurred out of office. For this reason, there was particular debate following the limited success of the two inter-war, minority Labour Governments (1924 and 1929-31) so that the ideas of Tawney, Cole, Laski, Durbin and Strachey can be viewed together. Strachey also provided one of the leading intellectual inputs in Opposition between 1951-64, alongside Crossman and Crosland. Stuart Holland provided further reflection following the 1970 General Election defeat and again after 1979, and so can be compared with his contemporaries including Owen and Hattersley. The political thought of Giddens and Brown is interesting since it has been developed in Government since 1997, although Brown's approach was shaped by his experience in Opposition following his election to Parliament in 1983. For purposes of academic analysis this raises an epistemological problem since this development of ideas was not just one of ideological contemplation, but was also an attempt to develop the political strategy of the Labour Party; that is to say to win elections. Ideas do not exist independently of political strategy and should not be analysed as such. However, this should not be taken to mean that ideas do not matter and the importance of a hermeneutic framework is that the individuals regarded themselves as developing the political thought of the Labour Party and not just as devising arguments capable of gaining votes.

The adoption of a hermeneutic understanding requires the use of particular sources. These can be divided in to three broad categories. Firstly, the use of published work, largely in the form of books which can be taken to be the most developed articulation of an individual's political thought, but also in terms of articles in periodicals such as *Encounter* or *Tribune* and newspapers and also in the form of pamphlets, notably in the case of the Labour Party published by the Fabian Society. The second broad range of sources, where available is the private collection of papers, which allows for an examination of the private views of the subject. In some cases, such private sources have later been published. Finally, where possible the authors have sought to interview key individuals.

One further methodological issue concerns the selection of individuals. Here the role of the authors is rather like that of the cricket fan, picking his or her all-time greatest team, albeit in this case there are twelve 'players'. The selection of the twelve subjects of this book has been based on objective criteria, as those who have deliberately sought to develop the political and economic thought of the Labour Party in a particular direction, although this selection has inevitably involved subjective assessments of *originality* and *impact*. Some of the individuals, Tawney and Crosland most notably, do not need to be justified and the same case could be made for others including Cole, Laski, Durbin, Strachey and Holland since they either made a substantial contribution to the thinking of the Party itself or influenced those who did. Owen and Hattersley are held to have offered two clear alternative responses to the New Right from the late-1970s and therefore can be used to analyse the evolution of contemporary social democracy. Finally, Giddens and Brown are held as providing the most significant contributions to such a contemporary social democratic perspective and additionally can be used to investigate current debates and likely future developments of social democracy, which is one of the purposes of the conclusion. Perhaps the most controversial inclusion therefore is that of Crossman, although this can be justified in two ways. First, Crossman regarded himself as an intellectual and had been a philosophy lecturer and also in the absence of other intellectual figures on the Labour left in the 1950s can be held to be the leading exponent of this position. Secondly, Crossman is usually held to be a 'failed thinker' and this claim can be analysed.

The choice of these twelve individuals can be further justified by examining the reasons as to why others have been *excluded*. Firstly, some were excluded because they were deemed to fall outside of the chronological focus of this book. The political thought of the Labour Party emerged gradually. There were four elements involved in the formation of the Labour Representation Committee from 1900 (the Labour Party from 1906) – the trade unions, the Marxist, Social Democratic Federation, the Fabian Society and the trade unions. The SDF had almost no influence and left shortly after the formation of the Party, which was essentially a compromise between the industrial concerns of the trade unions and the more intellectual concerns of the Fabians. This compromise could still be detected in 1918 Constitution and the limits to Labour's socialism by the Government's orthodox response to the economic crisis of 1929-31. Therefore, the intellectual deliberations of Tawney, Cole and others from the 1920s (slightly earlier in Cole's case) and during the 1930s can be seen as far more sophisticated than previous attempts to provide the Labour Party with a doctrine. For this reason, certain individuals were excluded from the book, notably the Webbs, Ramsay MacDonald[9] and Philip Snowden.

A second justification for excluding certain individuals is that they should be regarded as popularising the ideas of others, writing short books on, or making essentially journalistic contributions to, the thought of the Labour Party. Such individuals include Stafford Cripps, Aneurin Bevan – although the importance of his *In Place of Fear*[10] should not be underestimated – Michael Foot, Ian Mikardo and Tony Benn.[11]

Others provided a more substantial contribution, but this largely consisted of a contribution specific to a policy area or single political issue. This could be said to be the case with Hugh Dalton, who was highly influential in attracting a number of younger, intellectual figures in to the Labour Party[12], but whose own intellectual contribution largely related to matters of fiscal policy.[13] Herbert Morrison made a substantial contribution to the development of the Party's approach to public ownership but his limited attention to doctrine was well expressed in his frequently quoted belief that "socialism is what the Labour Party does."[14] Moreover, Denis Healey made a significant contribution to Revisionism in the 1950s, but this largely related to foreign and defence policies.[15] Others such as TH Marshall[16], Richard Titmuss[17] and Michael Young[18] contributed to welfare policy issues. Ken Coates provided distinctive ideas relating to industrial democracy and Michael Barratt Brown made sustained arguments for the continuing relevance of public ownership.[19] A group of intellectuals associated with the *New Left Review* operated either outside of the Party or on the fringes of it but provided a critique of parliamentary activity as a way of introducing socialism and therefore of much of the Labour Party's *raison d'être*.[20] The contribution of others was limited in various ways, although this should not diminish their wider achievements – such figures would include John Mackintosh[21], who may well have made a substantial contribution (in either the SDP or on the Labour right) in the 1980s. Similarly, David Marquand provided a major contribution to the political thought of the SDP, but his most important contribution was made during his time outside of the Labour Party; while his association with Blair once he returned to the Labour Party prior to the 1997 General Election was brief.[22] Finally, the response of left-wing academics to the New Right was of vital importance. However whereas Raymond Plant is the subject of discussion in relation to Roy Hattersley and can be seen to have influenced others on the Labour right at that time, Bernard Crick's contribution tends to be limited to a long-term association with David Blunkett, who is not considered here to have provided a major contribution to social democratic thought.[23]

Despite all of these criteria, further justification is required for the exclusion of chapters focusing on Douglas Jay and Roy Jenkins. Both made a sustained contribution to Labour's political thought, but are not included for several specific reasons. In the case of Douglas Jay, his first significant work *The Socialist Case*[24] was influential in the Party's discussion on issues of political economy in the 1930s and as will be discussed influenced Strachey in particular. However, it did not provide as significant a contribution as Durbin's *The Politics of Democratic Socialism*[25] to social democratic theory, instead focusing largely on the issue of redistribution. His second book, *Socialism in the New Society*[26] did contain a more theoretical discussion but this was written in the early 1960s and so lacked the originality of Crosland's *The Future of Socialism*[27] as a contribution to Revisionism. In a similar way, Jenkins made a sustained contribution from the early 1950s onwards, but his earlier work was arguably less significant than other contributions to social democratic literature in the 1950s[28], and in particular compared to that of Crosland and Strachey. In terms of his later contribution to British social democracy one could argue that his work lacked the originality of that of Owen.[29] Indeed, Jenkins can be said to have made a more important contribution as a historian than as a social democratic theorist.

Structure of the Book

In addition to this introduction and the conclusion, the book is divided into twelve substantive chapters, each focusing on an individual thinker.

R.H. Tawney is widely regarded as making the most substantial contribution to the ethical basis of British socialism. This contribution came from Tawney's philosophy of Christian socialism which is present in his major books *The Acquisitive Society* and *Equality*.[30] The chapter evaluates the theological underpinnings of his Christianity and then asks why his faith led him to democratic socialism.

G.D.H. Cole was concerned primarily with the nature of libertarian socialism and workers' control of industry which he addressed through his Guild socialist ideas and publications. The chapter explains Cole's Guild socialism and charts its demise. An evaluation of the revision of Cole's thought from Guild socialism to parliamentary socialism on the Labour left is provided. The chapter concludes by assessing Cole's principles of workers' control and anti-statism in the thought of the New Left and David Owen.

Harold Laski it has been said was the pre-eminent socialist, public intellectual of his generation. The chapter evaluates this claim and charts his radical, ideological credentials from Fabian socialist to Labour left activist to Marxist socialist during the 1930s. Additionally, Laski's radical and libertarian socialism is compared to that of Cole.

Evan Durbin, so it is argued in this book, is a complex figure who is not capable of being pigeonholed in the usual left-right spectrum. He was critical of the increased influence of Marxist ideas on the Labour left and also of the 'underconsumptionist' ideas of J.A. Hobson[31] in the Independent Labour Party, but advocated a greater role for the state in economic planning. A particular focus for this chapter is on his wartime patriotism, an attitude more often associated with the right in British politics.

John Strachey offers an interesting example of an individual who substantially revised his thinking. In the late-1930s he gradually moved away from his earlier Marxism, which he advocated after a close association with Oswald Mosley. The chapter goes on to examine the nature of his post-war thought. As with many on the Party's right-wing he accepted that the reforms of the Attlee Government had led to major social and economic change but at the same time continued, as did many on the Labour left, to advocate further public ownership. The chapter asks first if Strachey succeeded in defining a position distinct from both the revisionists and from the Labour left and secondly if this position was a valid one.

Of all the thinkers discussed in this book the most widely criticised is Richard Crossman. Seen by many as a dilettante, Crossman has also received little by way of academic attention. This chapter seeks to redress this, to some extent, by asking what did Crossman mean by socialism, was there a distinct principle or political approach to which Crossman held in his writing on socialism and activity in the Labour Party and whether anything more positive than the usual accounts can be said in his defence.

A useful comparison can therefore be made between Strachey, Crossman and the most prominent of the post-war revisionists, Tony Crosland. The chapter will outline his perception of social and economic change and his position on both ends and means in socialist thought. In the course of this discussion it will be asserted that a good deal of scholarship misrepresents Crosland's socialism, which some see as calling for the acceptance of the post-war settlement. Instead, it is argued that he held to a radical notion of equality and also had more to say on public ownership than is sometimes suggested.

The first major intellectual response to the dominant revisionist paradigm from the Labour left was made by Stuart Holland in his book *The Socialist Challenge*[32] published in 1975 and other works. The chapter seeks to analyse Holland's thought looking in particular at the extent to which it offered a coherent and consistent critique of Revisionism and the degree to which it influenced the shift to the left in the late 1970s and early 1980s.

David Owen is included as a thinker due primarily to his contribution to British social democracy in the early 1980s. The chapter discusses his approach to social democracy around the time of the formation of the SDP and goes on to ask if his thought marked an acceptance of the New Right paradigm and/or the extent to which he was a proto-New Labour thinker.

Roy Hattersley is interpreted as the leading Labour right thinker of the 1980s. Hattersley's contribution is best seen as an attempt to update Crosland's ideas in the face of the challenge of the New Right, specifically by trying to defend a democratic socialist conception of freedom. The chapter will ask if this response to the New Right was valid and the extent to which his ideas have remained consistent particularly given his subsequent critical attitude to New Labour.

Anthony Giddens has had substantial influence both internationally and nationally as the pioneer of the 'Third Way' notably, in the context of the Labour Party, on Tony Blair. This chapter will initially outline what the Third Way is and then go on to explore in greater depth the Third Way conception of equality. It will be argued that the Third Way offers a revision of ends as well as means, despite claims that it holds to traditional social democratic conceptions of equality (and other values), but questions the extent to which this new conception of equality is valid.

Finally, a discussion of Gordon Brown's approach to social democracy brings us up to date. It is argued that more than anybody else in the current Government, Brown has provided the ideational foundations of contemporary social democracy not just in terms of economic policy but also for welfare reform. The chapter seeks to discover the nature of Brown's conception of equality in light of New Labour alleged ambiguity on the subject.

By way of conclusion, the authors evaluate the configuration of contemporary social democracy[33] by asking what are the likely future developments within both social democracy itself and the academic study of social democracy over the next few years.

[1] See G. Foote, *The Labour Party's Political Thought: A History* (Macmillan, Basingstoke, 1997) and N. Thompson, *The Political Economy of the Labour Party* (UCL, London, 1996)

[2] E. Bernstein, *Preconditions of Socialism*, edited by H. Tudor (Cambridge University Press, Cambridge, 1993)

[3] This view is not just held by left-wing critics of the Labour Party but is also used by Steven Fielding in an attempt to show that there is actually nothing new about 'New' Labour. S. Fielding, *The Labour Party: Continuity and Change in the Making of 'New' Labour* (Palgrave, Basingstoke, 2003)

[4] J. Rawls, *A Theory of Justice* (Oxford University Press, Oxford, 1999, 1st edition 1971)

[5] A. Arblaster, 'Liberal Values and Socialist Values' in R. Miliband and J. Saville (eds.) *Socialist Register* (Merlin, London, 1972)

[6] Although the classical liberals have only a limited use for the concept of community

[7] The best recent account of the complexity of the ends-means relationship is offered by Raymond Plant. See his 'Blair and Ideology' in A. Seldon (ed.) *The Blair Effect* (Little, Brown, London, 2001) and 'Ends, Means and Political Identity' in R. Plant, M. Beech and K. Hickson (eds.) *The Struggle for Labour's Soul: Understanding Labour's Political Thought* (Routledge, London, 2004)

[8] For a discussion of hermeneutics and its application to political analysis see A. MacIntyre, 'A Mistake About Causality in Social Science' in P. Laslett and W. G. Runciman (eds.) *Philosophy, Politics and Society* (Blackwell, Oxford, 1972)

[9] Although it may be argued that MacDonald had provided his own distinctive contribution to socialist thought from the early 1900s onwards there was apparently little evidence that this offered sufficient intellectual armoury to provide a socialist response to the economic crisis from 1929. See, Foote, *The Labour Party's Political Thought*, pp.57-64 and B. Barker (ed.) *Ramsay MacDonald's Political Writings* (Allen Lane, London, 1972)

[10] A. Bevan, *In Place of Fear* (Heinemann, London, 1952)

[11] The clearest exposition of Benn's political views are his books, *Arguments for Socialism* (Penguin, London, 1980) and *Arguments for Democracy* (Cape, London, 1981)

[12] Including Hugh Gaitskell, Douglas Jay and Evan Durbin, although in reality these individuals influenced one another in developing a Keynesian, or at least a corporate socialist approach to economic policy in the mid to late 1930s.

[13] See especially H. Dalton, *Practical Socialism for Britain* (Routledge, London, 1935)

[14] For a brief discussion of Morrisonian corporate socialism see Foote, *The Labour Party's Political Thought*, pp.174-176

[15] Notably, D. Healey, 'Power Politics and the Labour Party' in R.H.S. Crossman (ed.) *New Fabian Essays* (Turnstile, London, 1952) and *Neutralism* (Ampersand, London, 1955)

[16] T. H. Marshall, *Citizenship and Social Class* (Cambridge University Press, Cambridge, 1950)

[17] For a selection of Titmuss's main works see B. Abel-Smith and K. Titmuss (eds.), *The Philosophy of Welfare: Selected Writings of Richard Titmuss* (Allen and Unwin, London, 1987)

[18] M. Young, *The Rise of the Meritocracy* (Thames and Hudson, London, 1958)

[19] See for example, K. Coates and T. Topham, *The New Unionism: The Case for Workers' Control* (Owen, London, 1972) and Michael Barratt Brown, *From Labourism to Socialism: The Political Economy of Labour in the 1970s* (Spokesman, Nottingham, 1972)

[20] The most important contribution here was R. Miliband, *Parliamentary Socialism* (Allen and Unwin, London, 1961)

[21] See D. Marquand (ed.) *John P. Mackintosh on Parliament and Social Democracy* (Longmans, London, 1982)

[22] D. Marquand, *The Unprincipled Society* (Cape, London, 1988) and *The Progressive Dilemma: Lloyd-George to Blair* (Phoenix, London, 1997, 2nd edition)

[23] For Crick see his pamphlet *Socialist Values and Time* (Fabian Society, London, 1984). Blunkett's most important contribution is, *Politics and Progress* (Politicos, London, 2001)

[24] D. Jay, *The Socialist Case* (Faber and Faber, London, 1937)

[25] E. Durbin, *The Politics of Democratic Socialism* (Routledge, London, 1940)

[26] D. Jay, *Socialism in the New Society* (Longmans, London, 1962)

[27] C.A.R. Crosland, *The Future of Socialism* (Cape, London, 1956)

[28] Notably R. Jenkins, *The Pursuit of Progress* (Heinemann, London, 1953)

[29] See R. Jenkins, *What Matters Now* (Fontana, London, 1972) and *Partnership of Principle* (Secker and Warburg, London, 1985)

[30] R.H. Tawney, *The Acquisitive Society* (Bell, London, 1921) and *Equality* (Allen and Unwin, London, 1931)

[31] See Foote, *The Labour Party's Political Thought*, pp.125-135 for a useful summary of Hobson's economic thought

[32] S. Holland, *The Socialist Challenge* (Quartet, London, 1975)

[33] For a more detailed examination of these issues see M. Beech, *The Political Philosophy of New Labour* (IB Tauris, London, 2006)

2

R.H. TAWNEY

'The essence of all morality is this: to believe that
every human being is of infinite importance, and
therefore that no consideration of expediency can
justify the oppression of one by another. But to
believe this it is necessary to believe in God.'[1]

It is our contention that no volume on the Labour Party's
most influential thinkers could omit Richard Henry Tawney.
Tawney merits inclusion in this volume because he is still
regarded more than forty years after his death as one of the
most influential socialist writers and philosophers in the
Labour Party's history. The purpose of this chapter is
threefold. Firstly, it attempts to explain Tawney's
widespread appeal in diverse corners of the Labour Party.
Secondly, it aims to understand Tawney's moral philosophy
– namely his Christian beliefs. Third and finally, the chapter
hopes to locate the religious motivations for Tawney's
socialism. Thus, this chapter seeks not to repeat arguments
that have been well made in previous scholarship on
Tawney. The existing scholarship[2] provides answers to most
of the pertinent questions, bar perhaps one. Namely, what
role did Tawney's Christian faith play in his choice of
political creeds? In other words, if his metaphysical
commitment was to his God in the form of Jesus Christ –
why was his temporal commitment to democratic socialism?
Due to the limits of an essay and the complex nature of the
question only the beginnings of an answer can be fathomed.

The Ubiquitous Mr Tawney

Tawney is arguably Labour's most influential thinker. Problems arise instantaneously whenever such statements about an individual are made but in Tawney's case the argument defending such a claim is made somewhat easier by the diverse array of socialists who cite him as their main intellectual or political icon. Ross Terrill describes those socialist sects and tendencies that have acknowledged Tawney and in so doing provide his work with almost universal appeal:

'... the one twentieth-century British socialist thinker who can be saluted from every quarter; Bevanite left, Gaitskellite right, guild socialist, Marxist, Fabian, Christian socialist – the philosopher who has most nearly provided an overall framework for socialism in British conditions and according to the British temper.' [3]

The Old Left, the Old Right, the 'Centre', the New Left and New Labour (which we understand to be the new right-wing of the Labour Party) [4] have all doffed their caps to Tawney the socialist and to specific elements in his work more generally. For example, *The Acquisitive Society* was very important and influential on the Labour left in the 1920s in general, as it suggested a robust critique of laissez-faire capitalism and its underlying ethic of acquisitiveness that Tawney argued had become a pseudo-religion amongst many. [5] Also it was a boon for the non-Marxist Labour left as in one sense it provided them with a definitive statement of all that was wrong with capitalist society without the requirement of endorsing Communism. On the other hand, if any period of Tawney's career can be interpreted as being close to some of the solutions to capitalist society provided by Labour Marxists, then it is the 1920s. *The Acquisitive Society* is as Marxist as Tawney got. He does talk of state transformation and he waxes lyrical about public ownership and planning.[6] Though he stops short of being a Labour Marxist due to his belief that private property *per se* was not immoral, nor was it un-socialist. Simply, for Tawney, the function of property is the measure of its moral worth. If it is functionless and the class of citizens who own such property lives idly from the pecuniary benefits that rent supplies then this is wrong and must be addressed by the state.[7] His centrist or 'labourist' appeal lay in his work with the Workers' Educational Association from 1912-1914 in Lancashire and the Potteries. But Tawney the man was a friend of the working class rather than just its teacher. He refused a commission in the British Army and served as a private during the First World War and was severely wounded on the first day of the Battle of the Somme. Equal to this was his life of simplicity and his distinct lack of ostentation. The Old Right has staked the most fervent claim to Tawney. This must be because they see him as embodying their core view that socialism is a political philosophy centrally concerned with the value of equality, through arguments set out in his book *Equality* (1931). Hugh Gaitskell made the following statement at Tawney's memorial service at St. Martin-in-the-Fields on Thursday 8th February 1962:

'I always think of him as the Democratic Socialist *par excellence* – an idealist who was rationalist, a believer in liberty and equality – a man who loved his faith.'[8]

In one sense the Old Right see Tawney as the figure who taught - the Labour Party from the 1930s - that the chief 'end' of socialism was to create a more equal and fair society in the way Anthony Crosland in the 1950s and 1960s argued for certain means (redistributive politics and comprehensive education) over others (public ownership and widespread economic planning) as the correct tools to use when building the 'New Jerusalem'. The Old Right place Tawney near the beginning of the canon of social democratic thinkers, perhaps only just behind Eduard Bernstein, that includes Douglas Jay, Evan Durbin (wrongly)[9], Anthony Crosland and Roy Hattersley to cite but some of them. New Left figures like Tony Benn see Tawney as having advocated their cause in an earlier time against the common enemy – capitalism. In his Foreword to the 1981 edition of *The Attack and Other Papers* Tony Benn states:

'For some years Tawney has been quoted extensively by the right-wing of the Labour Party who have seemed to appropriate him as the Father of their own school of thought. The Social Democrats, whether they have left the Party to fight socialism from the outside, or whether they have stayed to fight socialism from within the Party, have both laid claim to be Tawney's true disciples and then to use his name to represent the socialist majority in the Party as being a new breed of socialists who are outside the democratic tradition.'[10]

In the contemporary era New Labour has re-emphasised social responsibilities and the principle of community as fellowship that Tawney sought to instil in all socialists through his writings. Moreover, New Labour it has been noticed admire Tawney's communitarian approach to social thought.[11] It is for these reasons plus Tawney's ecumenical persona that all of the notable groupings in the Labour Party appear to have laid claim to him and have at least rated his contribution to British socialist thought. Interestingly, few have openly endorsed Tawney's full moral and political doctrine of Christian socialism. Perhaps, the former Labour leader John Smith came closest in that he sought to marry his Christian faith to democratic socialism through the twin ideas of social justice and community as fellowship.[12] Tawney's doctrine of Christian socialism has suffered partly as Britain has become in one crude sense a less Christian society with the rise of secularism; the reduction in church membership; and with the proliferation of other religions forcing Christianity to compete in the spiritual marketplace. The Labour Party is careful to try and represent all faiths and those with no faith and in doing so represents none. In spite of this, socialists of all shades of opinion have believed that Tawney was one of their own because they accept the general ethical basis of his thought without agreeing with his religion. Perhaps he is best explained as being the Labour Party's moral philosopher.

Tawney's Moral Philosophy

To understand Tawney's moral philosophy there are three notable sources one must consult. Two of them are the well-established biographical studies of Tawney namely Ross Terrill's 1973 book, *R.H. Tawney and His Times* and Anthony Wright's 1987 book simply entitled, *R.H. Tawney*. Both Terrill and Wright in their biographical works provide informative narratives on Tawney's early life and his emerging socialism at Oxford and in the ensuing time he spent at Toynbee Hall. They chart his times as a tutor in economic history at the Workers' Educational Association (WEA) and his involvement in the trenches of the Somme during World War One with the British Army. But they also rightly note the centrality of his religion and the part it played in his life and his thought. The third source is Tawney's diary from 1912-1914 that has been edited by Jay Winter and David Joslin and is entitled, *R.H. Tawney's Commonplace Book*. In the introduction to the book the editors assert the character of Tawney's moral philosophy and the significance of the *Commonplace Book*:

'Richard Henry Tawney was a man of deep Christian beliefs and powerful emotions, and nowhere can we gain as full a view of his mind and temperament, of the limitations of his ideas as well as their strengths, as in the *Commonplace Book* or diary which he kept at Manchester from 1912 to 1914. This document is a unique record of the assumptions which supported Tawney's life-long work as a socialist and as a scholar.'[13]

The *Commonplace Book* can be seen as Tawney's first foray into explaining his moral philosophy to an audience of one, as he never intended it to be published. It was therefore a place that he could retreat to and exercise the connections in his mind between his Christian faith and his passions for social justice and the reform of the capitalist system. The writings in the *Commonplace Book* though fractured and unsystematic bear witness to the intellectual development of his Christian socialism. This Christian socialism was unchanged by the prospect of war or by the rise of Communism or anything else. As the diary ends on 2nd December 1914, a month after Tawney had volunteered in the British Army, one can note the closing of a work that formulated and fermented his moral and political thought.

Thus far it has been established that philosophically, Tawney was a Christian. In fact it would be more helpful to classify him specifically, especially in these post-modern times when the term 'Christian', like many others, is open to widespread interpretation. Tawney was a committed Christian in the Protestant tradition. He worshipped in the Anglican Church and his views were doctrinally orthodox and Bible based.[14] By orthodox I mean that his theology was that of an evangelical Anglican.[15] I employ a widely accepted definition of evangelicalism that emphasises the Reformation principles of *sola scriptura* (by Scripture alone), *sola gratia* (by grace alone), and *sola fide* (by faith alone) that

typifies the nature of this type of Protestant Christianity. [16]
It is a school of Protestant theology that has its antecedents
in Luther, Calvin, Zwingli through Jonathan Edwards, John
Wesley and George Whitefield. In addition, the foundational
document of the Anglican Church (of which Tawney was a
practising member) the Thirty-Nine Articles is a fully
evangelical document. In the words of Wright:

'It is not just that he (Tawney) believes in the existence of
God (as a fact of experience), nor in Christianity as the
personification of God, revealing his nature, but that he
holds these beliefs to be the indispensable basis for a true
morality...Tawney may have a view of man as a species as
'only a little lower than the angels', but his view of actual
man is informed by a heavy dose of original sin. Believing
that 'what goodness we have reached is a house built on
piles driven into black slime and always slipping down into it
unless we are building night and day' he was unlikely to take
an over-sanguine view of the ease with which moral, and
therefore social, advance might be accomplished.'[17]

This is in itself interesting because for much of the
twentieth century those Christians who had sympathy with
Tawney's concern for the poor and for some if not all of his
politics, in many cases would not have agreed as much with
his orthodox doctrines of the Christian faith. As Terril
states:

'But 'social Christianity' was not really separable from the
basic doctrinal deposit of Christianity. Tawney took the
doctrine for granted (he was taught it by a more evangelical
generation). By the 1950s, Christian social action had lost
the connection with Christian doctrine that it had when
Tawney first encountered Toynbee Hall and the Charity
Organisation Society. The question was no longer
evangelism or social action. If it was not both, it could not

be either.   Because Christian belief had withered, social
Christianity had less to offer socialist thought.'[18]

   These convictions often placed him alongside liberal
Christians[19] or those for whom association in and with the
Christian community of their local parish church provided
them with something whilst not requiring them to truly take
seriously the *raison d'etre* of the Church, namely its worship of
what Tawney viewed as the true and living God.[20]   The
author understands that 'liberal Christian' is a problematic
term. Of course disagreement amongst Christians is nothing
new and in terms of secondary or tertiary theological issues
such debates do not tend to result in schism. However, in
the Protestant church in general as in the Anglican Church
in particular, the liberal tradition is well established. From
the nineteenth century German Protestant theologian,
Friedrich Schleiermacher to contemporary Anglicans such as
the American, John Selby Spong and the Scot, Richard
Holloway, orthodox Protestantism has been critiqued.
Moreover, it is often hard to define accurately what a liberal
Christian believes.   Some common liberal theological
propositions include: denying that the Bible is inerrant;
denying the doctrine of original sin, the fall and mankind's
need for salvation; denying the Virgin Birth and by
implication suggesting that Christ is solely human and not
divine; denying the miraculous nature and power of Christ in
his ministry; denying the bodily Resurrection and Ascension;
denying the doctrine of the final judgement and of hell;
emphasising the cultural context of certain scriptural
pronouncements - thus stating that said pronouncements no
longer apply to the Church today such as the spiritual edict
forbidding homosexual relationships. Terrill comments on
Tawney's religious convictions:

   'He remained Christian, attending church conferences and
sitting on church committees concerned with the church's

role on political questions… Tawney's significance was that amidst the decay of the faith and authority of the church he formulated the most influential case from the socialist side for an expression of Christianity in political terms…In Christian terms, man achieves his fullness only in relationship with God, and his relationship with God is expressible only through the human relations of men who are 'members one of another'.[21]

From Christian to Christian Socialist

All Christians are first and foremost followers of Christ in the sense that their Christian faith is more than a set of cultural norms but a philosophy of life based around the teachings Christ.[22] This point is clearly made by Tawney in the essay 'Christianity and the Social Order':

'There is a distinctively Christian way of life…This way of life is not, as appears often to be supposed, identical with what is called 'goodness'; for there have been, and are, many admirable pagans, and Christianity is a religion for sinners…Christianity does not merely bear witness against the failures and vices of contemporary morality. It repudiates conventional morality's values, objectives and standards of success.'[23]

Thus, according to Tawney one's relationship with Christ is central to every other situation, relationship, attitude and moral choice that Christians face. The remainder of this chapter seeks to answer the following question: 'what role did Tawney's Christian faith play in his choice of political creeds?' There appear to be several reasons why democratic socialism appealed to Tawney. Firstly was the fact that this variant of socialism was by definition democratic. It regards individuals as ends in themselves and permits dignity to all humans on account of their common humanity. This very notion is a small side step from the central Christian doctrine of the equality of mankind before the eyes of God. So if Tawney's theology of the moral equivalence and sinfulness of mankind erred him to democracy it also erred him to socialism. If all are made equal in moral worth then it is immoral to permit some to be treated as if they are sub-human. This is where the context of Tawney's life affects his politics. Tawney soon realised that the new century was continuing and in some ways worsening the exploitation and poverty that had occurred in industrial societies since the industrial revolution:

'Christians are committed by their creeds to a view of man, and of his place in the universe, which makes tolerance of class advantages and class disabilities - let alone the idealisation of them customary in England – an essay in blasphemy. On that view, man is at once infinitely great and infinitely small. He is a little lower than the angels, the child of God and the heir to eternal life. He is also a fallen creature, helpless without God's aid, and in need of the redemption which God offers those who turn to Him.'[24]

Christians have lived and acquiesced under non-democratic regimes but the notion of democracy while not biblical is neither counter-biblical. It is *adiaphora* neither theologically right nor wrong and thus permissible. Yet the rights and dignity that western democracy entails provide the defence of individual rights including the right to freedom of expression and assembly and liberty to worship. The concept of democracy derived from the Ancient Greeks was gradually Christianised coming to fruition in the mid to late nineteenth century and early twentieth century. Christianity is not democratic as a philosophy and nothing would be more absurd than to expect the Creator and Sustainer of the universe to be on equal terms with His creation but as a temporal institution it preserves the rights of individuals and treats them as beings of innate moral value. The Christian teacher or minister preaches the same message of equal worth in his Sunday sermons. Either way, democracy as a temporal institution is commensurable with a Christian political philosophy.

In Tawney's case he regarded democratic socialism - when applied to his Christianity - as a commensurable political philosophy for a Christian. On its own democratic socialism is not enough to change the world for the better. It can ameliorate some of the ills of capitalism and social squalor but it cannot ameliorate or resolve the desperateness of the human condition. So, for Tawney democratic socialism is only viable because it flows from his Christian faith. Terrill expands upon this point when he says that:

'Tawney did not equate the task of the church with the quest for socialism, nor urge the church to declare its allegiance to the Labour Party. Nevertheless, he thought a proper statement of Christian social principles would carry strong socialist implications.... Tawney did not try to make a synthesis of Christianity and socialism. True, he thought Christians ought to lean to the socialist side, and chided his friend William Temple when Temple, out of a desire to be impartial, resigned from the Labour Party on being made Bishop of Manchester.'[25]

Tawney's Christian socialism meant that he believed that humans could not make a perfect society, nor remove the sinfulness present in the human character. Concurrently, economic and social exploitation would always occur. But Christian socialists must strive to make society and the economy just, democratic and functional. Therefore, Tawney did not have a reticent view of social reform or an overly sanguine view of capitalism, in fact, it was one of the main themes to pervade his scholarship and it was his systematic attack on laissez-faire capitalism in *The Acquisitive Society* and in *Equality*[26] that supplied the Labour Party with a moral as well as economic prescription for British socialism. His antipathy for capitalism is demonstrated in an extract from 'Christianity and the Social Order':

'Capitalism is an ambiguous term...The character of that civilisation is to be judged, not primarily by what is said about it either by its admirers or its critics, but by the institutions which it creates, the relations between human beings which those institutions establish, and the type of character, individual and social which is fostered by those relations...Capitalism today, except in so far as qualified by influences derived from other sources and long resisted by it, is not so much un-Christian as anti-Christian, and not least anti-Christian when it summons Christianity to its defence. It has, indeed, like its totalitarian rival miscalled Communism, some of the characteristics of a counter-religion.'[27]

The following passage is perhaps Tawney's most acerbic assault on the moral depravity of capitalism. He believes it creates and perpetuates selfish behaviour in citizens and simultaneously promotes materialism and the possession of material wealth as social virtues. Tawney argues that this form of capitalism makes acquisitiveness a religion and one that is counter-Christian. Tawney is implying that certain ideals and practices are incommensurable with any sense of Christian morality:

'Its emphasis on the supreme importance of material riches; the intensity of its appeal to the acquisitive appetites, and the skill with which it plays on them; its worship of economic power, often with little regard to the ends which power serves or the means which it uses; its idealisation, not merely of particular property rights, but of property in general; its subordination of human beings to the exigencies, or supposed exigencies, of an economic system, as interpreted by other human beings who have a pecuniary interest in interpreting them to their own advantage; its erection of divisions within the human family based on differences, not merely of personal quality and social function, but of income and economic circumstances – these qualities are closely related to the end which capitalist societies hold to be all-important. In such societies, as the practice of the latter clearly shows, they are commonly regarded as not vices, but as virtues. To the Christian they are vices more ruinous to the soul than most of the conventional forms of immorality.' [28]

For Tawney the social ills engendered by laissez-faire capitalism in the 1920s were a product of Britain's history. In *The Acquisitive Society*, Tawney traces laissez-faire capitalism back to the seventeenth century when, for the first time, the ideas of individual rights and individual interests began to dominate political philosophy.[29] This in itself was caused by the departure of the Church from the heart of social and political ethics. The powerful were those with property and as the rights and interests discourse grew the sanctity of private property established its place at the core of such ideas. Public welfare, social harmony and communal responsibility in Tawney's view receded in the public consciousness. In his later work *Religion and the Rise of Capitalism* published in 1926 he expands and pinpoints this thesis. In the book Tawney suggests that the Protestant Christianity of the Puritans deeply influenced economic ideas and the concept of individualism - that stemmed largely from the theological perspective that they held which insisted that one has individual responsibility for the care of one's soul and the right to read and interpret Scripture and apply it how one's conscience dictates. This fostered an ethos of individualism that according to Tawney bred an overly atomised form of capitalism. Interestingly, his prescription to reform such a capitalism is based on doctrines from Scripture and yet he attributes the problematic ethos surrounding laissez-faire capitalism to fellow Christians reading and trying to apply their interpretation of the same doctrines in their society. Tawney would not wish to repudiate the faith of the Puritans, and he was not comfortable eschewing the sovereignty of the individual's conscience in deciding what is moral and he noted the goodness and charity in the lives of such Puritans as Richard Baxter.[30] Likewise he was not against the proper place that individual rights hold in social ethics. However, he did believe that there had been a disconnection between private interests and public interests and that this was of focal importance to the development and, ultimately, the dominance of the principle of liberty understood in its negative sense and the emergence of laissez-faire capitalism. As he says:

'During the last two centuries Europe, and particularly industrial Europe, has seen the development of a society in which what is called personal religion continues to be taught as the role of individual conduct, but in which the very conception of religion as the inspiration and standard of social life and corporate effort has been forgotten.'[31]

In addition, Tawney argued that the Non-conformist churches had the potential to fill the gap left by the Anglican Church in espousing Christian social ethics but their history was an impediment to this mission. In his view the fact that non-conformity was birthed in reaction against what he terms, '…an overgrown formalism, an artificial and insincere unity'[32] coupled together with the fact that many non-conformists were from the commercial and merchant classes meant that only a limited amount of comment on the social ethics evident in the New Testament occurred. Tawney argues that:

'Individualist in their faith, they were individualist in their interpretation of social morality. Insisting that the essence of religion was the contact of the individual soul with its Maker, they regarded the social order and its consequences, not as the instrument through which grace is mediated, or as steps in the painful progress by which the soul climbs to a fuller vision, but as something external, alien, and irrelevant – something, at best, indifferent to personal salvation, and, at worst, the sphere of the letter which killeth and of the reliance on works which ensnares the spirit into the slumber of death.'[33]

Therefore, for Tawney Britain in the early twentieth century was a country that was informed by Christianity and still largely Christian in a personal religious sense, but in terms of a public doctrine Christianity had long since abrogated much of its capacity to speak into the economic and social issues of the day.

Conclusion

In a way that is distinct to the other Labour thinkers included in this volume, Tawney brings religion to his political thought, to his democratic socialism. Although in a sense this is incorrect as he was a Christian prior to becoming a socialist. Thus it is more accurate to say that his political philosophy emanated from his moral philosophy. As has been noted, the centrality of the democratic method led Tawney to a parliamentary rather than a revolutionary brand of socialism. The valuing of democracy as an end in itself must not be underestimated especially in the 1920s and 1930s when many socialists flirted with, or joined the

Communist Party of Great Britain.[34] Simultaneously,
Tawney's moral critique of laissez-faire capitalism with its
protection of the idle rentier class; the economic freedom it
withheld from the masses who served it; and the ethos of
acquisitiveness that it venerated flowed from his beliefs in
the need for private property to be used for functional and
purposeful endeavours; the duty to utilise wealth for social
purposes; and the ubiquitous radical notion that economic
freedom was necessary for true liberty to be meaningful.
Such commitments are more indicative of Tawney's political
persuasion than cold, rationalist utterings about equality as
an abstract construct. This dual perspective of democracy
and an innate disgust of laissez-faire capitalism formed
Tawney's democratic socialist position. Simple summaries
are hard to ascertain when attempting to trace his religious
motivations. For example, it is unclear whether a particular
experience led Tawney to see his faith and socialism as
compatible. What is widely known is that whilst at Balliol
his thinking was influenced like several generations of
undergraduates by the propositions of Philosophical
Idealism chiefly through the ideas of T.H. Green. Though
long dead by the time Tawney and his close friend William
Temple went up to Oxford – the Greenian intellectual
climate[35] linked radical politics and the duty to serve the
community – especially the poor and ill educated. This was
not lost on the young Tawney who after Oxford lived and
worked in London's East End at Toynbee Hall and
subsequently became a tutor with the WEA as was stated
above. Though perhaps not a simple summary - as matters
of conscience seldom are - but a possible and appealing
factor when trying to locate the catalyst behind Tawney's
decision to commit his life to the cause of democratic
socialism exists in the pages of the *Commonplace Book*. This
source, his private diary over a two year period, seems to
indicate that his high view of Scripture and the teachings of
Christ were for him a signpost that pointed to the service of

the poor and concurrently, to the infinite value of human beings which for him was most powerfully demonstrated at Calvary in the grace of his God.

[1] J. Winter and D. Joslin, (eds.) *R.H. Tawney's Commonplace Book* (Cambridge University Press, Cambridge, 1972) p. 67.

[2] See T.S. Ashton 'Richard Henry Tawney 1880-1962' *Proceedings of the British Academy*, 1962 pp.461-482, J.R. Williams, R.M. Titmuss and F.J. Fisher, *R.H. Tawney: A Portrait by Several Hands* (Shenval Press, London, 1960), J.M. Winter, 'R.H. Tawney's Early Political Thought' *Past and Present*, May 1970 pp.71-96, R. Terrill, *R.H. Tawney and His Times* (Andre Deutsch, London, 1973), A. Wright, *R.H. Tawney* (Manchester University Press, Manchester, 1987).

[3] Terrill, *R.H. Tawney and His Times*, p.277.

[4] We understand these groupings to represent the main ideological tendencies in the Labour Party since 1945. For more see R. Plant, M. Beech and K. Hickson (eds.) *The Struggle for Labour's Soul* (Routledge, London, 2004), pp.1-4.

5 See M. Beech, *The Political Philosophy of New Labour* (I.B. Tauris, London, 2006), pp. 29-30.

6 R.H. Tawney, *The Acquisitive Society* (G. Bell and Sons, London, 1921), pp.137-156.

[7] Tawney, *The Acquisitive Society*, pp.36-54.

8 H. Gaitskell, 'An Appreciation' in R.H. Tawney, *The Radical Tradition* (ed.) R. Hinden (George Allen & Unwin, London, 1964), p.212.

[9] Evan Durbin is not easily pigeonholed in any tradition or school of Labour's political thought. In this sense he is similar to Tawney. What is argued later in this monograph is that Durbin has often been erroneously viewed as a thinker of the Labour right. This is not the case as he strenuously argued for the necessity of widespread nationalisation and economic planning if the Labour Party was going to transform Britain from a capitalist to a socialist economy.

10 T. Benn, 'Foreword to 1981 Edition' in Tawney, *The Attack and Other Papers* (Spokesman, London, 1981), p. xi.

[11] See M. Beech, 'New Labour' in Plant, Beech and Hickson (eds.) *The Struggle for Labour's Soul*, pp.93-96 and J. Harris, 'Labour's political and social thought' in D. Tanner, P. Thane and N. Tiratsoo (eds.) *Labour's First Century* (Cambridge University Press, Cambridge, 2000), p.39.

[12] See J. Smith, 'Reclaiming the Ground: R.H. Tawney Memorial Lecture 20th March 1993' in C. Bryant (ed.) *Reclaiming the Ground* (Hodder and Stoughton, London, 1993).

13 Winter and Joslin (eds.) *R.H. Tawney's Commonplace Book*, p.xiii.

[14] See N. Dennis and A.H. Halsey, *English Ethical Socialism* (Clarendon Press, Oxford, 1988), pp.171-176. Also see Tawney's letters to his wife

whilst a delegate at the International Missionary Council in Jerusalem, March 1925. His association with the International Missionary Council denotes at least sympathy for, if not a belief in evangelism. Tawney *Papers*, 20/7, Private correspondence - Jeanette Tawney, 26th and 29th March 1925, British Library of Political and Economic Science (BLPES), London.

[15] Maurice Cowling suggests that Tawney was a 'High Anglican'. In Anglican circles this term can refer to one's preferred form and style of worship. For example, quiet, responsorial liturgy with limited amounts of singing hymns of praise. It can also refer to one's churchmanship or theological perspective within Anglicanism and some use the term to denote an Anglo-Catholic theology. If the latter is what Cowling means, I disagree. Tawney's views in his *Commonplace Book* appear orthodox Protestant, especially with his references to Scripture, grace and the centrality of Christ. There appear to be no clues as to a Catholic Anglicanism in any of his published works or private papers. See M. Cowling, *Religion and Public Doctrine in Modern England: Volume Three Accommodations* (Cambridge University Press, Cambridge, 2001) p.275.

[16] Bebbington and McGrath have expressed evangelicalism in the following concepts, Biblicism, christocentrism, crucicentrism, conversionism and activism. See D. Bebbington, *Evangelicalism in Modern Britain from the 1730s to the 1980s* (Unwin Hyman, London, 1989), A. McGrath, *Evangelicalism and the Future of Christianity* (Hodder and Stoughton, London, 1995). For a good overview of evangelical precepts see J. Stott, *Evangelical Truth* (Inter-Varsity Press, Leicester, 1999).

[17] Wright, *R.H. Tawney*, pp.19-20.

[18] Terrill, *R.H. Tawney and His Times*, p.249.

[19] For notable works on contemporary liberal theology by Anglicans see J.S. Spong, *Born of a Woman: A Bishop Rethinks the Birth of Jesus* (Harper, San Francisco, 1992), J.S. Spong, *Resurrection: Myth or Reality? A Bishop's Search of the Origin's of Christianity* (Harper, San Francisco, 1994) and R. Holloway, *Doubts and Loves: What is Left of Christianity* (Canongate Books, Edinburgh, 2002) and R. Holloway, *Godless Morality* (Canongate Books, Edinburgh, 2004).

[20] For evidence of Tawney's belief in Christ, the Trinity and in the truth of Christianity See Winter and Joslin (eds.) *R.H. Tawney's Commonplace Book*, pp.78-79.

[21] Terrill, *R.H. Tawney and His Times*, pp. 265-268.

[22] Tawney's socialist works were written for his predominantly secular audience. Yet as one can see from the last chapter of *The Acquisitive Society* occasionally his religion spills through. He did write for a Christian audience at times – for example, 'Christianity and the Social

Order' is an essay from a collection of remarks presented at a conference discussing the Church's role in social ethics in 1937. See R.H. Tawney, 'Christianity and the Social Order' in Tawney, *The Attack and Other Papers*.
[23] Ibid. p.168.
[24] Ibid. p.182.
[25] Terrill, *R.H. Tawney and His Times*, pp.248 and p.268.
[26] R.H. Tawney, *Equality* (George Allen & Unwin, London, 1931).
[27] Tawney, 'Christianity and the Social Order' in Tawney, *The Attack and Other Papers*, pp.169-170.
[28] Ibid. p.170.
[29] Tawney, *The Acquisitive Society*, pp.12-15.
[30] Ibid. p.229.
[31] Ibid.p.227.
[32] Ibid. p.229.
[33] Ibid.
[34] See Dennis and Halsey, *English Ethical Socialism*, pp.150 and 168.
[35] See M. Carter, *T.H. Green and the Development of Ethical Socialism* (Imprint Academic, Exeter, 2003), pp.168-171.

3

G.D.H. COLE

'The essence of the Guild socialist attitude lies in the belief that society ought to be so organised as to afford the greatest possible opportunity for individual and collective self-expression to all its members, and that this involves and implies the extension of positive self-government through all its parts.'[1]

George Douglas Howard Cole was one of the Labour Party's most important thinkers especially in his role as a socialist theoretician in the pre-World War Two era. Alongside his contemporaries R.H. Tawney and Harold Laski he was one of the 'Red Professors'.[2] His early publications, *The World of Labour* (1913)[3], *Self-Government in Industry* (1917)[4], *Social Theory* (1920)[5], *Guild Socialism Re-Stated* (1920)[6], and *Chaos and Order in Industry* (1920)[7] significantly contributed firstly to the development and zenith of Guild socialism in the Labour Movement and secondly to a broader emphasis on workers' control of industry and on the anti-statist tradition in British socialist thought.[8] In the 1970s the New Left argued for greater democratisation of industry to be central to the socialist vision and in so doing implicitly rekindled Guild socialist arguments.[9] Also, whilst a leading Labour figure and then as a member of the Social Democratic Party, David Owen acknowledged his intellectual debt to Cole regarding a decentralist and anti-collectivist approach to socialist governance.[10] This chapter attempts to provide a basic outline of Cole's Guild socialism and to locate it within Labour's ideological heritage. Secondly, the chapter will evaluate the demise of the Guild socialist movement and comment on the second phase in Cole's socialist development, namely the move he made to embrace parliamentary socialism and 'Labourism'. Finally, the salience of Cole's socialist ideas will be analysed in light of some calls for a less state-centric form of democratic socialism.

Guild Socialism and the Labour Party

Cole was at root an individualist, this term is more helpful than the term 'liberal', because that term is exceedingly problematic as it has a plethora of connotations in social, economic and political theory.   In fact Cole's individualism is best described as libertarianism.   This term is also complicated implying different things in American and British discourse. In British terms, Cole can be understood as a libertarian because he was fundamentally concerned with protecting the liberty of the individual above all things; he was concerned about the centralisation of power in any sphere but especially in conjunction with the state; and he was suspicious of large organisations that required one to conform or to behave in a prescribed manner, hence his antipathy for religion, the military - and in his early activism – for Parliament. This innate libertarianism which is implied by a biographer[11] was a perennial characteristic throughout Cole's life and was made more interesting and distinctive on the arrival of his commitment to socialism. Cole became a socialist on reading *News From Nowhere*[12] by William Morris: 'I was converted, quite simply, by reading William Morris' 'News From Nowhere', which made me feel suddenly and irrevocably, that there was nothing except a Socialist that it was possible for me to be.'[13] Cole's socialism was a critique of laissez-faire capitalism especially the subjugation of the

individual worker through the absence of choice and
economic control over one's labour.   Added to this
libertarian socialism was a principle inherited from Morris
namely a desire for fellowship and as his thought developed
a belief in certain forms of autonomous groups or
communities – known as guilds that were inspired by the
medieval guilds brought to Cole's attention in the work of
Arthur Penty.   As Margaret Cole suggests of Penty's
motivation:

'...in essence it was a medievalist's plea for a return to
medieval standards of craftsmanship in production, and
more important for what followed, to the medieval tradition
of self-regulation and self-government in the different
occupations and through them of self-government in the
medieval cities - a tradition killed, so Penty believed, by the
unregulated scramble for production and profit-making
produced by the industrial revolution; and he gave a hint in
the modern world the trade unions might be agents of return
to a saner state of things.'[14]

For Cole the attraction of Penty's guilds was in the fact
that they demonstrated self-government and economic
control of labour for the workers, as well as corresponding
to the idea of socialist fellowship amongst workers that he
derived from the ethical socialist writings of Morris.
He began his formal association with democratic socialism
and the Labour Movement by joining the Oxford University
Fabian Society in 1907 but in 1915 after becoming
disillusioned by the collectivism and state socialist approach
of the Fabians, Cole and his friend William Mellor
established the National Guilds League which sought to
promote Guild socialism.   Guild socialism was a form of
democratic socialism and one can highlight four
foundational precepts that underpin its interpretation of
socialism. The first foundational precept is the injustice of

laissez-faire capitalism that not only exploits workers and treats them as means (labour) to an end (profit) but also, because the capitalist system denies them individual liberty over their work due to the mechanism of wage-labour, thus the worker is a slave albeit a remunerated slave who gets to go home at the end of his shift. The second of these precepts is that democratisation is central to socialism and this requires the working class and the industrial workers in particular, to democratically control their industries and the production of goods by their labour. The third precept is anti-collectivism. This placed Cole directly in opposition to the mainstream socialism of the Fabian Society that was thoroughly collectivist and statist in outlook and method. This anti-collectivism led Cole to call for the 'socialisation of industry' through a National Guild system as opposed to the nationalisation of industry by the state. Cole distinguishes between these two notions:

'...we have of late years ceased to distinguish between nationalisation and socialisation, and even dropped the latter word altogether. For there are clearly two directions the state may extend its power over industry. It may own more; and it may manage more. Nationalisation, in the true sense of the word, as it is used in common by capitalist and by Labour advocates, means national management; socialisation, whether in the mouth of a social democrat or of a hireling of the Anti-Socialist Union, means national ownership...Furthermore even if we go on to socialise, we couple national ownership with a system of controlling industry which Guild-Socialists hold to be both morally and economically wrong...If, after a voyage almost as lasting as the Flying Dutchman, we round in the end the cape of state capitalism, we shall only find ourselves on the other side in a Sargossa Sea of state socialism, which will continue to repress all initiative, clog all endeavour, and deny all freedom to the workers.'[15]

For Guild socialists, nationalisation meant that the state manages industry and by implication the capitalist is permitted to exist and own some of the means of production and distribution thus, merely functioning under a regulatory managerial state. On the other hand, socialisation implied the social ownership of industry by the state that encompasses the means of production and distribution and thus leads to the abolition of the capitalist. This initially appears as if Guild socialism is endorsing collectivism. However, according to Cole this is necessary so that guilds can be granted the autonomy to organise and the liberty to produce goods and sell them to the state. Therefore, socialisation of industry guarantees democratisation of industry for the industrial workers. In essence under this system the workers still have their procedural political rights but also industrial rights through the ownership of their industry. Cole makes the following point: 'Where now the state passes a Factory Act, or a Coal Mines Regulation Act, the Guild Congress of the future will pass such Acts, and its power of enforcing them, will be the same as that of the state.'[16]

Cole envisaged a national system of industrial organisation through guilds. 'National' for Cole did not refer to one, single centralised body that co-ordinated workers across a range of industries from the top down, for this would be collectivism and no different in character from the much maligned Fabianism of which Cole was the sharpest critic. He understood 'national' as meaning the nation-wide coverage of decentralised guilds: 'Decentralisation...begins at the centre – in this sphere, with the democratic, equalitarian, national, industrial Guild.'[17] The state as Cole described it in *Self-Government in Industry* is a territorial association. It is a body comprised of communities of individuals. Cole accepted that the democratic nation-state had political legitimacy although he grew to feel that greater democratic participation and power should be devolved to local and regional levels.[18] However, his Guild socialism instructed that true democracy was self-government of the individual in all spheres of social life: political and industrial and as democracy in its truest and fullest sense is a freedom, procedural representative democracy in the political sphere was insufficient:

'To deny state sovereignty in industry is not to reduce industry to a mere multiplicity of warring Guilds; it is to confront Parliament with an industrial body which has an equal claim to be representative of the nation as a whole. Neither Parliament nor the Guild Congress can claim to be ultimately sovereign: the one is the supreme territorial association, the other the supreme professional association.'[19]

The fourth precept is the necessity of guilds or as Cole saw them in the twentieth century – trade unions:

'Cole's grand discovery in *The World of Labour* was that the trade unions were the key agency both in the achievement of socialism and in industrial organisation of a socialist society. Thus trade union activity always had a dual purpose. On the one hand, it wanted to secure better wages and conditions; but at the same time it was the harbinger of a new industrial order rooted in worker control.'[20]

Cole suggested that specific guilds would operate in regions of the country and would themselves be made up of workers within districts where factories are situated and within the factories different sections or 'shops' would democratically elect their supervisors, foreman and managers.[21]

However, Guild socialism was not the only socialist doctrine advocating workers' control during the first two

decades of the twentieth century – the other was
Syndicalism. The challenge of Syndicalism as a theoretical
assault on Fabianism was a defining moment in the
development of what became Cole's Guild socialism.[22]
Geoffrey Foote links the Syndicalists to the Guild socialists
through the figure of Cole: 'It was to be G.D.H. Cole, a
close sympathiser with the class war ideas of the Syndicalists,
who was to blunt their revolutionary challenge and
demonstrate their similarity with, and political contribution
to, the Labour Party.'[23]   Syndicalism was a brand of
revolutionary socialism that was greatly influenced by
Marxism, if not categorised as a form of Marxism itself.[24]
The doctrines of class war culminating in a violent
revolution through the role of a militant industrial working
class and the ultimate subjugation of the bourgeoisie and
overthrow of capitalism with a workers' socialist republic –
clearly defines Syndicalism as a type of Marxist socialism.
Trade unions were the vehicles of industrial activism and it
was through these unions that economic power would be
gained via revolution.[25] As Foote suggests:

'In its destructive aspects – its opposition to state
socialism, union bureaucracy and representative democracy
– Syndicalism was a direct challenge to the Labourist
ideology underlying the Labour Party's political thought. It
was generally incompatible with British Socialism, and as
such had nothing to offer the Labour Party as it sought a
doctrine flexible enough to unite its various strands.'[26]

Having provided a brief evaluation of Guild socialism and
compared it to Syndicalism one is in a better position to
attempt to clarify Guild socialism within the political
thought of the Labour Party.   It is important to note that
the pre-1945 and post-1945 periods are distinct in Labour's
political thought though many of the post-1945 variants and
tendencies of socialist thought have their antecedents in

G.D.H. COLE   45

Labour's history before World War Two. One of its most distinctive characteristics is its non-revolutionary tenor. As has been stated above, this makes Guild socialism a notably different strain of socialism than its near relation Syndicalism. Some aspects of Guild socialism's intellectual foundations such as the centrality of the class-struggle, workers' control of industry and socialisation of industry are rooted in Marxist analysis. This evinces the fact that Guild socialism is a radical socialism but is separated from Marxism because it eschews any notion of the need for, or the inevitability of, a class war with a violent class-based revolution. So in the early twentieth century it is perhaps fair to assert that Guild socialism was the most radical democratic socialist position for those individuals who wanted to remain in the Labour Party, (compared to those who joined the Communist Party of Great Britain). In terms of social theory, Guild socialism was the leading anti-collectivist and anti-statist vision of socialism. Cole epitomised the decentralist tendency and the desire for democratisation within the economic sphere of life more than any other democratic socialist thinker in the Labour Party. These two aspects are radical in both senses of the word. Cole's political economy was the most left-wing prescription by a non-Marxist socialist and his proposed organisational format for achieving socialism was contrary to the dominant collectivist socialist outlook in both the pre-1945 and the post-1945 eras.

The Demise of Guild Socialism

The primary reason for the demise of the Guild socialist movement was the nature of the economic events in the early 1920s. The national economic slump which resulted in high unemployment significantly affected the outlook of large swathes of the Labour Movement.[27] A direct correlative of this economic context was the growing belief that Industrial Unionism[28] in both its revolutionary (Syndicalist) and democratic (Guild socialist) forms was insufficient and too remote a possibility to reduce the immediate poverty caused by mass unemployment and the disparate factionalism of trade unionism. By 1924 the first Labour Government - albeit a minority one – had won power and this signalled the success of the parliamentary route to start to establish democratic socialism in Britain. [29] Although its tenure was short and largely unfruitful, its significance was not lost on the majority of the Labour Movement. Thus, Guild socialism like its violent cousin, Syndicalism, was consigned to the era before the advent of parliamentary power by a government for the working class. This period marked a further development in the thought of Cole. The demise of Guild socialism prompted him to look for new ways in which to implement his socialist principles and to attempt to provide relevant policy solutions to the problems of industrial society in Britain. Cole still preferred the extra-parliamentary method for socialism in the period immediately after the demise of the Guild socialist movement and additionally he was hostile to the bureaucratic and centralising tendencies of the state as the organ of social and economic change for the Labour Movement. He stated that he would: '...sooner see the Labour Party not propose nationalisation at all than propose nationalisation in bureaucratic terms.'[30]

Critical of the newly formed Communist Party of Great Britain and of the efforts of the Labour Party in Parliament especially the minority Labour Government of 1924, Cole found himself politically homeless in an organisational sense. He was still an academic and found this a pleasing outlet for his political preferences especially during this period. As a propagandist within the British Labour Movement during the interregnum between Guild socialism and his later activism in the Labour Party he set himself the task of formulating ideas and programmes for socialism in Britain (which were non-communist but in his opinion at the time, more thoroughly socialist than the Parliamentary Labour Party would or could offer[31]) and then teaching them through his role as a tutor with the Workers' Educational Association. Wright comments that: 'At a personal level, he found in the WEA an arena of intellectual freedom, a scope for unorthodoxy, which the more propagandist schools would deny him.'[32] What is interesting in the ideological trajectory of Cole's thought is that by the time of the General Strike in 1926 which was arguably the high watermark of Industrial Unionism in the history of the Labour Movement in Britain, Cole was already convinced of the futility of the Guild socialist method (decentralised worker's control of industry) but he did not eschew its morality. Cole noted that Industrial Unionism could not defeat the modern state.[33] The trade unions no matter how aptly organised and motivated could not replace capitalism with socialism.[34]

To change capitalism into socialism a Labour Government had to control capital rather than industry. In terms of formulating a new and more carefully conceived political economy Cole was influenced during the late 1920s and early 1930s by the under-consumptionist ideas of J.A. Hobson and to an extent by the work of John Maynard Keynes as it was developing before *The General Theory*[35] was published.[36] This post-Guild period can be understood as a second phase in Cole's socialism and his opening piece of socialist writing (he had published poetry, novels and history books previously) in this period was his 1929 book entitled, *The Next Ten Years in British Social and Economic Policy*.[37] Cole noted that between the years 1910-1929 democratic socialist doctrine had undergone significant changes. Cole conceded that the Labour left demand for full socialisation of the economy had been abandoned.[38] Crucially for understanding the ideological journey of Cole, he asserted

that the Labour Party was united on the fundamental issue
of parliamentary socialism as opposed to attempting to
establish socialism by extra-parliamentary methods.[39] His
main proposals for a forthcoming programme of a Labour
government included the creation of a National Labour
Corps to temporarily harness the labour of the mass
unemployed to build houses, roads, railways, to clear slums,
drain land and for use in the ongoing national electrification
process.[40] Other proposals were the establishment of a
Board of National Investment to restore and invest in
industry; the extension of nationalisation including the Bank
of England and extension of state-control over certain
private organisation such as the joint-stock banks and the
extension of state-management of other companies and
industries.[41] Thus, Cole saw the merits of three forms of
state intervention in the economy. Regarding workers'
control, Cole proposed: 'That the Guild socialist case for the
management of industry on functional lines and an effective
voice for the workers in the conditions of their work, hold
good.'[42] He proposed that income tax should be raised to
fund social programmes such as a system of Family
Allowances especially through supertax on the rich and
through the collection of death duties in the hope of
ultimately abolishing inherited wealth.[43]

Guild Socialism Rekindled?

Ideas similar to some Guild socialist precepts have been
recovered by elements of the New Left.[44] However, such a
rekindling of ideas that were similar to Guild socialism does
not necessarily mean that a new Guild socialist movement
was nascent across European democracies. Nor does it
imply that Cole was re-read and thus, reclaimed by a new
generation of activists and socialist thinkers. This thought is
appealing for those interested in intellectual histories, but

often the re-discovery of ideas is accidental rather than deliberate. As Wright notes:

'A new activism in society (symbolised in France, by the events of May 1968) was paralleled by a new control-minded militancy in industry (symbolised, in Britain, by the work-in at Upper Clyde Shipbuilders). The demand was for 'participation' in society and 'democracy' in industry, terms which were both loosely defined and momentous in their implications.'[45]

Therefore, it would appear that the decentralist tendency dormant in democratic socialism for the preceding forty years was brought once again to the fore partly in response to the increasing build up of power of multi-national corporations and in part to the perceived failure of state socialism in redistributing power in any meaningful sense to certain sections of society, namely the trade unions. Transference of industrial power from managers to workers through bodies known as workers' councils that were directly elected by individual workers themselves was a major aspect of the New Left.[46] This demand in one sense had never left sections of the British Labour Movement but by the mid-1960s and arguably from the Seamen's Strike of 1966 trade unions in Britain began to re-emphasise the demand for industrial democracy. A socialist organisation committed to ideas of workers' control was the Institute of Workers' Control based at Nottingham University under the influence of Ken Coates.[47] The Institute of Worker's Control was formed in 1968 and it had significant union support in the form of the Transport and General Workers' Union leader Jack Jones and the Amalgamated Engineering Union's leader Hugh Scanlon. As the New Left developed within the Labour Party its supporters eventually gravitated around the figure of Tony Benn by the mid-1970s. The Bennite New Left agenda from the mid-1970s until the early

1980s had, as one of its centre pieces of policy, the idea of worker's control of industry. This notion was not in the revolutionary form of the Syndicalists but it appeared to have more in common with Cole's Guild socialist approach. The statement below by Tony Benn reads remarkably similar to statements made by Cole during the heyday of Guild socialism:

'Whatever problems may lie ahead, no one in the movement doubts that progress must be made, first to bring labour into a truly equal partnership in controlling industry and then in reorganising, so that those who actively create the wealth can shape the processes by which it is done and determine (within the framework of law and the needs of the nation) how the surpluses should be applied to develop our manufacturing, productive and service industries...Political democracy wrested the control of Parliament from those who owned the lands and factories. Industrial democracy is a logical and necessary development of it.'[48]

Therefore, in terms of expressing a desire for greater workers' control of industry the Bennite New Left was the most recent section of the Labour Party to ally themselves with this Guild socialist ideal. However, if one broadens out Cole's principle of decentralisation of power from the collectivist state then other sections and figures within the Labour Party have shared this sentiment. For example the anti-statist tradition in socialist thought was restated by David Owen whilst a senior Labour politician and as a member of the SDP. He embraced what he called the '...radical democratic libertarian tradition of decentralised socialism...'[49] this is a wordy expression but perhaps it is most easily explained as an anti-centralist and anti-collectivist tendency in social democracy. Thus more centrist elements within British democratic socialism saw merit in a less state-centric form of governance. Owen went so far as explicitly citing Cole and the decentralist tradition that was embodied in Guild socialism.[50] In addition some may be tempted to argue that if decentralisation of power is a sign of this anti-centralist tendency then New Labour deserve to be included as they have created devolved government in London, Scotland, Wales and Northern Ireland as well as unsuccessfully trying to give England regional assemblies. In one sense, according to Dilys Hill, there is some merit in this view but the relationship between the plethora of devolved bodies and central government is unclear:

'New Labour has given little consideration to the constitutional position of local government in a political system based on parliamentary sovereignty…The emphasis now is on decentralisation to front-line services rather than to elected local councils…But the debate on the constitutional role of local government, the relations between the several countries of the UK, the regions, local councils and Westminster, remains not only unresolved but largely unexpressed.'[51]

This perhaps exposes the fact that contrary to the devolution legislation New Labour are traditionally statist and reluctant to devolve economic power from the centre. Thus, regarding the decentralisation of economic power they have more in common with Fabian socialism than with Cole.

Conclusion

As the twentieth century progressed and the Labour Movement finally gained a majority government in Clement Attlee's administration of 1945, Cole grew more and more resigned to the fact that the Labour Movement was correct to follow the political path, as opposed to the path which desired worker's control of industry and was embedded in a

Marxist belief that capitalism would collapse. During those formative years from the mid-1920s until the mid-1940s Cole's antipathy towards the Labour Party faded and his suspicion towards the Fabian collectivist approach receded. Perhaps more notable was the fact that he consciously and explicitly distanced himself from Marxism particularly in the form of the Communist Party of Great Britain. [52] Cole's distrust of meta-narratives survived – and thus he was not inclined to leave democratic socialism for Marxist socialism or its progeny Communism. Perhaps a good example of the ideological distance travelled by Cole is the following quotation in which he implies that democratic socialism is value-driven and the value he enunciates is fairness: 'The world of 1947 may seem a chilly place; but there is promise in it. Even now, amid crisis and shortage, the poor and the weak in Great Britain are getting a fairer deal than ever before.'[53] Vague and ambiguous as the term 'fairer deal' is, the quotation demonstrates a second phase in Cole's socialist thought which was value driven rather than both value-driven and policy specific. His Guild socialist days were simultaneously value-driven in terms of individual liberty and fellowship and also policy-specific suggesting that socialism was chiefly about worker's control and the socialisation of the means of production and distribution. This was a gradual but significant philosophical revision in his socialism. His Industrial Unionism was replaced by 'Labourism' but the inclinations for libertarian socialism never left him as he maintained his belief in the virtues of decentralisation of power and protecting individual liberty in a socialist context. [54] Cole's Guild socialism was neither greatly influential nor enduring but the emphasis he placed on certain aspects of socialist thought certainly was. This sentiment would be challenged by Julius Braunthal who stated in the 'Introduction' to *A History of Socialist Thought: Volume V Socialism and Fascism 1931-1939* that Cole was internationally influential as a socialist scholar and thinker:

'G.D.H. Cole was a great figure of international socialism no les than British socialism... For example, his *Self-Government in Industry*, published in 1917, and translated into German and Swedish, was a source of inspiration for the architects of socialist reconstruction in Germany and Austria when the revolutionary upsurge at the end of the First World War posed the problem of socialisation of industries in these countries.'[55]

Cole, his wife maintained, was a committed Guild socialist until the end of his life.[56] However he was realistic enough to have charted its nadir and its growing irrelevance for a desperate, unemployed industrial working class. Viewed with hindsight the Guild socialist movement appears a romantic ideal of workers' control of industry. Moreover, Guild socialism did not provide a robust political economy that was able to suggest ways of replacing markets and Cole had to rely heavily on the state to socialise industry so the National Guild Congress could deal solely with the state. Thus an entire sector of his political economy was dependent upon a statist and collectivist approach. Questions of freedom of choice for consumers, efficiency and lack of competition under a Guild socialist system were unsatisfactorily addressed. These points and the reticence towards the parliamentary method destined Guild socialism to be an interesting crucible of ideas for pluralistic forms of socialism and as a mouthpiece for the principle of workers' control, without in reality ever threatening to succeed. Reconciling himself with the Labour Party despite his antipathy for its state-centrism and collectivism, Cole demonstrated pragmatism in his thought in the post-Guild period. There is little doubt that taken as a canon of scholarship Cole's socialist thought is fascinating, original and contradictory. Cole's contribution as Guild socialist theoretician and then as Labour Party intellectual is indicative of the breadth and diversity of the British Labour Movement.

[1] G.D.H. Cole, *Guild Socialism Re-Stated* (Leonard Parsons, London, 1920), p.13.

[2] Julius Braunthal notes that the works and ideas of Cole, Laski and Tawney had become well known to intellectuals in Tokyo, Hong Kong, Jakarta, Singapore, Rangoon and Delhi whether, '...active in the Labour Movement or teachers at universities or working in the administration of their countries.' This demonstrates the influence of these three socialist academics from the 1920s onwards. See J. Braunthal, 'Introduction' in G.D.H. Cole, *A History of Socialist Thought: Volume V Socialism and Fascism 1931-1939* (Macmillan, London, 1961), p.xii.

[3] G.D.H. Cole, *The World of Labour* (G. Bell & Sons, London, 1913).

[4] G.D.H. Cole, *Self-Government in Industry* (G. Bell & Sons, London, 1917).

[5] G.D.H. Cole, *Social Theory* (Methuen, London, 1920).

[6] Cole, *Guild Socialism Re-Stated*.

[7] G.D.H. Cole, *Chaos and Order in Industry* (F.A. Stokes, New York, 1920).

[8] Cole published a huge amount and wrote many other books some of which were in his role as an academic and others in his role as a Labour activist. For a thorough bibliography see M. Cole, *The Life of G.D.H. Cole* (Macmillan, London, 1971), pp.289-292 and A. Wright, *G.D.H. Cole and Socialist Democracy* (Clarendon Press, Oxford, 1979), pp.283-296.

[9] See T. Benn, *Arguments for Socialism* (Spokesman Books, London, 1979), pp.64-73.

[10] See, D. Owen, 'Labour's Co-operative Way Forward' 26th May 1980, *The Guardian*, David Owen Papers, University of Liverpool, D709 2/10/5 and D. Owen, *Face The Future* (Oxford University Press, Oxford, 1981), p.19.

[11] Cole, *The Life of G.D.H. Cole*, p.35.

[12] W. Morris, *News From Nowhere* (Longmans, London, 1896).

[13] G.D.H. Cole, 'British Labour Movement: Retrospect and Prospect' in *Ralph Fox Memorial Lecture* (Fabian Society, London, 1951), p.3.

[14] Cole, *The Life of G.D.H. Cole*, p.51.

[15] G.D.H. Cole, 'Nationalisation and the Guilds' *The New Age*, 10th September 1914, p.438.

[16] Cole, *Self-Government in Industry*, p.28.

[17] Ibid. p.173.

[18] See Cole, *Social Theory* and *Guild Socialism Re-Stated*.

[19] Cole, *Self-Government in Industry*, p.17.

[20] Wright, *G.D.H. Cole and Socialist Democracy*, p.29.

[21] Cole, *Self-Government in Industry*, p.184.

[22] For a good history of Guild socialism see, N. Carpenter, *Guild Socialism* (D. Appleton, London, 1922).

[23] G. Foote, *The Labour Party's Political Thought* (Macmillan, Basingstoke, 1997), p.99.

[24] The syndicalism referred to here is British syndicalism present in the first two decades of the twentieth century. It is the syndicalism of Tom Mann and Noah Ablett. See Foote, *The Labour Party's Political Thought*, pp. 84-99.

[25] J. Corina, 'Introduction to the 1972 Edition' in G.D.H. Cole, *Self-Government in Industry* (Hutchinson Educational, London, 1972,) p.xix.

[26] Foote, *The Labour Party's Political Thought*, p.94.

[27] Wright, *G.D.H. Cole and Socialist Democracy*, p.142.

[28] This term implies a type of militant unionism that sought to gain industrial and political power through action taken by trade unions. It is borrowed from an unpublished paper on the life and thought of G.D.H. Cole by John Saville. See, J. Saville, G.D.H. Cole, Unpublished paper, DLB/11/15, Dictionary of Labour Biography Archive, University of Hull.

[29] Wright, *G.D.H. Cole and Socialist Democracy*, p.138.

[30] G.D.H. Cole, 'About Nationalisation' *New Standard*, July 1924, in Wright, *G.D.H. Cole and Socialist Democracy*, p.140.

[31] See Cole's articles in the *New Statesman, New Standards, Labour Monthly* and *Labour Magazine*.

[32] Wright, *G.D.H. Cole and Socialist Democracy*, p.145.

[33] Cole, G.D.H., 'Some Lessons of the Late General Strike' *New Statesman*, 19th June 1926, in Wright, *G.D.H. Cole and Socialist Democracy*, p.153.

[34] Ibid.

[35] J.M. Keynes, *The General Theory of Employment, Interest and Money* (Macmillan, London, 1936).

[36] Wright, *G.D.H. Cole and Socialist Democracy*, p.186.

[37] G.D.H. Cole, *The Next Ten Years in British Social and Economic Policy* (Macmillan, London, 1929).

[38] Ibid. p.421.

[39] Ibid.

[40] Ibid. p.424.

[41] Ibid. p.427.

[42] Ibid.

[43] Ibid. p.428.

[44] Wright, *G.D.H. Cole and Socialist Democracy*, p.1.

[45] Ibid. p.279.

[46] Margaret Cole implies that Guild socialist ideas were still present in British society in the late 1960s. See Cole, *The Life of G.D.H. Cole*, p.50.

47 See K.Coates and T. Topham, (eds.) *Readings and Witnesses for Workers' Control* (Spokesman, London, 1968).
48 T. Benn, *Arguments for Socialism* (Spokesman, London, 1979), p.43.
49 Owen, *Face the Future*, p.1.
50 Ibid. p.27.
51 D. Hill, 'Constitutional Reform' in R. Plant, M. Beech and K. Hickson, (eds.) *The Struggle for Labour's Soul* (Routledge, London, 2004), p.211.
52 Wright, *G.D.H. Cole and Socialist Democracy*, p.275.
53 G.D.H. Cole, *A History of the Labour Party From 1914* (Routledge and Kegan Paul, London, 1948), p.478.
54 Wright, *G.D.H. Cole and Socialist Democracy*, p.13.
55 Braunthal, 'Introduction' in Cole, *A History of Socialist Thought: Volume V Socialism and Fascism 1931-1939*, pp.xi-xii.
56 Cole, *The Life of G.D.H. Cole*, p.50.

4

HAROLD LASKI

'Communism has made its way by its idealism not its realism, by its spiritual promise, not its materialistic prospect. It is a creed in which there is intellectual error, moral blindness, social perversity. Religions make their way despite these things.'[1]

'Proletarian dictatorship is not an inevitable stage in social evolution. It is not merely the outcome of special economic conditions; it is also the outcome of great leaders who, like Lenin, have the eye to see, and the hand to execute, the requisite strategy at the appropriate moment.'[2]

Harold Laski warrants inclusion in this volume for two main reasons. The first reason is that it is well known that Laski was influential on the left in Britain and America during the 1920s and 1930s as an academic and a journalist; as a Labour Party activist and as a tutor in the Workers' Educational Association; and as a colleague and friend to some of the most remarkable political and legal figures of the day such as Sidney and Beatrice Webb, Ramsay MacDonald, George Lansbury and Stafford Cripps and Supreme Court Justices Holmes, Frankfurter and Brandeis. Secondly, Laski is worthy of examination because his political thought is fascinating in itself. A steadfast libertarian in social thought, a pluralist political scientist at the beginning of his career; and as his political commitment to socialism developed his thought gradually evolved through three phases and the transition from Fabian socialism to Labour left socialism to Marxist socialism is indicative of the travails of the Labour Party in the 1930s. This chapter has two aims; the first is to provide a summary of Laski's education, career and activism in the Labour Party and the second is to chart Laski's ideological trajectory as a socialist intellectual in the Labour Party.[3] The conclusion will discuss the extent to which Laski's thought has influenced succeeding generations of socialists in the Labour Party and the extent to which his main ideas have endured.

Political Scientist and Labour Activist

When attempting to provide a summary of Laski's education, career and activism in the Labour Party one can divide his life in to distinct periods. The first period is his adolescence and his Oxford years from 1911-1914. The young Laski became politicised mainly through Frida, his then girlfriend and subsequently his wife, and the causes they supported were concerned with the extension of liberty. Frida was a militant suffragette and Laski became heavily involved in the suffrage movement. Whilst an undergraduate, he spoke in favour of motions at the Oxford Union and actively campaigned for female suffrage. Through the suffrage movement Laski was introduced to G.D.H. Cole and the University branch of the Fabian Society. Laski initially showed some enthusiasm for Guild socialist ideas as they expressed the right for liberty in decision-making in the work-place for the working class. As Herbert A. Deane notes:

'It is interesting to note that the political movements which made the deepest impression on Laski in his undergraduate days, and to which he constantly referred in his early books and activities, were the women's suffrage

movement, the growing radicalism of the approach of
syndicalism of some of the trade unions, and the alliance
between Ulster and a section of the Conservative Party to
sabotage the Liberal's Home Rule legislation for Ireland.[4]

   Michael Newman in his biography of Laski argues that he
was mistaken to claim that: 'I have, I suppose, been a
socialist in some degree ever since the last years of my
schooldays.' [5] Newman asserts this because Laski's
conversion to socialism was a gradual process. Newman
implies that Laski was always interested in radical politics,
dissatisfied with Edwardian liberalism and was committed
above all principles to the protection and extension of
liberty. Thus, Laski was a left-leaning libertarian rather than
a socialist.[6]
   The second period begins with the outbreak of the First
World War and ends with the fall of MacDonald's Labour
Government. After trying to join up, Laski failed the army
medical and subsequently he and Frida spent the years 1914-
1920 in North America. Initially they went to Montreal,
Canada where Laski held a Lectureship in Political Science at
McGill University and then from 1916-1920 they moved to
Cambridge, Massachusetts where Laski was appointed
Assistant Professor in Government at Harvard University.
His early academic works published in this period such as
Studies in the Problem of Sovereignty[7]; *Authority in the Modern State*[8];
and *The Foundations of Sovereignty and Other Essays*[9] were all part
of a research project that sought to critique the sovereign
legitimacy of the modern nation-state and question the
concomitant duties that its citizens were obliged to
demonstrate. Laski was intellectually indebted to J.N. Figgis
and his major work *Churches in the Modern* State[10] and was
influenced by Cole and French syndicalist ideas whilst
conducting his research on the state.[11] Laski termed his
approach the critique of 'mystic monism' in *Studies in the
Problem of Sovereignty* and Deane elucidates this point:

'Laski's earliest political writings are a constant polemic against what he terms 'mystic monism' in political thought – the conception that the state is to political theory what the Absolute is to metaphysics, that it is mysteriously One above all other human groupings, and that, because of its superior position and higher purpose, it is entitled to the undivided allegiance of each of its citizens.'[12]

Therefore, Laski's underlying assumptions as a political scientist were pluralistic in that he believed the state must be decentralised and that its huge power and influence required dissipation and dilution through various bodies at sub-state level. Moreover, he desired that political power should be placed in the hands of many groups so to protect individual liberty from an over-powerful state controlled by elites. It was in this sense that Laski's view of power and who should wield it was pluralist as opposed to elitist or Marxist. As a pluralist political scientist Laski was sceptical not only of the claims to sovereignty of the traditional nation-state but also to claims concerning the legitimacy of elite state actors:

'His desire to prevent the force of the state from being concentrated at any single point within it leads him to attack the idea of the state's sovereignty; he wants to see power split up, divided, set against itself, and thrown widespread among men by various devices of decentralisation, and he wants to be certain that the civil, economic, and social rights of individuals and groups are ensured against the encroachments of those who exercise power.'[13]

Therefore, as a libertarian Laski was unsurprisingly hesitant about the centralisation of political and economic power, a view he shared with Cole. Yet Laski, unlike Cole, was not a committed Guild socialist and though he found some syndicalist ideas interesting his antipathy to the state came much later when he believed that the state was inherently a device of capitalists. Anthony Wright suggests the similarities of two of the three 'Red Professors': 'Although Laski never called himself a Guild socialist, his own radical anti-statism put him very much under the same theoretical umbrella.'[14] Laski and Frida returned to England in 1920 and Laski immediately took up a Lectureship at the London School of Economics which he was associated with for the rest of his life becoming Graham Wallas Professor of Political Science in February 1926.   During the 1920s Laski's political thought was firmly in the Fabian socialist tradition and his academic publications, journalism and teaching reflected the radical tradition often associated with the British intelligentsia.

The third notable period is from 1931 until his death in 1950.   This was the period when Laski's thought changed significantly save his commitment to libertarianism. After the MacDonald 'betrayal' of 1931, Laski became increasingly disillusioned by the perceived advantages of pursuing socialism through parliamentary mechanisms. He came to feel that the capitalist state was structurally opposed to socialism, even if a Labour government was in power. It was after the fall of MacDonald's Government and during the throes of the Depression that Laski's drift towards Marxism gained pace. The words of other biographers of Laski, Isaac Kramnick and Barry Sheerman, recount his reticence for trying to achieve socialism through the institutions of the democratic capitalist state:

'If, then, finance-capital could act so powerfully on the minor issue of the level of dole, what would it do if a duly elected government truly sought to introduce socialism?...This was the issue for Laski in the 1930s, - a tug of war in his political soul between this logic and his scholarly and activist instincts that preferred social transformation through constitutional parliamentary processes.'[15]

During the Second World War Laski's writings evinced an inconsistency which one can argue stayed with him throughout the rest of his career. This does not refer to the tension between libertarianism and the strong state that needs to nationalise industries and finance to guarantee socialism in Britain. The inconsistencies referred to here pertain to Laski's conception of Marxism and his attitudes towards the democratic capitalist state in Britain. For example, from the mid-1930s onwards Laski extolled Marxist socialism in a number of publications [16] and simultaneously criticised parliamentary democracy as inadequate for realising socialism and being in essence a bourgeois instrument. Then, during the Second World War Laski began to espouse the virtues of the British democratic tradition in his wartime book, *Where Do We Go From Here?*[17] The language and sentiment are very similar to Evan Durbin's own short, wartime book, *What Have We to Defend?*[18] As Deane correctly notes, that as German fascism began to wane and the Allied victory appeared more likely Laski reinitiated his pre-war attitude present in *Faith, Reason and Civilisation*:[19] '...he tended to revert to his earlier analysis of Fascism and to fall back on the simple dichotomies of good and evil, socialism and capitalism, the progressive and peace-loving Soviet Union and the reactionary and imperialistic capitalist world led by the United States.'[20]

The Socialist Intellectual

In the first section of this chapter it has been asserted that Laski began as a left-leaning libertarian. As a political scientist his approach in his writings was initially pluralist, this changed on arrival back in Britain and as his political thought changed so did his theoretical approach as a political scientist. Laski's first major piece of socialist thought was *A Grammar of Politics* which can bee seen as representative of his initial democratic socialist phase, he described himself during this period as a Fabian socialist.[21] In *A Grammar of Politics*[22] Laski argued for nationalisation[23] and set out a strategy for socialism. Laski's pluralist approach to the state was replaced with a collectivist approach. It should not however, be assumed that Laski abandoned his libertarian principles when he discarded his pluralism. Newman says Laski was still a libertarian but not a pluralist because he was opposed to the centralised state but as a socialist saw the potential of the state particularly in economics. In the words of Kramnick and Sheerman: 'His ideal was a revival of the older Fabian principle of a "civic minimum", the provision by the state of a sufficient share of the primary material wants – food, shelter, health, education and employment.'[24] Laski was convinced of the merits of using the central state as a tool to secure specific socialist ends. He believed that if the state was used in such a way, it could simultaneously avoid the prospect of revolution and influence and affect the economy.[25] At this time and for much of his career Laski was fiercely critical of Bolshevism and the Russian Revolution of 1917 because of its violent class-war and the ensuing 'dictatorship of the proletariat'. Laski's liberal democratic ideals meant that he deplored the means used by the Communists to secure their ends.

The second period worth noting when charting the ideological trajectory of Laski is when he gradually moved away from moderate Fabian socialism to a more radical state socialism indiciative of the non-revolutionary Labour left of the late 1920s and early 1930s.[26] It is important to note that the Labour left was not a unified block but a plethora of socialist factions including the Independent Labour Party of Maxton and Christian socialist pacifists such as Lansbury, Marxists and of course the more conventional, non-revolutionary Labour left of Tawney, Cole and Attlee. It was this latter group that Laski moved in and most closely aligned himself with.   Interestingly, Newman claims the outcome of the General Strike did not further radicalise Laski but he also argues that at a similar time in the mid-1920s Laski was, '...now wrestling more constructively with the threat that communism presented to his own position.'[27] Newman says that Laski became associated with the left-wing of Labour in the early 1930s[28] but it can be suggested that after the outcome of the General Strike and his concerns with the domestic conduct of Soviet Russia and the persistent moderation of MacDonald, Snowden and Thomas as leading figures in the Labour Party, Laski was already becoming more radical than his earlier period as a Fabian socialist.   Many of the key figures on the non-revolutionary Labour left including Laski eventually became members of the Socialist League: 'The Socialist League emerged out of the inveterate disposition on the Left to form new groups to meet old problems, a tendency aggravated by the uneasiness with MacDonald just before and after his betrayal.'[29]   The inception of the Socialist League came when Cole, his wife Margaret and Lance Beales organised a weekend away with fellow Labour intellectuals to radicalise the left and to respond to what they viewed as acommodationism with the capitalist state and the ever-present gradualism and reformist liberalism of the Labour moderates. [30]   The Society for Socialist Inquiry and Propaganda was established in 1930 but it did not exist for long, because in 1932 the Independent Labour Party disaffiliated from the Labour Party and a group of ILP members decided to join the SSIP and merging together they formed the Socialist League under the Chairmanship of the ILP member E.F. Wise and following his death a year later he was succeeded by Stafford Cripps.[31]   The nature of the Socialist League is aptly demonstrated in a pamphlet authored by Laski entitled, *The Labour Party and the Constitution.*[32] As Kramnick and Sheerman note:

'The platform included the immediate socialistion of essential industrial enterprise and the financial system, but equally imperative were the legislative strategies to confront capitalist obstructionism. An Emergency Powers Act would give Parliament authority to take all necessary steps to deal with an emergency financial crisis or panic, through ministerial Orders of Council.'[33]

In this pamphlet Laski called for a range of policy prescriptions that represented radical, left-wing socialism. However, Socialist League members including Attlee, Cripps, Cole, Margaret Cole and (at that time) Laski were firmly within the traditions of democratic socialism advocating radical, but not proletariat revolutionary proposals:

'The Socialist League and Laski sought a revolutionary change in the British economy and social structure, but not as those to their left, like Strachey, advocated through a proletarian uprising. Although the popular Tory press helped to convince many that the League was bent Lenin-like on violent revolution and dictatorship (which lots of Labourites accepted as well), nowhere in the League's or Laski's literature is there the least suggestion of anything other than Parliament as the arena of political and social change.'[34]

The third and final period worth noting when charting the ideological trajectory of Laski's thought is from around 1933 when Laski's democratic socialism underwent a significant revision and arguably became a form of Marxist socialism.[35] His 1933 book, *Democracy in Crisis*[36] is perhaps the most interesting publication of Laski's career. It is indicative of his ideological journey and in it he openly attacks the nature and mechanisms of the capitalist state. This is noteworthy as it marks the final step away from his Labour left parliamentary socialism which stressed gradualist socialist measures through the existing constitution and state apparatus. Although evolutionary, the development of his political thought reaches something of a crossroads in this book. One can see the ever-present commitment to democratic traditions and the mode of parliamentary socialism by parties of the left and a pessimistic view which thought that the state was inherently capitalist and profoundly hostile to socialism, to the point that civil war would ultimately occur when the Labour Party pursuing socialism would clash with the interests of capital. Thus Laski felt that the only way to implement socialism was through a violent overthrow of the present system which would eventually manifest itself as communism:

'But even before January 1933 and the establishment of the Nazi regime in Germany, a deep-seated pessimism had superseded his vision of peaceful change, and he implied that the economic crisis was more likely to lead to revolution or a Right-wing dictatorship.'[37]

By 1937, Laski viewed Ernest Bevin and fellow right-wingers of the Labour Party like Hugh Dalton and Herbert Morrison as having become reformist ameliorators concerned only with mitigating the ills of capitalism. Laski felt that the moderates had ceased to be socialists committed to the transformation of British capitalist society.[38] Laski attempted to argue that he was not a Marxist understood as synonymous with communism and the totalitarian regime present in the Soviet Union, but that he was a Marxist socialist. As Kramnick and Sheerman suggest:

'In 1939 he wrote in the Nation "Why I am a Marxist". But, difficult as these distinctions might be for ordinary people to fathom, Laski was adamant he was a Marxist socialist and not a Marxist communist, by which he meant a Leninist or Stalinist. To be a Marxist, on the one hand, was for Laski, to be a real socialist as opposed to a social reformer.'[39]

In theoretical terms, Laski had become a Marxist socialist. That is, he had accepted Marx's theory of history as he felt it accurately accounted for contemporary British political events including the crisis of capitalism in the form of the Great Depression; bourgeois resistance to socialist advance in the form of the King bypassing Parliament and asking MacDonald to form a non-socialist National Government; and the rise of fascism in Europe in the form of Hitler and Mussolini and in Britain in the form of Mosley's British Union of Fascists. Deane maintains that Laski never desired a proletarian revolution even if he came to think that it was inevitable.[40] He further notes that Laski's most overtly Marxist statement came in an article entitled, 'A Key to Communism'[41] whereby he appears to endorse the explanatory power of Marxism in view of the collapse of capitalism in democratic states and the futility of social democratic parties in attempting parliamentary reformism.[42] In 1938 Laski authored *Parliamentary Government in England*[43] which advocated his Marxist socialism and concomitantly stressed his liberal democratic values of tolerance, liberty, free speech, free press and freedom of association.[44] A different interpretation of Laski is provided by Peter Lamb in his monograph on Laski's thought in which he argues that Laski was a Marxist not in the classical sense of endorsing the orthodox tenets of Marx (namely historical materialism, the labour theory of value, the inevitability of the collapse of capitalism, the establishment of the dictatorship of the proletariat and the eventual withering away of the state ushering in communism) but that he was broadly influenced by Marx:

'...being a Marxist can either mean holding every one of the beliefs that Marx considered to be his most important, or holding that one's own most important beliefs stem from the work of Marx. Laski was a Marxist in the latter sense.'[45]

However, this is an unsatisfactory and a sympathetic reading of Laski. By the mid-1930s Laski was evangelising the merits of Marxist socialism.[46] Lamb argues that Laski always believed that constitutional measures must be attempted meaning that socialism should be sought through parliamentary means.[47] What Lamb is correct in asserting is that Laski was never comfortable with, and never desired, violent revolution and the forcible overthrow of capitalist democracy, even if he believed at times that it would inevitably occur. Herein is the greatest weakness in Laski's political thought. Laski wrote too much, too quickly and failed to develop a robust position between orthodox or classical Marxism on the one hand and social democracy on the other. In addition, Laski's political activism and role as a socialist public intellectual led him to respond to everything, constantly writing and campaigning with little time to reflect and think deeply about the implications and often the inconsistencies of his work. This in itself is the main reason why his political thought has not been as enduring as Tawney's who wrote much less and developed his Christian socialist thesis over many years. This is not to say that Tawney did not advocate widely different policy prescriptions at given periods in time. However, Tawney's general thesis of wanting to create a more free and fraternal society through the reduction of material inequalities and through the abandonment of acquisitiveness in British culture, never changed very greatly.

Foote makes a pertinent point in the following extract. It is a point which accepts that Laski never ceased to hold the libertarian ideals of his early academic publications and that he admitted that the development of a 'socialist' society with such principles was a harder task than he previously had thought:

'In a new preface to (*A Grammar of Politics*), he made it clear that he had not rejected the libertarian principles first laid down there – indeed, time had reinforced their truth – but that he had overestimated the ease with which such a society could emerge.'[48]

What is more difficult to accept is that Laski's Marxism could ever be compatible with his libertarian principles and the underlying worth he often implicitly gave to democracy. In some ways Laski's thought can be seen as a forerunner to the neo-Marxism of the mid-twentieth century. To the revisionist Marxists who wanted to endorse the transformative power of Marxist socialism and the values of equality and fraternity amongst the working class but who simultaneously eschew violent revolution and class-war. In effect such later socialists were trying to articulate a democratic Marxism. To some, such a phrase is oxymoronic. Nevertheless, this was Laski's dilemma and the central weakness in the final ideological period of his thought.

Conclusion

Harold Laski was a complex figure whose writing contained stark tensions and conflicts. Kramnick and Sheerman sum up the tensions and conflicts in Laski's life: 'He was a collectivist and an individualist, a Marx and a Voltaire...He

loved America and fiercely criticised it. He saw Soviet
Russia as the harbinger of a new civilisation and its crimes
broke his heart.'[49] To an extent philosophical tensions are
present in all political thought, but they were especially
prevalent in the thought of Laski. Especially the tension
between centralisation versus decentralisation of state power
and between non-violent democratic processes versus
Marxist revolution of the proletariat. It is fair to say that
Laski was a central figure in the policy debates that shaped
the Labour Party from the 1920s until the Second World
War but by the time of his death in 1950 the Attlee
Government had implemented historic and significant social
and economic changes. Laski's thought and his ideas did
not, after his death, live on in the debates that shaped the
Labour Party in the post-war era. This is not to say that in
his life-time he was not influential. As a teacher he was
immensely popular and inspirational to a generation of
politically interested students: 'Michael Foot remembers
that when he went to Oxford some years later, "we all read
Laski's *Communism*, the first real book on communism by an
English critic." It also led many Tories like Baldwin to see
Laski as the major intellectual influence of the Labour
Party.'[50] In terms of influencing the Labour Party, he did so
again as a teacher: '…among the Labour MPs elected in the
landslide of 1945 sixty-seven had once studied with him as
either university students, trade unionists in workers
educational courses or officers in wartime courses.'[51] He
reached the minds of many students who later became
politicians such as Pierre Trudeau and Krishna Menon and
students who became notable academics and thinkers
themselves like C.B MacPherson, Ralph Miliband, Bernard
Crick and John Saville.

As a socialist academic Laski's partisan works also reached
many people. This was partly because of his well connected
American friends who enabled his work to reach a large
transatlantic audience. It was also partly because of his

indefatigable work ethic which kept him delivering lectures, speeches, authoring pamphlets, newspaper articles, journal articles and writing dozens of books. Moreover, it was because Laski genuinely cared about teaching and enjoyed debating with his students so much, that he and Frida opened their home to his students for dinner and debates throughout his career. If Laski did not win people over through the moral force of his arguments then he often won them over through his personality and his passion for the free exchange of ideas. It is not hyperbole to assert that Laski was the pre-eminent British socialist public intellectual of the 1920s and 1930s.

Nevertheless and similarly to Cole, Laski's thought has not endured in the Labour Party in the way that Tawney's has. This is partly because Tawney's thesis is essentially moral and provided the ethical critique of capitalism and the normative case for a society to be designed around principles such community as fellowship and a diminution of inequalities in income and wealth. The postwar settlement implemented by the Attlee Government made Britain a more democratic socialist nation and the subsequent period often dominated by years of Conservative rule engendered a new and different range of problems for democratic socialists to address. The emergence of the Cold War exposed Laski's Marxist socialist position to widespread scrutiny and criticism inside and outside the Labour Movement. He favoured the Marxism of the Soviet Union but detested its totalitarianism and he was fond of America and Americans – many of whom were his closest friends – but deplored it as the citadel of laissez-faire capitalism. Max Beloff famously wrote that: '...the future historian may talk of the period between 1920 and 1950 as the "Age of Laski".'[52] This is certainly a tribute though perhaps an overstatement. A more objective observation is that Laski, despite his philosophical shortcomings, was without doubt the pre-eminent British, socialist public intellectual of his generation.

[1] H. Laski, *Communism* (Thornton Butterworth, London, 1927), p. 250.

[2] H. Laski, *The State in Theory and Practice* (George Allen & Unwin, London, 1935), p.318.

[3] Thorough assessments of Laski's political thought have been undertaken in two notable monographs; see H. Deane, *The Political Ideas of Harold J. Laski* (Columbia University Press, New York, 1954) and P. Lamb, *Harold Laski: Problems of Democracy, the Sovereign State and International Society* (Palgrave Macmillan, Basingstoke, 2004). These two books present different accounts of the validity and consistency of Laski's thought. It is partly because of contribution of these monographs that this chapter does not seek to evaluate Laski's main works in detail and, partly because Laski's canon is too vast to analyse in a single chapter.

[4] Deane, *The Political Ideas of Harold J. Laski*, p.5.

[5] M. Newman, *Harold Laski: A Political Biography* (Macmillan, Basingstoke, 1993), p.16.

[6] Ibid. p.30.

[7] H. Laski, *Studies in the Problem of Sovereignty* (Yale University Press, New Haven, 1917).

[8] H. Laski, *Authority in the Modern State* (Yale University Press, New Haven, 1919).

[9] H. Laski, *The Foundations of Sovereignty and Other Essays* (Harcourt Brace and Co., New York, 1921.

[10] J.N. Figgis, *Churches in the Modern State* (Longmans, London, 1913).

[11] Newman, *Harold Laski: A Political Biography*, p.55.

[12] Deane, *The Political Ideas of Harold J. Laski*, p.14.

[13] Ibid. p.17.

[14] A. Wright, *G.D.H. Cole and Socialist Democracy* (Clarendon Press, Oxford, 1979,) p.14.

[15] I. Kramnick and B. Sheerman, *Harold Laski: A Life on the Left* (Allen Lane, London, 1993), p.300.

[16] Laski's books from his Marxist socialist perspective include: H. Laski, *Democracy in Crisis* (George Allen & Unwin, London, 1933), H. Laski, *The State in Theory and Practice*, London (George Allen & Unwin, London, 1935), H. Laski, *Parliamentary Government in England* (Viking, New York, 1938), H. Laski, *Reflections on the Revolution of Our Times* (Viking Press, New York, 1943), H. Laski, *Faith, Reason and Civilisation* (Viking Press, New York, 1944), H. Laski, *The American Democracy* (Viking Press, New York, 1948), H. Laski, *Trade Unions in the New Society* (Viking Press, New York, 1949).

[17] H. Laski, *Where Do We Go From Here?* (Penguin Books, London, 1940).

[18] E. Durbin, *What Have We To Defend?* (George Routledge and Sons, London, 1942).

[19] H. Laski, *Faith, Reason and Civilisation.*

[20] Deane, *The Political Ideas of Harold J. Laski*, p.239.

[21] Newman, *Harold Laski: A Political Biography*, p.78.

[22] H. Laski, *A Grammar of Politics* (George Allen & Unwin, London, 1925).

[23] Newman, *Harold Laski: A Political Biography*, p.83.

[24] Kramnick and Sheerman, *Harold Laski: A Life on the Left*, p.228.

[25] Newman, *Harold Laski: A Political Biography*, p.75.

[26] A letter from MacDonald requesting Laski's help in campaigning in the 1929 General Election in Seaham where Harry Pollit was staying and the fact that he responded demonstartes Laski's loyalty to the Labour Party and that even whilst a Labour left figure he was determined to challenge Marxism in the form of the Communist Party of Great Britain at that time. See Letter to Laski from MacDonald, 16th April 1929, DLA/43, Laski Papers, University of Hull.

[27] Newman, *Harold Laski: A Political Biography*, p.103.

[28] Ibid. p.133.

[29] Kramnick and Sheerman, *Harold Laski: A Life on the Left*, p.304.

[30] Ibid.

[31] Ibid. p.305.

[32] H. Laski, *The Labour Party and the Constitution* (Socialist League, London, 1933).

[33] Kramnick and Sheerman, *Harold Laski: A Life on the Left*, p.308.

[34] Ibid. p.318.

[35] For a good discussion of Laski's journey from democratic socialism to Marxism see Deane, *The Political Ideas of Harold J. Laski*, pp. 201-218.

[36] H. Laski, *Democracy in Crisis.*

[37] Newman, *Harold Laski: A Political Biography*, p.147.

[38] Kramnick and Sheerman, *Harold Laski: A Life on the Left*, p. 378.

[39] Ibid. pp.360-361.

[40] Deane, *The Political Ideas of Harold J. Laski*, p.205.

[41] H. Laski, 'A Key to Communism' Review of *Marxism and Modern Thought* by N. Bukharin et al, *The New Statesmen and Nation*, X, July 20th 1935.

[42] Deane, *The Political Ideas of Harold J. Laski*, p.201.

[43] Laski, *Parliamentary Government in England.*

[44] Kramnick and Sheerman, *Harold Laski: A Life on the Left*, pp.382-383.

[45] Lamb, *Harold Laski: Problems of Democracy, the Sovereign State and International Society*, pp. 8-9.

[46] Evidence of the radicalisation of Laski's political thought by the mid-1930s and his commitment to Marxist socialism can be found in the chapter 'The Revolutionary Claim' in H. Laski, *Democracy in Crisis*, pp. 234-266. Another pertinent source is a letter from F. Gousev on behalf of Stalin thanking Laski for his efforts in trying to strengthen relations between the UK and the Soiviet Union. See Letter to Laski from F. Gousev, 15th June 1945, DLA/43, Laski Papers, University of Hull.

[47] Lamb, *Harold Laski: Problems of Democracy, the Sovereign State and International Society*, p.26.

[48] G. Foote, *The Labour Party's Political Thought* (Macmillan, Basingstoke, 1997), p.150.

[49] Kramnick and Sheerman, *Harold Laski: A Life on the Left*, p.590.

[50] Ibid. p.259.

[51] Ibid. p.587.

[52] M. Beloff, 'The Age of Laski', *Fortnightly Review*, June 1950, p.378.

5

EVAN DURBIN[1]

'There is more unity expressed in the sharpest and angriest debate in the House of Commons, than in all the marching and counter-marching and shouting enthusiasm of a National-Socialist Rally or an All-Soviet Party Conference in Moscow. There is more unity in a querulous House because the Opposition is present, because men of different opinions may meet and argue and quarrel, and yet appreciate the common good and live to serve it.'[2]

Evan Durbin was one of the most influential British thinkers of the 1940s and one of the Labour Party's most able advocates of democratic socialism, yet he is relatively overlooked by historians of Britain.[3] This chapter seeks to do several things. Firstly, it attempts to provide a short review of Durbin's democratic socialism.[4] Secondly, it attempts to explain and position Durbin's socialism within the ideological groupings of the Labour Party. Thirdly, and most significantly the chapter attempts to appraise the role of patriotism in Durbin's socialism and to try and understand the debate socialists had about the concept of patriotism in the context of the 1930s and 1940s.

Durbin's Democratic Socialism

The Politics of Democratic Socialism was first published in 1940, and written between 1938-1939. In the eyes of Donald Sassoon Durbin's book is the exemplar of democratic socialism.[5] Durbin believed that democracy and socialism were inextricably linked. You could not have socialism without democracy. Such was Durbin's attitude towards the ethical basis of socialism as democratic in nature that Chapter 4 of *The Politics of Democratic Socialism* is given to examine the relationship between these ideas. He opens this chapter with the following question: 'If the method of dictatorship is an unlikely way to secure social justice, what alternative method is open to us? I wish to argue that the only conceivable route to a better social order lies in the pathway of democracy, and that the political method of democratic government is an essential principle, not an accidental accompaniment, of any just society.'[6]

Durbin was passionately against Marxism and Labour Marxist ideas prevalent in the Party in the 1920s and 1930s. In particular he challenged their class analysis of the state and the need to attack the financial power of the ruling class for socialism to 'truly' be realised. As a democratic socialist he firmly believed in gradual social change and felt that democracy was far too valuable to risk losing. Brian Brivati records that when Durbin and Gaitskell embarked on their academic careers and were associating with leading socialists in the Labour Movement such as Hugh Dalton and Nicholas Davenport of the XYZ Club Durbin's democratic credentials found him considerable respect:

'In the early 1930s Gaitskell was somewhat compromised in Dalton's eyes by his association with G.D.H. Cole and his brief Marxist period. In contrast, Durbin had always made a comparison between the fascist and the Soviet style of politics, refusing even to join Tots and Quots or the 1917

Club[7] because they contained too many Marxists, and had worked out a coherent theory of democratic socialism which he published in 1940...'[8]

This democratic foundation in Durbin's thought led him to conclude that despite Britain's gross economic inequalities and the divisive class system, there was more that united British citizens (in terms of their democratic rights and responsibilities) than there was that divided them (in terms of cultural or ideological differences). He declared that the central task for democratic socialists was '...the control of industry and the distribution of income....'[9] The transfer of economic power from private interest in to the hands of the state and the redistribution of real income from the rich to the poorer classes. He said that four types of strategic measures existed and needed to be implemented if a socialist government wanted to fully transform Britain's capitalist society:

1. Ameliorative measures: extension of social services to ameliorate poverty.[10]
2. Socialisation measures: nationalisation of industry and the acquisition of economic power by the state for central planning.[11] (Although he did suggest that there might be 'half-way houses' which would transfer substantial control to the state without changing the ownership of industry.)[12]
3. Prosperity measures: legislative and administrative acts to maintain and increase the 'volume of industrial activity'.[13] (Durbin felt that socialist economists had overlooked the importance of maintaining production especially in the period of transition from a capitalist to a socialist society that could take a very long time).
4. Egalitarian measures: aimed at changing the inequality between classes towards a fairer

distribution of income and wealth. Use of
inheritance tax and progressive income tax.[14]

Defining Mr. Durbin

When trying to define Durbin two interesting questions
arise. What type of democratic socialist was he and what
ideological grouping, if any, did he fit into in the Labour
Party? Durbin is difficult to pigeonhole in terms of
ideological groupings in the Labour Party. This is partly
because his life and thought spans the pre-1945 and post-
1945 eras. Labour historians tend to analyse Labour ideas in
these eras. During the cross-over of this period the centre
of gravity shifted in the national Labour Party and in British
politics generally due to factors such as the defeat of Nazi
Germany, the emergence of the Soviet Union as a
totalitarian socialist superpower, the achievements of the
Attlee Government such as the welfare state and full
employment and the economic consensus between the
Conservative and Labour Party towards Keynesian demand
management. So, where does that leave us with
understanding Durbin's political loyalties?

Durbin could be viewed as occupying several strands of
thought in the Labour Party; on the centre-left, as an early
right-wing revisionist or as a centrist in the Labour Party of
the 1930s and 1940s. By centrist I follow Noel Thompson
in understanding that the term represents the '...matrix of
values, aspirations, analysis and prescriptions to which at any
point in time, a critical mass of the Party gravitates.'[15]
According to Geoffrey Foote, Durbin understood the
differences in the debate between those who followed
Hobson and those who applied Keynes's ideas over the
appropriate type of political economy for democratic
socialism in the 1930s. In his book *Purchasing Power and Trade
Depression*[16] he critiqued Hobson's ideas of under-

consumption of the economy from a type of Keynesian viewpoint. The Labour left held Hobson's economic prescription at the time and Durbin roundly criticised them for their flawed assumptions. Yet at the same time, his own economic solutions could be regarded as radical. Foote states that in Durbin's mind:

'...the failure of a planless economy to respond to a rise in savings by converting those savings to investment would cause a general depression, since the hoarding of capital would lead to a contraction of consumption goods and, therefore, capital goods (which Durbin believed to be totally dependent on the market for consumption goods)...This would bring about a general contraction of the economic system, leading to unemployment and social insecurity. Only a planned socialist economy - where government, banking, industrial and trade union action was centrally co-ordinated - would be able to overcome the trade cycle of boom and slump which had come to characterise capitalism.'[17]

Therefore, Durbin's position on central planning was a centre-left position within the Labour Party. Durbin was won over by the arguments for economic organisation as a means to bring order out of the chaos of laissez-faire capitalism. As time passed and the inefficiencies of the Soviet planned economy became more apparent, the idea of widespread central planning as the way to transform a capitalist society in to a socialist society became a more marginalised idea but remained as an important economic prescription along with widespread nationalisation for the post-1945 Labour left led by Nye Bevan and underpinned by Richard Crossman in his book *Planning for Freedom*.[18]

The reason it is suggested that Durbin held a 'type of Keynesian viewpoint' is that his political economy was not conventional Keynesianism that his friends Gaitskell and Jay later implemented in government in the 1940s and early 1950s.[19] This is because Durbin desired greater control of economic decision-making for the state. He argued for a supreme economic authority, which could undertake economic planning and widespread nationalisation of finance and industry. In this sense his political economy was more similar to Strachey than it was to Gaitskell or Jay. One could class Durbin as a 'Keynesian planner' because he emphasised a macroeconomic strategy of central planning and state ownership as well as Keynesian fiscal policy. His political economy was not that of market orthodoxy espoused by figures such as MacDonald and Snowden in the early 1930s, nor was it the Labour Marxism that talked of abolishing the private sector of the economy and nor was it simply conventional Keynesianism. At heart, Durbin straddled the traditions of the Fabian technocrat seeking to solve macro-economic problems and the socialist who trumpets the need for social ownership as the only realistic countermeasure to the market.

Keynesianism was not Labour economic policy until the late 1940s and because of this it did not receive widespread acceptance until its implementation under the Attlee Government. One could argue that this was in part due to Keynesianism's apparent lack of transformative impetus which made it seem like an economic doctrine that was designed to ameliorate the harsher aspects of capitalism rather than one that socialists would use to gradually change Britain's capitalist economy into a socialist economy. Durbin's desire to change Britain's capitalist economy by using a variety of measures including Keynesian demand management, central planning and nationalisation was in stark contrast to the moderate socialist ambivalence of Dalton and Morrison towards large-scale nationalisation and planning and their satisfaction in utilising Keynesian demand management and the redistribution of wealth. Thus, Durbin's political economy should be seen not as of the revisionist right but of the centre-left in the Labour Party of the 1930s and 1940s.

Durbin had a long-term, explicit hostility to communism. He was in no way predisposed to Soviet sympathies which meant that he was firmly in the centre of Labour thought. So why is he regarded as being overtly a rightwing revisionist? Firstly, Durbin regarded himself as a moderate in the Labour Party of the 1930s[20] but this merely meant he was not a Labour Marxist or a fellow traveller. Secondly, it has been largely an error of hindsight. Durbin's influence on Gaitskell and Dalton is remembered and as the domestic Labour Party context evolved these individuals became leading exponents of the revisionist right with its commitment to conventional Keynesian demand management. Thus, by association Durbin became a figure or honorary member of Labour right revisionism.

Thus, Durbin's stands out as holding a unique position to the point where the centre-left of the 1930s; the centrist tendencies of the 1940s; and posthumously the revisionist right of the 1950s and beyond could lay claim to aspects of his thought. Of the three ideological groupings the claim of the revisionist right is patently the weakest of the arguments and yet because of his multiple associations with varying strands of democratic socialist thought no one ideological grouping can fully claim him. Durbin was a democratic socialist who believed a socialist society would need to involve widespread economic planning and nationalisation; he was consistently hostile to Marxist thought and Soviet communism; and he influenced some significant future politicians on the revisionist right in the Labour Party.

Now we turn to the next purpose of the chapter, namely to understand the role of patriotism in Durbin's socialism. We begin by evaluating the few, but notable statements of patriotism in Durbin's main work, *The Politics of Democratic Socialism*. Then move on to consider *What Have We To Defend?* a book that sought to argue for patriotism and for the moral necessity of war. This investigation has not been undertaken before and it continues the project of restoring the ideas of Durbin, arguably one of Britain's most influential thinkers of the 1940s to the mainstream of British history and discusses the connection between patriotism and democratic socialism in the Labour Party.

Patriotism in *The Politics of Democratic Socialism*[21]

Within the essays that make up *The Politics of Democratic Socialism* there are several patriotic references and some passages that are overt statements of patriotism.[22] Durbin was writing the book when Britain had declared war on Nazi Germany. He had observed the build up of Hitler's Nazis in the 1930s and the development of Stalin's Russia throughout the 1920s. With this political backdrop it is understandable that Durbin felt that it was possible for Britain to be defeated in World War Two.

Some of the prose in *The Politics of Democratic Socialism* is evocative and appears at times to be a rallying cry to stand and fight for British democracy and peace. Durbin's patriotism emanated from the value he placed in Britain's democratic institutions, its peace and its liberties. He believed in them and also saw the need to defend them from the growing domestic political parties that promulgated fascism and communism: 'We could not walk quietly in our traditional paths of liberty if either of our violent parties grew to power, or if we were on the losing side in the present European war.'[23] Describing his faith in the British parliamentary, democratic process compared to the alleged 'national unity' offered in Hitler and Stalin's states he asserted:

'There is more unity expressed in the sharpest and angriest debate in the House of Commons, than in all the marching and counter-marching and shouting enthusiasm of a National-Socialist Rally or an All-Soviet Party Conference in Moscow. There is more unity in a querulous House because the Opposition is present, because men of different opinions may meet and argue and quarrel, and yet appreciate the common good and live to serve it.' [24]

However, a footnote in *The Politics of Democratic Socialism* pertaining to patriotism appears to cast doubt on the logic of why Durbin is an advocate of patriotism. In the following passage Durbin seems to suggest that it is not desirable that national unity be preserved in order to affect individual well-being:

'It appears to me to be obvious a. that the happiness of the individual must always depend, objectively and subjectively, upon the unity and health of some social group, b. that the dominant group of the historical period in which we live is the nation-state. Hence it is essential, for the continuation of individual well-being, that national unity should be preserved. In saying this I am not contending that these things are desirable. Loyalty to the nation is not in my view the greatest or finest loyalty. Unless it becomes the channel through which greater loyalty to mankind can flow, national patriotism is exclusive and dangerous. But we have to deal with people as they are, and to admit the power and contemporary importance of loyalty to the national group.'[25]

He appears to justify this view by arguing that loyalty to the nation (patriotism) is not the 'greatest' or 'finest' loyalty and unless 'it becomes the channel through which greater loyalty to mankind can flow' it remains 'exclusive and dangerous'. If Durbin means that for many British citizens loyalty to the nation is 'exclusive and dangerous' because it is a loyalty solely to Britain and its people instead of equal loyalty to humanity including citizens of Russia or Germany, then Durbin has misunderstood what patriotism means. This is because it is an idea that prides the nation one is from, and values it as one's homeland and values one's fellow citizens as in some sense an immediate community (which is comprised of one's family, extended family, close friends, colleagues, neighbours and acquaintances). It places loyalty and value to a nation's way of doing things, its culture, history, language, and territory to name but a few factors. Thus, of course patriotism places special value on a single nation-state say on Britain instead of Germany because British people are from Britain and to a large extent Britain has made them what they are (Durbin previously argues this very point).[26] So what else could he have meant?

It is possible that Durbin was trying to distinguish between openly xenophobic ideas disguised as 'honest patriotism'. It is contended here that he was suggesting that there is good and bad patriotism. For example, if patriotism merely promotes loyalty to the nation state at any moral cost it then becomes fascism. If this is why Durbin felt that loyalty to humanity was the ultimate form of loyalty then he is right. If this was not what he was trying to say then his logic is flawed and two philosophical problems arise from this. Firstly, it is very difficult to distinguish feelings of value and warmth towards one's nation-state and feelings of superiority over other nation-states. One can love Britain and be patriotic towards it as a nation-state whilst not believing it to be racially superior to other nation-states. But one can feel glad to be born in Britain and on reflection would not choose to be anything else but British. One gets to this view because as Durbin himself noted Britain has shaped the outlook of its people. For example, two individuals can wave the Union flag with equal fervour but have different reasons for doing so and could be morally opposed to each other. This is why it is crucial to define what patriotism is and is not. It is why it is important to explain what an individual like Durbin thought of the merits of 'good patriotism'. The second problem is related to the first namely, that not all nation-states are democracies and not all of them uphold human rights. Thus we make value judgments on what makes a good nation-state and why. Durbin clearly believed that despite its flaws Britain was a better nation-state than Germany or Russia and that there were bad individuals in those nation-states causing them to behave immorally. In short, this confusing footnote of Durbin's exposes him to philosophical criticism and this it is argued is where *The Politics of Democratic Socialism* is at its weakest. Durbin's book provides - largely speaking - robust economic and political arguments for democracy and socialism. In *The Politics of Democratic Socialism* the philosophical justification for patriotism needed to be stronger and more analytical but *What Have We To Defend?* - the book to which we now turn - is a cogent argument for patriotism and for the necessity of war.

Patriotism in *What Have We To Defend?*

In *What Have We To Defend?* Durbin's patriotism is clear. The book's main thesis is to articulate the ethics of the British way of life and in particular, to highlight the value of what he calls the 'British social tradition'. In essence it is an apologia for Britain and its *raison d'etre*. When discussing Durbin and patriotism this is the fundamental text and it is also the last significant publication of his life and was published two years after *The Politics of Democratic Socialism* in 1942. Durbin's tone is unashamedly patriotic and emotive. He did not have to write in such a style to generate support for the War effort as Britain was fully mobilised at the time. Nor was it engineered in such a way to challenge widespread dissent that occurred during the conflict, as only 2% of

Britons were conscientious objectors.[27]   In fact he did not have to worry about many people reading it as people were deeply involved in the war effort and paper was rationed so the level of circulation was thin.   Several letters written to him by friends note the disappointment that so few copies were published and were in circulation.[28]   The only option left for us to conclude is that Durbin was a patriotic socialist.

What Have We To Defend? was a project Durbin felt he ought to write, partly as a justification for war and partly to declare the righteousness of a just war to defend the existence of a nation that in many ways was good, but - in his view - with potential to be better.   Durbin's patriotism was in large part based on reasoned argument rather than romanticism though there are examples of romanticism and exaggeration in the following quotations from *What Have We To Defend?*: 'We are not tolerant through carelessness. Instead we are united in a community of a positive and creative affection – of love for one another – in turbulent brotherhood.'[29]   '…I repeat my claim that British society is one of the finest that men have yet built for themselves.'[30] 'These greater Englishmen of the future will do splendid things.   They will abolish inferiority in the dignity of Englishmen, seeing that no child born in this land falls short of equal access to the means of happiness.'[31]

In one of Durbin's preparatory notes when drafting *What Have We To Defend?* he poses bold questions about the forthcoming war, and asks, 'Is it worth the struggle?   For what are we fighting?'[32]   In the context of writing it one can appreciate why he raises such questions.   He is not therefore thinking the unthinkable - weighing up whether life would really be better living under German colonial rule or as slaves in a labour camp called *England*.   He is using the questions as rhetorical devices to set out an argument for war.   He cites preserving Britain's national existence as a democratic and free nation-state.   This is patriotism in the face of death.   It is first-order patriotism in the face of possible national, cultural, and political annihilation. The following quotation from one of his unpublished private papers clearly demonstrates this:

'...I believe it is our duty to fight in this country, for the preservation of our national existence. I should not feel such an obligation if I were the citizen of a dictatorially governed nation – whether Fascist or Communist. But living in a country that has slowly built up a system of responsible government, I believe that it is worth our while to die in order to preserve the way of life that has become natural to us.'[33]

Although it may occasionally sound nostalgic or romantic in tone Durbin's patriotism was not blinkered. It was not the unquestioning patriotism that asserts that one's nation can do no wrong. In chapter 3 of *What Have We To Defend?* Durbin outlines four characteristics of British social life that he finds morally offensive and classes as 'national faults'. These are the unjust distribution of wealth; the class system; modern vandalism against Britain's national heritage both in the town and the countryside; and limitations in the understanding and imagination of British society.[34] Nor was his patriotism the 'High-Tory' patriotism that displayed reverence and nostalgia for the days of empire. In *What Have We To Defend?* Durbin has a chapter on empire and his views seem complex. On one hand he states: 'Large parts of the Empire – India and the Colonies – have not yet reached a satisfactory independence, we remain ignorant of our great responsibilities to their native people and we have not surmounted the prejudice of colour.'[35] From this it is clear he is not an imperialist. That said, he does not feel that Britain's current prosperity (in 1940) is dependent upon 'political conquest or control...'[36] His argument states that, 'We did approximately 54 per cent of our export trade with foreign countries in 1938; and another 34 per cent with the

Dominions and India which possess complete sovereignty in the regulation of their trade and use their power to impose tariff barriers against us…Again it is true to say that the whole of this trade might disappear overnight and we should scarcely notice any difference in our domestic prosperity.'[37] Thus making his views appear at best naïve and at worst ambivalent to the price paid by the former colonies and their peoples, to guarantee Britain its wealth and power.

Furthermore, Durbin's patriotism was not a belief that Britain was racially or morally superior to other nations. If it was anything more than first-order or wartime patriotism – and by that I mean the realisation that one must fight against the evil of Nazism or see one's country capitulate – it appears to have been patriotism based on the value of what he calls the British social tradition. He states the conventions of contested elections, relative social peace, civil liberties, political dissent and toleration - as values worth defending and to be proud of. Democracy for Durbin involved several factors: government chosen by the people, legal opposition to the government and an implicit undertaking between the parties contending for power in the nation state not to persecute each other, and peaceful alternation of parties in government. Therefore, it can be seen that what Durbin truly valued was the social tradition of British parliamentary democracy and its concomitant principles.

Anti-Patriotism and Socialism

It is accurate to say that some socialists and Marxists oppose the connection between patriotism and socialism. According to Marx, group pride and loyalty are part of the identity one feels with one's class not the nation-state that according to him is an instrument of bourgeois repression.[38] In his 1916 book *Imperialism: The Highest Stage of Capitalism*[39],

Lenin tried to understand the problem facing Marxism during World War One namely, why Marxists were choosing to fight for their nation-state rather than in solidarity with their class in their own nation and in the other nations embroiled in the war. For example German Marxists voted for the war budget and Lenin faced the fact that Marx's predictions of the imminent collapse of capitalism and the revolutionary character of the proletariat was incorrect.[40] The working classes across Western Europe including many Marxists followed the call to patriotism and to fight and possibly die for one's nation-state. In the words of George Sabine and Thomas Thorson:

'The outbreak of World War One in 1914, and more especially the support of the war by socialist parties of Western Europe, turned Lenin's thought in a new direction...The war put Marxism into the context of national and international politics, and the defection of Marxists from their internationalist and anti-patriotic professions proved that these were matters of primary concern for the strategy of revolution.'[41]

In a 1937 article in the *Daily Herald* Durbin wrote *Why I'm Not A Marxist* an opposition piece to John Strachey's *Why I Am A Marxist*:

'...the more important mistake made by Marxists, and particularly by communists, is their repudiation of continuous democracy...Marxists have always argued that revolution and the subsequent 'dictatorship of the proletariat' are the only method of doing it (ending the class struggle). I am not a Marxist because I do not believe that a just or decent society can be set up that way...A revolution means civil war, and quite apart from the question as to who would win such a war in England, it could never lead to greater social justice. The victorious party, if it were the

Communist Party, could only govern by force. It could only hold opposition by the instrument of political terror – by victimisation, torture, shooting and all the hideous paraphernalia of a secret police. It would substitute one form of injustice for another. Whatever else is gained social justice is not gained by such expedients as these.'[42]

As a democratic socialist Durbin firmly believed in gradual social change and felt that democracy was far too valuable to risk losing and he realised that national unity and national sentiment was a reality which transcended class boundaries and that it was important to many people.[43] George Orwell[44] echoed Durbin's view, a view which was in stark contrast to the orthodox Marxist analysis of patriotism and class: 'Patriotism is usually stronger than class-hatred, and always stronger than any kind of internationalism.'[45] Durbin moved further in this analysis by suggesting whether it is liked or not, the community of the nation-state has formed its citizens and it is this bond which ignites loyalty in the citizen towards the nation-state.[46] What is interesting is that Durbin seems to imply that it does not matter who the state is governed by providing it remains a democratic nation-state. This is because many of its citizens will remain loyal to it as an idea and will perpetuate deep-seated feelings of connection towards it. He suggests that:

'The Fascist says, and says rightly, that national unity is one of the first necessities of political life. Rightly or wrongly, our primary loyalties are directed towards, and some of our deepest passions stirred by, the life and character of the geographical and racial group to which we belong. We grew up in its culture. It has entered into our bones and made us what we are. In a very real sense it is part of us. As a consequence, much of the wealth, security and derivative well-being of the individual depend objectively upon the unified and successful administration of the nation state, and subjectively the happiness of the individual may be bound up with the unity of the nation.'[47]

Writing in his Labour Marxist phase (before his conversion to a moderate, democratic socialism) John Strachey asserted in *The Theory and Practice of Socialism* that patriotism in one's country before it becomes a socialist country is futile: 'The immediate denunciation as a traitor to his country of everyone who questions the capitalists' absolute power is evidence that what the capitalists are intent that the people should defend is a country which belongs lock, stock and barrel to them...Thus socialists and communists do not question the right of men to defend their country; but we do recommend that they should first acquire a country to defend. Till then we are bound to protest and to struggle against the exploitation of nationalist sentiment by the capitalists for their own benefit.' [48] Therefore if one's country was not yet socialist as Britain was not when Strachey penned these views, the question which is begged becomes 'Should workers living in a capitalist democracy not fight, defend and die for their liberty?' and also 'Is not capitalist democracy better than fascism?' It was this type of attitude which Durbin, in his private papers regarded as a '...lot of nonsense talked by the left...'[49] with regard to patriotism and value in the nation-state. He further berated the anti-military mindedness of left intellectuals: '...the wicked neglect by intellectuals of the left like myself – of military service – of my position at the LSE – the WEA...'[50] This does suggest a remnant of guilt in not serving in frontline duties because between 1940-1942 Durbin was placed in the Economics Section of the War Cabinet Secretariat and from 1942-1945 he served as personal assistant to Deputy Prime Minister Clement Attlee. In addition, he feels that the British intelligentsia are responsible yet again but this time for failing to grasp the contemporary nature of international relations and in particular the rise of Hitler and the Nazi rearmament of the 1930s: 'We knew nothing of the basis since 1933 of international relations.'[51]   In this regard he feels the intellectuals above all others should have alerted the public and the politicians to the threat of Hitler. Later in the same paper he broadens the burden of responsibility for what he calls 'the disaster – our plight in June 1940'[52] and cites the follies of Chamberlain's Government and the Labour Opposition implying the woeful lack of preparedness for war with Hitler and for misjudging the Munich agreement: 'The government for no armaments, the Opposition for opposing armaments, all of us because we are free people. The real truth…the slowness of the change of opinion after 1933 - the fundamental turning point.'[53]

Frank Pakenham was another like-minded socialist critical of the anti-patriotism that emanated from elements of the leftist intelligentsia. During wartime such criticisms became elevated and its impact was heightened as national unity and solidarity became crucially important for morale at home and abroad.   In his review of *What Have We to Defend?* Pakenham says: 'The taunt has often been levelled at socialists that they love every country but their own, and, though the charge was usually untrue and on occasions such as Munich has been returned with interest; the Left have admittedly kept singularly quiet about patriotism in the past. The Tories prudently appropriated such national symbols as the Monarchy, the Flag, and Empire, putting heart into their tamest meetings with the National Anthem and leaving Labour to fall back on the Red Flag and the International.'[54] Though not an intellectual in the vein of Durbin or Orwell, Pakenham, an educated, thoughtful socialist affirmed Durbin's logic for the need to fight the war and affirmed a secondary purpose, which was to debunk anti-patriotism prevalent amongst the intellectual elites of the British left. Orwell also criticised a certain faction of English socialist intellectuals for their contempt towards patriotism regardless of its purpose. Orwell's following remarks from *The Lion and the Unicorn* show his contempt for the 'fashionable', Bloomsbury ideas which to him were harmful and distasteful: 'During the past twenty years the negative, *fainéant* outlook which has been fashionable among English left-wingers, the sniggering of the intellectuals at patriotism and physical courage, the persistent effort to chip away English morale and spread a hedonistic, what-do-I-get-out-of-it attitude to life, has done nothing but harm.'[55]

Conclusion

In all of Durbin's work his views on patriotism are present in parts of *The Politics of Democratic Socialism* and most obviously in his argument for war against Nazi Germany in *What Have We To Defend?*. The rest of his books concern themselves with economic problems and arguments for a socialist political economy. In one sense, this makes it straightforward to classify Durbin's patriotism as first-order patriotism. The belief in fighting for Britain in what appeared in 1938-1939 (when he was writing *The Politics of Democratic Socialism*) as an impending war and what by 1942 (when *What Have We To Defend?* was published) was nothing short of a desperate fight to retain British sovereignty, contending for the liberties enshrined in the 'British social tradition'.

It is especially clear from Durbin's tone in *What Have We To Defend?* that the certainty of victory against the Nazis was a mirage and had no place in his determined and often sober arguments for patriotism. This was not the smug patriotism found in the mouths of those secure in victory. Yet Durbin's patriotism was deeper still. A second-order principle was that patriotism - rightly understood - was acceptable amongst democratic socialists. As a democratic socialist he believed that Britain had distinctive characteristics that one ought to be proud and ashamed of but, undeniably, a democratic socialist future would guarantee Britain's greatness. For Durbin, democratic socialism was ethically superior to other political philosophies and because it sought to benefit British society as a whole, it had morality on its side and was therefore righteous. The step from striving for a righteous society to being patriotic towards one's nation is small. Durbin's Christian heritage and moral imperatives that are foundational to such a tradition of democratic, ethical socialism sit comfortably with patriotism. In some of his language in *What Have We To Defend?* one detects the oratory of the Baptist lay preacher[56] with passion and conviction in spiritual certainties. For Durbin, patriotism is morally neutral and can be used for just and unjust purposes and likewise it can be blind and ignorant as well as observant and informed in how it values a nation and its customs. Above all, the democratic socialist in Durbin ascribed value to the British social tradition to its parliamentary democracy, civil liberties, social peace and tolerance. Durbin's work in the 1940s contributed to a strand of democratic socialist thought that endorsed patriotism (rightly understood) and believed that when fully democratic in economic as well as political spheres Britain would be moving towards socialism and would be on the road to becoming a more ethical society.

1 This chapter contains new research on the political thought of Evan Durbin and his place in Labour Party thought, but the sections pertaining to his patriotism appeared as an article entitled, 'Evan Durbin: Assessing a Patriotic Socialist' in the U.S. *Journal of International Twentieth Century Studies*. Therefore, I would like to express my gratitude to the publisher Cantadora Press for allowing me to use parts of the article within this chapter.

2 E. Durbin, *The Politics of Democratic Socialism* (Jonathan Cape, London, 1940), p.253.

3 For more of Durbin's lesser known corpus see E. Durbin, 'The Importance of Planning' in G. Catlin (ed.) *New Trends in Socialism* (Lovat Dickson & Thompson, London, 1935), 'The Social Significance of the Theory of Values' Economic Journal (1935), 'Democracy and Socialism in Britain' Political Quarterly (1935), 'The Response of the Economist' in (ed.) T.H. Marshall, *The Ethical Factor in Economic Thought* (London, 1936), *The Economic Basis of Peace* (London, 1942), 'Socialism: the British Way' in (ed.) Donald Munro, *The Socialist Experiment carried out in Great Britain by the Labour Government of 1945* (London, 1948).

4 For more on Durbin's political and economic ideas see, S. Brooke, 'Revisionists and Fundamentalists: The Labour Party and Economic Policy during the Second World War' *The Historical Journal* 1, (March 1989), 157-175, S. Brooke, 'Problems of Socialist Planning: Evan Durbin and the Labour Government of 1945' *The Historical Journal* 3 (Sept. 1991), 687-702, E. Durbin, *New Jerusalems* (Routledge & Keegan Paul, London, 1985), and N. Thompson, *Political Economy and the Labour Party* (UCL, London, 1996), pp.89-94.

5 See D. Sassoon, *One Hundred Years of Socialism: The West European Left in the Twentieth Century* (Fontana Press, London, 1997), p.245.

6 Durbin, *The Politics of Democratic Socialism*, p.235.

7 The 1917 Club was a Marxist social club that Gaitskell joined in 1929 before he joined Tots and Quots that was a dining club of socialist intellectuals and scientists many of whom were Marxist socialists. Brivati notes that '...they met to discuss the social aspect of scientific affairs from a broadly left-wing perspective.' See B. Brivati, *Hugh Gaitskell* (Richard Cohen Books, London, 1997), p.31.

8 Ibid. p. 54.

9 Durbin, *The Politics of Democratic Socialism*, p.291.

10 Ibid.pp.292-294.

11 Ibid.pp.294-295.

[12] At the time of his death Durbin had began making notes on *The Economics of Democratic Socialism* but they were not cogent chapters. Thus, the book was never completed nor have the notes been published.

[13] Durbin, *The Politics of Democratic Socialism*, pp.295-297.

[14] Ibid.p.297.

[15] N. Thompson, 'The Centre' in R. Plant, M. Beech and K. Hickson (eds.) *The Struggle for Labour's Soul: Understanding Labour's Political Thought since 1945* (Routledge, London, 2004), p.48.

[16] E. Durbin, *Purchasing Power and Trade Depression* (Jonathan Cape, London, 1933).

[17] G. Foote, *The Labour Party's Political Thought* (Macmillan, Basingstoke, 1997), p.161.

[18] See R.H.S. Crossman, *Planning for Freedom* (Hamish Hamilton, London, 1965).

[19] I owe this and the related points of classifying Durbin's political economy as of the centre-left in the Labour Party of the 1930s and 1940s to Noel Thompson. He raised this point in a paper I gave to the staff of the Department of History at the University of Wales, Swansea entitled: *Democratic Socialism and Patriotism in the thought of Evan Durbin*.

[20] Durbin, *The Politics of Democratic Socialism*, p.320.

[21] For a good essay on patriotism and British socialism see, M. Taylor, 'Patriotism, History and the Left in Twentieth-century Britain' *The Historical Journal* 4 (1990), 971-987.

[22] For example see Durbin, *The Politics of Democratic Socialism*, pp.280 and 333.

[23] Ibid. p.333.

[24] Ibid. p.253.

[25] Ibid. p.250.

[26] Ibid.

[27] E. Durbin, *What Have We To Defend?* (Labour Book Service, London, 1942), p.2.

[28] British Library of Political and Economic Science (BLPES), London, *Evan Durbin Papers*, 7/7, Private Correspondence - from Reginald Bassett and Frank Pakenham.

[29] Durbin, *What Have We To Defend?*, p.43.

[30] Ibid. pp.53-54.

[31] Ibid. p.91.

[32] Durbin, *Papers*, 4/1, Unpublished preparatory notes for *What Have We To Defend?*

[33] Ibid.

[34] Durbin, *What Have We To Defend?*, pp.13-34.

[35] Ibid. p.67.

[36] Ibid. p.62.

[37] Ibid.

[38] See K. Marx, *The Communist Manifesto* (Peking Books, London, 1974), p.26.

[39] V.I. Lenin, *Imperialism: The Highest Stage of Capitalism* (Lawrence and Wishart, London, 1948).

[40] G. Sabine and T. Thorson, *A History of Political Theory* (Dryden Press, Illinois, 1973), p. 747.

[41] Ibid.

[42] E. Durbin, 'Why I Am Not A Marxist', *Daily Herald*, 16th February 1937.

[43] Durbin, *What Have We To Defend?*, p.6.

[44] For a good essay on Orwell's views of patriotism see, S. Lutman, 'Orwell's Patriotism', *Journal of Contemporary History* 2, (April 1967), 149-158.

[45] G. Orwell, *The Lion and the Unicorn* (Secker and Warburg, London, 1941), p.27.

[46] Durbin, *The Politics of Democratic Socialism*, pp.184-185.

[47] Ibid. p.250.

[48] J. Strachey, *The Theory and Practice of Socialism* (Gollancz, London, 1936), p.259.

[49] Durbin, *Papers*, 1/9, Notes on Nationalism.

[50] Durbin, *Papers*, 4/1, Unpublished preparatory notes for *What Have We To Defend?*.

[51] Ibid.

[52] Ibid.

[53] Ibid.

[54] Durbin, *Papers*, 7/7, Private Correspondence - Frank Pakenham, 'The Patriotism of the Left' *Observer* London, 8th November 1942.

[55] Orwell, *The Lion and the Unicorn*, p.115.

[56] As a young man and whilst a student at Oxford, Durbin was a Baptist lay preacher. Some biographical accounts suggest that he lost his faith in Christ at some point in his post-Oxford years and that democratic socialism became his central philosophy. When reading his private notebook what is palpably clear is that Durbin was a Christian and believed in spiritual certainties. See Durbin, *Papers*, 10/7, Notebook of Speeches and Sermons (1924-1929).

6

JOHN STRACHEY[1]

'Capitalist society in 1955 is a very different thing from
what it was 100 years ago when the socialist *critique* of
it was first undertaken, or even from what it was 50
years ago when most of the current socialist
conceptions of it were first formulated. Socialists will
not succeed very well in their task of social
transformation until and unless they form a clear idea
of what capitalism has become and is becoming.'[2]

It is very easy to criticise John Strachey for his inconsistency.
In the 1920s Strachey was a prominent critic of Fabian
gradualism, then joined the New Party formed by Oswald
Mosley, before leaving that Party to become a leading British
Marxist of the 1930s. His perspective at this time was
strongly orthodox communist. He then shifted ground once
again, influenced by Keynesian economic theory in the late-
1930s. After the Second World War Strachey served in the
Attlee Administration, although his ministerial record was
less than impressive.[3] Strachey's thought during the 1950s
appeared to some commentators to be essentially the same
as the emerging revisionist paradigm.[4] There were
similarities, but also crucial differences that will be examined
later.

This chapter will seek to show an element of underlying
consistency in Strachey's thought, which remained constant
throughout the various adaptations to his political economy.
This can be briefly described as a radical commitment to end

the unfairness of the capitalist economy, and the promotion of what Strachey thought were the most effective means to achieve high and sustained economic growth, high levels of employment and the reduction of poverty and inequality. It was this concern which lay at the centre of Strachey's politics. Hence, the first aim of the chapter is to trace the development in Strachey's thought up to 1951. The second aim is to examine in more detail Strachey's post-war position. It will be shown that his position during the debates of the 1950s is more complex than sometimes assumed. Although Strachey was a prolific contributor to writings on British socialism, his most important work is *Contemporary Capitalism* (1956). The chapter will therefore examine this work in more detail in the belief that it casts light on the nature of the debates over the future direction of socialism in the 1950s, and will therefore form a basis for further discussion on Richard Crossman and Tony Crosland in the following two chapters. The argument here, and against the views expressed in the most authoritative study of Strachey's political economy to date by Noel Thompson[5], is that Strachey's response to the revisionists is ultimately inadequate.

The Evolution of Strachey's Political Economy to the 1950s[6]

Strachey adopted a critical position on the Labour left from the mid-1920s as the economic situation deteriorated. Strachey had been associated with Oswald Mosley from this time when he had written *Revolution by Reason* in 1925, an expanded version of Mosley's policy for economic expansion as advocated in the so-called 'Birmingham proposals'.[7] When Mosley presented a radical programme of government intervention in the late-1920s, Strachey again supported him. The primary focus for criticism was the conduct of economic policy under the Labour Government after 1929, when Prime Minister Ramsay MacDonald and Chancellor of the Exchequer Philip Snowden defended orthodox economic policy. This led eventually to the formation of the New Party. Strachey joined as he supported the radical fiscal expansion advocated by Mosley. Indeed, Strachey did much to provide the New Party with its economic policy by writing *A National Policy: An Account of the Emergency* with, among others Aneurin Bevan.[8] *A National Policy* was written before the New Party was formed but was published afterwards. Bevan decided to remain in the Labour Party, believing that a more radical programme could be encouraged within the Party. Strachey, however, believed that the Labour Party was no longer the best vehicle for the development of a more radical economic programme. Strachey then became discouraged by what he regarded, correctly, as the emergence of fascism within the New Party. He disliked the emphasis on charismatic leadership and the increasingly personalised style of leadership under Mosley, together with the increased emphasis on nationalism in the economic and other policies of the New Party. For Strachey, the true ideological basis for a radical politics in Britain was not fascism but communism and he wrote two books *The Coming Struggle for Power* and *The Menace of Fascism* to outline his position as it stood in the early 1930s.[9] The latter was intended in part as a rejection of the Mosley position and hence an admission that the New Party had not offered a basis for socialism.

The Coming Struggle for Power represented the first in a series of works by Strachey which marked him out as a leading advocate of communism in Britain in the 1930s, perhaps the most intellectually credible advocate of that position. Strachey argued that the Labour Party and the trade unions had become "the principal and essential bulwarks of capitalism."[10] The real choice was not therefore between capitalism and parliamentary social democracy, since the inability of the Labour Party to manage capitalism effectively had been shown vividly with the collapse of the MacDonald Government. Instead, the real choice was between capitalism and communism. Britain, Strachey argued, was a "particularly favourable ground for communism,"[11] since there was a large and relatively well-educated industrial working class, a small agricultural sector and the failures of capitalist management had become clear. Moreover, the relatively small geographical area of the UK made it much more likely that communism could be realised. All of this led Strachey to conclude in 1932 that, "the struggle for communism can surely be won by the workers of Britain, unshakeably allied to the workers of all the world."[12]

This book was followed by *The Nature of Capitalist Crisis*[13] and *The Theory and Practice of Socialism*[14], both of which sought to elaborate on these themes. The Labour Party was singled out for criticism, from the familiar Marxist critique of social democratic politics: "the writers, thinkers and spokesmen of the British Labour Party, who chiefly influence the British masses, consistently hold out the illusion of a pleasant, easy and non-revolutionary issue from the present crisis... This counsel is the deadliest of all the poisons which can be administered to the workers."[15] It is worth emphasising that Strachey's commitment in his published work to communism was total at this stage. He argued that the only true course open for the salvation of the working-class was Marxism: "for nowhere and never have workers' movements succeeded unless they have mastered and applied the scientific discoveries of Marx, Engels and Lenin."[16] Indeed, Strachey sought to adhere to the official Soviet position and defended Stalin's regime: "Stalin's claim to rank as one of the decisive figures in history is that he found the way to overcome the extraordinary difficulties which ten years ago stood in the way of establishing socialism in the Soviet Union."[17] The most effective means for the realisation of communism was to combine industrial activity with political activity through the Communist Party of Great Britain, which since its formation, "represented this alternative policy within the British working class movements."[18] What was apparent here was that Strachey's commitment to communism had reached its completion. He argued, with the certainty of a dogmatic Marxist, that a popular front was required - bridging the gaps between the trade unions, the Labour Party and the Communist Party of Great Britain - to allow for the realisation of Marx's final stage of history.

However, it is worth emphasising one crucial issue over which Strachey disagreed with many orthodox Marxists. It had been argued by sections of the Communist Party of Great Britain that social reform designed to reduce the worst excesses of poverty and capitalist inequity should not be part of a communist struggle for power. Any attempt at social reform would only bolster the position of the capitalists since it would reduce proletarian discontent. The object of communism should therefore be not to introduce ameliorative social reforms but to organise for the seizure of power, at which point capitalism could be overthrown. An early statement that showed that Strachey was beginning to distance himself from the Marxist viewpoint was contained in *What Are We To Do?* published in 1938.[19] He argued that both the social democratic ameliorators and the Marxist critics of social reform were incorrect since social reform could be introduced as the first stage in a wider process of the transfer of social and economic power that would result in socialism. Strachey argued that what was required in the conditions of the late-1930s was the resolute leadership of a united left-wing political party with a strong attachment to democracy in terms of the defence of Parliament, local government and the public ownership of industry as a force against the fascist threat. In terms of specific policies, Strachey advocated nationalisation, an increase in the spending power of workers through minimum incomes and social security, a programme of public works and a national

investment board. These policies were not the statement of
a full programme for socialism, as those on the Labour right
argued, but the first stage in the transfer of power since it
would lead to a real improvement in the conditions of
workers, mobilise the working class and therefore lead to
class conflict. Hence, Strachey argued that the choice
between moderate social reform and Marxist transformation
was a false one since "the Labour movement must choose
the most favourable ground on which to fight the inevitable
struggle with those who rule society to-day; and the most
favourable ground is precisely the struggle for the simplest,
most elementary, social reforms and ameliorations. For
events will show fast enough that even those reforms and
ameliorations today involve a large measure of socialism."[20]

Strachey's pre-war position is often contrasted with his
post-war position as if he moved, under the impact of war,
from a Marxist analysis to a revisionist position.[21] Such a
view is mistaken however, since his view began to change
before the War and as we will see below his post-war
position, despite some similarities, was distinct from the
Gaitskellite revisionists. The clearest indication that
Strachey was moving away from Marxism came in his 1940
publication *A Programme for Progress*.[22] This book sought to
answer the question, "how, precisely and practically, is the
struggle for a better social and economic order – for
socialism – to be carried on?"[23] This book is important
since in it Strachey concedes that it is possible to remove the
worst effects of capitalism through state activity and in so
doing create a different, fairer, social and economic
structure. There are several reasons, suggested by his
biographers, why Strachey changed his mind at this time.[24]
The first is undoubtedly the decision of Stalin to ally himself
with Hitler. Following this, Strachey found it increasingly
difficult to accept the Soviet case for war. The later Nazi
invasion of the Soviet Union did not lead him to revert back
to the Communist Party of Great Britain and he formally

rejoined the Labour Party in 1942. Moreover, the impact of war led him to adopt a much more patriotic tone, arguing that a working-class movement needed to continue in its campaign for social and economic transformation but primarily to fight against Hitler since the former could not result without first defeating fascism.[25] However, it would be wrong to suggest that Strachey's opinions were changed just as a result of war. He had been in the process of revising his earlier Marxist thought in the late-1930s after witnessing the improvement in social and economic conditions as a result of the New Deal programme in America. He had initially been highly critical of such a policy since it amounted, he had argued, to a revival of capitalism[26], but as the beneficial impact of the New Deal was recognised Strachey became more positive: "I have come to believe that expansionist measures, if they do form part of such a general progressive programme can be an indispensable step in the right direction."[27] Moreover, he was influenced at this time by Douglas Jay, who helped to persuade Strachey of a 'Keynesian solution' to economic stagnation if public spending was directed to largely peaceful production.[28] Hence by 1938, Strachey was able to argue, in stark contrast to his argument in the early 1930s, that state activity could stimulate the economy for a longer period of time: "Roosevelt in practice and Keynes, in theory, have shown us that powerful weapons are at the disposal of a resolute, progressive movement which is confronted with a slump whether deliberately provoked or not."[29] The argument developed at this time was that, in contrast to Marx, democracy had shown itself capable of reforming the economic system and hence was able to 'control' economic forces rather than be controlled by them. It was this argument that is central to an accurate understanding of Strachey's post-war position.

The six-point programme outlined by Strachey can therefore be seen as the position he had reached during wartime. The programme called for a pattern of extensive public and mixed public and private investment in the economy, lowering of the rate of interest, substantial redistribution of income through a range of measures, but most notably the introduction of death duties, increased pensions and allowances, a public banking system and control over foreign payments. It is important to recognise that this position rested on a particular view of the economy, derived in part from his earlier Marxist sympathies, but interestingly also having some similarities with the position of Hayek.[30] The central economic problem rested on the tension between production for 'use' and production for 'profit'. Since the capitalist enterprise produced solely for profit and took no account of social use in what was being produced there was a need for a future left-wing government to introduce public ownership in order to shift from an economic system based on profit to one based on use. Attempts to socialise the economy without reference to ownership would create strains in the economy, as both Hayek and Strachey suggested. However, whereas the former used this argument to justify a free market, so Strachey used it to justify nationalisation, arguing that redistribution alone would be insufficient. In addition to this argument, Strachey, showing the influence of Keynesian ideas on him, also argued that public ownership would reduce unemployment through the multiplier effect.[31]

Arguably, the ideas of corporate socialism developed in the 1930s by Strachey and others influenced the policy of the Attlee Government between 1945-51. The nationalisation programme is usually seen as being carried out for pragmatic reasons, taking in to public ownership those industries that had been decimated in wartime. However, it could also be argued that the Attlee Government was influenced by the intellectual development of socialism in the 1930s. In a sentence, this was the belief that a programme of redistribution and public works as advocated by Keynes would be insufficient without public ownership since the state would lack sufficient economic power and the private sector would retain sufficient power to act as a barrier to progressive reform. By the end of the Labour Government in 1951, approximately one-fifth of industry had been taken in to public ownership. A key debating point in the 1950s, in addition to a range of foreign and defence policy issues, was therefore what role should there be for further public ownership under a future Labour government.

The 'Great Debate'

Strachey's position in the 1950s is often interpreted as being revisionist. Strachey was not one of the leading Gaitskellites, being one of the three key figures[32] in the 'Keep Calm' movement – a centrist grouping, which sought to maintain ideological unity within the parliamentary party. However, his 1951 publication *The Just Society: A Reaffirmation of Faith in Socialism* (republished later the same year in *New Fabian Essays*)[33] would appear to suggest that he had accepted the revisionist position. He accepted that his views had changed radically since the earlier 1930s when he held a Marxist position and listed his key influences: "this (Marxism) way my own view until about 1938. About 1938, I began to modify these views. It was the work of a new school of economists – notably, of course Keynes' *General Theory*, but also works like Douglas Jay's *The Socialist Case* – which affected my mind."[34] He argued that the 1945-51 Government had "in fact appreciably modif(ied) the nature of British capitalism."[35] Specifically, these changes included full employment and higher levels of investment, exports and agricultural production. This amounted to a substantial reform of capitalism in which the power of monopoly capitalists had been eroded. However, these changes did not equate to the introduction of socialism, "our present economic and social arrangements are essentially transitional. We must push on to socialism or, inevitably, in the end we shall be pushed back to unreformed, pre-war capitalism."[36] This would require a future Labour administration to carry out a further programme of nationalisation and in particular to socialise the joint stock corporations, where power was still retained by capitalists. Finally, Strachey was upbeat about the possibilities of such reform given the achievements of the Attlee Government, the unity of the Labour Movement and the high level of government expertise.[37]

These arguments were further developed in what was arguably Strachey's greatest publication, *Contemporary Capitalism*, published in 1956, the same year as Crosland's *The Future of Socialism* and so inevitably subject to comparison.[38] Strachey sets out, with some considerable sophistication the political economy of Marx and Keynes. The book appears more of an academic analysis rather than a political tract. It could therefore be argued that Strachey provides a more sophisticated analysis of political economy than does Crosland, and certainly in a detailed intellectual biography of Strachey written by Noel Thompson a more favourable interpretation of Strachey is offered.[39] However, it could also be argued that the strengths of Strachey's book are also it weaknesses since the book arguably lacks the clarity of *The Future of Socialism* in terms of offering a political programme for a future Labour government and in my opinion suffers from a number of conflicting arguments as will be set out at the end of the chapter.

As seen in the opening quotation, Strachey in *Contemporary Capitalism* argued that capitalism was something radically different from what had been analysed by Marx. Specifically, there had been a series of trends in capitalism that had developed since Marx's analysis of the economic system in the nineteenth century.[40] There had been an increase in the basic size of the individual corporate unit, although this differed from sector to sector and in different economies. This had allowed for managerial autonomy and the separation of ownership and management. In addition, there had also been a growth in the economic functions of the state, in particular events had demonstrated that democratic authority could control the means of production in sharp contrast to what Marx had argued. Hence, a number of the predictions made by Marx in relation to the nature of the capitalist economy had been proven false by subsequent developments. Strachey argued the reason for this lay in the fact that Marx had sought to identify in a scientific way, laws capable of proof and refutation. In fact, social reality had demonstrated itself to be too complex for such a mode of analysis. Many of the features that Marx identified within capitalism were present as 'tendencies' but not as 'laws' and, in particular, the countervailing tendency towards democratisation had been more powerful in social and economic development in the West.[41] The Marxist attempt to demonstrate scientific laws in the economy and society led, according to Strachey, to dogmatism, exemplified by neo-Marxists who sought to prove Marx's predictions in the post-war period, ignoring evidence to the contrary.[42] Hence, one of the themes of *Contemporary Capitalism* is the repudiation of Strachey's earlier Marxist commitments, as David Reisman has argued, "in acclaiming the future of moderation, it is clear, Strachey was also bidding farewell to the God that failed."[43]

However, although Strachey sought to distance himself from Marxism, he was not a straightforward revisionist. The main theme within *Contemporary Capitalism* is the ongoing tension between capitalism and democracy.[44] Capitalism is anti-egalitarian and demands the centralisation of power in non-democratic corporations. It is therefore in conflict with democracy, which requires the dispersal of power in a more egalitarian society. As already discussed, Strachey argued that there had been significant economic change, but in contrast to Crosland, Strachey argued that this marked a transformation *within* the capitalist economy rather than the transformation *of* capitalism. As will be shown in a later chapter, Crosland argued that the economic trends identified by himself and by Strachey – the separation of ownership and control of industry and the increased power of the state and organised labour – had created a post-capitalist society. Crosland initially called this 'statism' but later rejected this term. Although he could not find another appropriate term he continued to argue that capitalism had been replaced. In contrast, as the title of his 1956 book indicated, Strachey argued that the economy was still fundamentally capitalist. The post-war economy was a transitional phase, the last stage of capitalism, which needed a further push to create a socialist society.   Hence, Crosland and Strachey both accepted that the combination of longer-term economic trends and the reforms of the Attlee Government had created an economic structure which was notably different from the free-market capitalism that Marx had analysed in the nineteenth century, and both emphasised that democratic pressures had been able to produce real economic change.

This agreement, however, co-existed with a fundamental disagreement over the nature of the post-war economy. This appears in the terminology used to describe the post-war economy – either as 'contemporary capitalist' or as 'post-capitalist'.[45] This disagreement was not just a semantic one.   Crosland believed that laissez-faire ideas had been removed from the political agenda for good, as summed up with his argument that "no one of any standing now believes the once-popular Hayek thesis that any interference with the market mechanism must start us down the slippery slope that leads to totalitarianism."[46] However, Strachey in a much more measured, and as it proved to be in the longer-term more accurate, way argued that the fundamental tension between capitalist ownership and democracy had not yet been permanently settled: "democracy and last stage capitalism undoubtedly pull in opposite directions. Their co-existence constitutes a state of antagonistic balance. They co-exist in the same way that the two teams in a tug-of-war co-exist upon a rope. Such a form of co-existence can hardly be permanent."[47]   Indeed, this fundamental argument made by Strachey in *Contemporary Capitalism* suggests a significant disagreement between Crosland and the other revisionists on the one hand and Strachey on the other, as Noel Thompson has suggested: "for Strachey, then, capitalism, continued to exist... It was here, as Strachey saw it, that *The Future of Socialism* was fundamentally flawed."[48] Strachey's argument here is similar to the view expressed by the Bevanites, in particular Richard Crossman (see the following chapter) and Aneurin Bevan in his famous book *In Place of Fear.*[49]

The differences between Crosland and Strachey are most identifiable in Strachey's review of Crosland's *The Future of Socialism.*[50] Strachey is initially sympathetic, "the first thing to say about the book is that it is very good indeed... It is a major work and no-one must in future take part in the current and, I trust, growing and continuing controversy on socialism without having read it."[51]   He shares the view expressed by Crosland that the central limitation of policies pursued by the Attlee Government was the amount of inequality which remained in the 1950s and that therefore the main aim of policy under a future Labour administration must be the pursuit of greater equality.   As discussed in depth in a subsequent chapter, Crosland argued that this should be done through fiscal and educational reforms primarily.   He placed little emphasis on ownership, since ownership had become separated from the control of industry so that the state had sufficient power to create a more egalitarian society without recourse to further nationalisation. This argument was rejected by Strachey for reasons already outlined – namely the tension between concentrated ownership and socialist pressures for greater democracy. Hence, Strachey argued that "in a word Mr Crosland's sincere equalitarianism[52] is quite inconsistent with his economic analysis,"[53] since for Strachey, "the ownership of the means of production is the most important single, though certainly not the sole, determinant of the structure of society. I shall continue to believe that the social ownership of the decisive part of the means of production is the only permanent basis for a socialist, classless society."[54] Hence for Strachey the commitment to public ownership is central to the very idea of socialism, "if socialists lose sight of the central importance of the ownership of the means of production, they will cease in a very real sense to be socialists at all: they will subside into the role of well-intentioned, amiable, rootless, drifting, social reformers."[55]

Conclusion

Hence, despite some clear similarities between Strachey's political economy in the 1950s and revisionism, there are some very real differences also. By way of conclusion it is important to ask the question, was Strachey correct to argue that public ownership of industry remained essential for the realisation of socialism in the 1950s? There is no easy answer to this question since it relies on an accurate understanding of the relationship between ends and means (values and policies). The first issue is to ask what did Strachey believe public ownership was for? Here it could be argued that, despite appearances, Strachey was actually rather vague by the time of his 'mature thought' in the 1950s. It would appear from his review of *The Future of Socialism* discussed above that public ownership remained the true objective of socialism. This was a distinctively 'socialist' goal, without which socialists would become "well-

intentioned, amiable, rootless, drifting, social reformers."
Without a commitment to public ownership socialists were
not actually socialists at all. However, it would be worth
asking in this instance why this should be so, given the
distinction between means and ends outlined by the
revisionists and notably by Crosland.[56] If the aim of
socialism is an ethical one, as both the revisionists and
Strachey suggested when they said a socialist society required
less inequality than existed in the 1950s, then socialism was
to be defined not by how much public ownership there was
but by how much equality there was. Both agreed that the
Attlee Administration had failed to create a significantly
more egalitarian society and that the success of a future
Labour government would be measured in terms of the
extent to which economic and social inequalities would be
reduced. If this was not the case and socialism was about
the pattern and nature of corporate ownership, as Marx had
suggested, then Strachey's critical analysis of Marxism in the
early chapters of *Contemporary Capitalism* would seem rather
out of place.

By examining the argument that Strachey makes in the
early chapters of *Contemporary Capitalism* we can therefore see
that public ownership was to be regarded not as the *objective*
of socialism but as a *necessary means* to the achievement a
socialist society, which could best be seen as a more
democratic and equal society. However, this is not the end
of the issue since it then becomes necessary to ask why
public ownership should be seen as a *necessary* means? There
are in fact several reasons why Strachey regarded public
ownership as indispensable for socialism.[57] These could be
briefly listed as efficiency[58], democracy, power and equality.
However, in each of these aspects it should be stressed that
the revisionists provided strong and – in the case of this
author at least – ultimately convincing arguments why public
ownership was not a *necessary* objective of socialism.[59] First
then, in terms of efficiency Strachey argued that public

ownership led to greater economic efficiency since increased output could be re-invested rather than going into dividend payments and also due to economies of scale. In contrast, revisionists argued that profit was required in order to attract investment funds and many private sector corporations had shown themselves to be more cost efficient due to competitive pressures. However, some revisionists, notably Crosland, did argue that the state could seek to extend public ownership in the form of competitive public enterprises, which could be used to increase efficiency in sectors of the economy where private sector investment had failed to raise efficiency as will be discussed in relation to Crosland later in the book.

As already discussed, Strachey placed a good deal of emphasis on democracy and argued that public ownership was central to any attempt to increase democracy and alter the dynamics of power from capitalism to socialism. It was only through a change in ownership that the power of owners could be reduced in favour of increasing the power of the state. Strachey, although optimistic about changes in the economy up to 1950, also expressed concern that underlying capitalist power still remained strong and that a future economic crisis would lead to the revival of the 'forces of reaction' in the capitalist economy and the Conservative Party. Given that Strachey here placed emphasis on the arguments of T.E. Utley, it is interesting that Utley became one of the key thinkers of the New Right in Britain in the 1970s.[60] It has been argued by Thompson that Strachey's caution seemed more appropriate in the context of the 1980s than Crosland's optimism.[61] However, the validity of the specific arguments made by Strachey that further public ownership was required in order to extend democracy and to secure the power of non-capitalist forces is less clear. First, there had been little attempt to increase industrial democracy in the industries nationalised between 1945-51. This required further reform – to appoint elected worker and/or trade union representatives to management boards – which could be applied to the public or private sector. In fact, Crosland continued to oppose calls for industrial democracy until the 1970s since he thought that the role of trade unions in protecting the interests of workers would be compromised by attempts to introduce high level industrial democracy. The revisionists also argued that there had been a transfer of power from owners of industry to corporate managers, trade unions and the state, which had gained power through public ownership of key industries and also through the adoption of Keynesian economic techniques. The important points here are first, that Strachey identified these trends in his critique of the neo-Marxists, which rather conflicted with his argument that power still remained in the hands of capitalists. Secondly that when a crisis did come in the British economy this only indirectly related to the relative power of capitalism to the state since it took the form of international pressure (largely from the U.S. government acting through the IMF) on sterling (largely in 1975-6, culminating in the IMF agreement in December 1976)[62] and it is not clear here that a further round of public ownership in the 1960s would have helped, indeed it may well have increased the economic problems faced by the Government in the 1970s.

Finally, in terms of equality, revisionists argued convincingly that public ownership had limited effects on the distribution of wealth due to the principle of 'fair compensation'. The favoured means for the pursuit of greater economic and social equality were fiscal and educational reforms and more will be said here in later chapters.

Hence, just as Strachey had been critical of Crosland's *The Future of Socialism* so the revisionists sought to reject Strachey's thesis.[63] It could be argued that despite producing a highly elaborate and scholarly perspective on the nature of both capitalism and socialism in the 1950s in his seminal book *Contemporary Capitalism*, Strachey's thought had several unresolved tensions, not least concerning the role of public ownership in the economy. It will be discussed in the following two chapters whether either Richard Crossman or Tony Crosland was able to provide a more complete synthesis of British socialism at this time, before returning to a number of the themes of this chapter in our discussion of Stuart Holland, who again raised the issue of public ownership in socialist political economy.

[1] The chapter benefits considerably from comments from Noel Thompson, whose biography of Strachey offers the best account of his thought to date, although I adopt a more critical stance on Strachey's contribution to British socialism, especially during the 1950s. John Strachey has in fact been subject to three biographies – H. Thomas, *John Strachey* (Methuen, London, 1973), M. Newman, *John Strachey* (Manchester University Press, Manchester, 1989) and N. Thompson, *John Strachey: An Intellectual Biography* (Macmillan, Basingstoke, 1993)

[2] J. Strachey, *Contemporary Capitalism* (first published by Gollancz, London, 1956; all references taken from D. Reisman [ed.] *Theories of the Mixed Economy Vol. VIII, Contemporary Capitalism* (William Pickering, London, 1994), p.11.

[3] Not least for the so-called 'groundnuts affair' for a discussion of which see Newman, *John Strachey* pp.111-118.

[4] See Thompson, *John Strachey* p.186 for a list of such commentators.

[5] Ibid.

[6] This discussion follows the three biographies of Strachey mentioned above.

[7] J. Strachey, *Revolution by Reason* (Leonard Parsons, London, 1925).

[8] A. Bevan, W.J. Brown, J. Strachey and A. Young, *A National Policy, an account of the emergency programme advanced by Sir Oswald Mosley* (Macmillan, London, 1931).

[9] J. Strachey, *The Coming Struggle for Power* (Gollancz, London, 1932) and *The Menace of Fascism* (Gollancz, London, 1933).

[10] Strachey, *The Coming Struggle for Power* p.293.

[11] Ibid. p.361.

[12] Ibid. p.396.

[13] J. Strachey, *The Nature of Capitalist Crisis* (Gollancz, London, 1935).

[14] J. Strachey, *The Theory and Practice of Socialism* (Gollancz, London, 1936).

[15] Strachey, *The Nature of Capitalist Crisis*, pp.370-371.

[16] Strachey, *The Theory and Practice of Socialism* p.437.

[17] Ibid. p.432.

[18] Ibid. p.445.

[19] J. Strachey, *What are we to do?* (Gollancz, London, 1938). However, it is worth emphasising that here Strachey was seeking to forge, in line with Communist Party policy at this time, a 'popular front' and so was seeking to stress areas where social democrats could agree with communists. See, Thompson, *John Strachey*, pp.126-147.

[20] Strachey, *What are we to do?*, pp.354-355.

[21] See note 4 above.

[22] J. Strachey, *A Programme for Progress* (Gollancz, London, 1940).

[23] Ibid. p.6.

[24] See Thompson, pp.148-167.

[25] Ibid. p.176.

[26] Ibid. p.82.

[27] Strachey, *A Programme for Progress*, pp.127-128.

[28] For this see Strachey, *A Programme for Progress*, esp. p.73. But note the cautionary remark that Keynesian ideas could lead to rearmament rather than social progress, see Newman, *John Strachey*, p.88.

[29] J. Strachey, 'We are all reformists now' *New Fabian Research Bureau Quarterly* November 1938, p.18, quoted in Thompson, *John Strachey*, p.132.

[30] See in particular, F. A. Hayek, *Prices and Production* (Routledge, London, 1931).

[31] Strachey, *A Programme for Progress*, esp. chapter 3.

[32] Along with George Strauss and Michael Stewart.

[33] J. Strachey, 'The Just Society: a reaffirmation of faith in socialism' (Labour Party, London, 1951) and J. Strachey, 'Tasks and Achievements of British Labour' in R.H.S. Crossman (ed.) *New Fabian Essays* (Turnstile, London, 1952).

[34] Strachey, 'Tasks and Achievements of British Labour', p.182.

[35] Ibid. p.182.

[36] Ibid. pp.197-198.

[37] The emphasis on unity and bureaucratic ability is significant – first because as already noted Strachey was part of the 'Keep Calm' group emphasising the need for Labour Party unity and second because Strachey has been characterised as a bureaucratic elitist by Newman, see Newman *John Strachey* passim.

[38] Strachey *Contemporary Capitalism*; C.A.R. Crosland, *The Future of Socialism* (Cape, London, 1956, subsequent references are to the 1963 edition).

[39] Indeed Thompson argues that Strachey produced a work of political economy and Crosland a work of social politics, which amounted to a series of *ad hoc* measures only so that "it is small wonder that Strachey should have stuck to its economic variant." Thompson, *John Strachey*, p.219.

[40] Strachey, *Contemporary Capitalism*, pp.20-39.

[41] Ibid., pp.82-100.

[42] Ibid., pp.131-148.

[43] D. Reisman, 'Introduction' in Strachey, *Contemporary Capitalism*, p.x.

[44] Strachey, *Contemporary Capitalism*, passim, but esp. the final two chapters.

[45] Crosland set himself the question 'Is this still capitalism?' to which he answered 'No.' *Future of Socialism*, p.42.

[46] Crosland, *The Future of Socialism*, p.343.

[47] Strachey, *Contemporary Capitalism*, p.255.

[48] Thompson, *John Strachey*, p.197.

[49] A. Bevan, *In Place of Fear* (Heinemann, London, 1952). Thompson, *John Strachey*, pp.198-9.

[50] J. Strachey, 'The New Revisionist' *New Statesman and Nation* October 6, 1956.

[51] Ibid.

[52] Strachey's word, but in this book the more common term 'egalitarianism' is preferred.

[53] Strachey, 'The New Revisionist'.

[54] Ibid.

[55] Ibid. This broadly remained Strachey's view according to Thompson and his final publications were primarily concerned with foreign and defence issues. See Thompson, *John Strachey*, pp.226-247. The most important of Strachey's final works are *The End of Empire* (Gollancz, London, 1959); *The Strangled Cry* (Bodley Head, London, 1962) and *On the Prevention of War* (Macmillan, Basingstoke, 1962).

[56] Crosland, *The Future of Socialism*, pp.64-67.

[57] See Strachey, 'Tasks and Achievements of British Labour'; 'The Objects of Further Socialisation' *Political Quarterly* January-March 1953, pp.68-77 and *Contemporary Capitalism*, pp.254-295.

[58] Strachey also argued here that the inefficiency of capitalist production would not be able to keep up with more efficient communist production. Strachey, *Contemporary Capitalism*, pp.196-7.

[59] The most notable accounts are, Crosland *The Future of Socialism*, pp.312-340; H. Gaitskell, 'Public Ownership and Equality' *Socialist Commentary* June 1955 and *Socialism and Nationalisation* (Fabian Society, London, 1956) and D. Jay, *Socialism and the New Society* (Longmans, London, 1962).

[60] Strachey, *Contemporary Capitalism*, pp.270-271. The other person who Strachey emphasised in this regard was Enoch Powell who he described as being "by far the most considerable figure" on the "lunatic, anti-democratic fringe of the (Conservative) Party." Quoted in Thompson, *John Strachey*, p.209.

[61] Thompson, *John Strachey*, pp.221-222.

[62] K. Hickson, *The IMF Crisis and British Politics* (IB Tauris, London, 2005).

[63] See Douglas Jay's review of *Contemporary Capitalism* in *Forward* 7 September 1956 and Strachey's reply in the same edition.

7

R.H.S. CROSSMAN

'How can the Labour Party regain its sense of direction? My contention…is that it cannot be done so long as politicians are content to rely on their 'hunch' and empirical experience. The Labour Party has lost its way not because it lacks a map of the new country it is crossing, but because it thinks maps unnecessary for experienced travellers.'[1]

'For the first forty-five years of this century the left remained on the offensive in the field of letters, and the role of Conservative writers was to defend unsuccessfully a series of last ditches. It was on territory conquered by these socialist books that the practical politicians of the Labour Government won their victory in 1945; and if a further advance towards socialism is ever to be made, the party machine will not make it unaided. The ground must first be cleared by another offensive, conducted by the socialist irregulars – the partisans of Labour – dons, intellectuals and men of letters.'[2]

These two quotations show us the importance attached to ideas by Richard Howard Stafford (Dick) Crossman. His argument was that significant advance had been made up to 1945 when Labour won its first majority and then proceeded to introduce a range of radical measures. However, if the aim of the Attlee Government had been to introduce socialism it had ultimately failed. It failed, according to Crossman, since it lacked a distinctly socialist theory – it had instead, in keeping with the British political tradition – been largely empiricist, pragmatic, cautious: it lacked, that is to say, a 'map' to guide it to socialism. On this, Crossman was clear. He was much less clear, however, as to what this map should look like. He is often seen as a dilettante, and has been widely criticised.

The aim of this chapter is to examine Crossman's contribution to the development of British socialism in the 1950s from a survey of his published articles, his diaries and his private papers as well as two biographical studies of Crossman and various other sources.[3] In so doing primary emphasis will be placed on his views on domestic issues. It is therefore worth emphasising what this chapter is *not* concerned with: it will not deal, except where it touches on the main theme, with either foreign policy issues or with the Labour Government of 1964-70. Some readers will find this disappointing, since Crossman spoke regularly on international affairs and served as a Cabinet minister after 1964. However, the focus for this chapter can be validated in two ways. First, there already exist a number of accounts of the debates over international and defence issues in the Labour Party at this point.[4] Secondly, there also exist a number of detailed accounts of the Wilson Government (1964-70).[5] In contrast, there is relatively little by way of academic evaluation of Crossman's philosophical and economic ideas[6], allowing for greater originality in this chapter. Moreover, this focus allows for comparison with John Strachey in the preceding chapter and Tony Crosland in the next. The fluidity of socialist ideas in the 1950s becomes apparent from such a comparison – Strachey is often seen as a revisionist, but as said in the previous chapter he has some striking similarities with the Bevanite left while Crosland was of course a leading revisionist thinker throughout the period. As will hopefully be demonstrated in this chapter, Crossman held to elements of the fundamentalist conception of socialism but also sought for a time to position himself close to Hugh Gaitskell. Therefore, the extent to which he provided a consistent and coherent viewpoint will be the subject of examination.

The chapter will firstly discuss the frequently negative perspectives on Crossman. This will be followed by a discussion and evaluation of Crossman's contribution to socialist debates. Crossman was critical of several approaches to British socialism – essentially the empirical tradition, Labour Marxism and Revisionism – so that it is easier to identify what he was *against* than what he was actually *for*. It is therefore necessary to investigate Crossman's critiques of other socialist writers before tracing his own views on both the Labour Party and British socialism. The chapter concludes with an evaluation of his ideas. Crossman is presented as a Labour Party 'centrist' and also as holding to a radical commitment to democracy, positions which were not always compatible.

Perspectives on Crossman

One of the most cutting statements on Crossman came from the Liverpool MP, Bessie Braddock. Braddock had been a radical left-wing councillor on Liverpool City Council and held similar views when first elected to Parliament. However, by the mid-1950s she had become a staunch Gaitskellite MP. She was frequently involved in clashes with the left and in one statement sought to ridicule Crossman's reputation as an intellectual: Crossman was "a man of many opinions, most of them of short duration."[7] This idea of Crossman as a dilettante is one widely expressed by both politicians and academic commentators. In itself, this is not surprising since this was the common view held by the

Gaitskellites. In his diary, Crossman noted that Gaitskell had said to him that, "your great fault is not getting on to bandwagons but jumping off them."[8]   In a similar way, David Marquand in his influential book, *The Progressive Dilemma* argues that Crossman was a man of limited intellectual focus.[9]   Moreover, Denis Healey, held to the view that Crossman lacked serious commitment to any principle he happened to be arguing for at that particular moment.[10]   However, such a view was not limited to Gaitkellites.   Geoffrey Foote in his detailed intellectual history of the Labour Party expressed the view that, "Crossman himself was in many ways a political dilettante flitting from idea to idea without ever considering the full practical consequences of committing himself fully to fighting for them."[11]   As shown in *The Struggle for Labour's Soul* a distinction can be drawn between the 'Old left' of the 1950s – with which Crossman is usually associated – and the 'New left' of the 1970s and early 1980s.   The New left is seen to be more intellectually consistent and confident – championing the Alternative Economic Strategy and with the intellectual foundations provided by Stuart Holland – and sought to distance itself from the older generation of left-wing Labour politicians.[12]

This is not to say that Crossman did not contain these aspects to his personality.   His famous statement when asked to describe his political views was that he possessed a "bump of irreverence"[13], which was no doubt derived from his upbringing in an upper-middle class household.   His father was a firm establishment figure, being a High Court judge with solid right-wing opinions, while his mother, who Anthony Howard sees as the dominant influence on the young Crossman, encouraged him to think radically and independently.   What this 'bump of irreverence' amounted to was a radical, free-thinking, anti-establishment attitude, although it was expressed in a very casual manner.   Moreover, in his diaries, Crossman expressed his sentiments regarding the limited impact of his main collection of political essays, *Planning for Freedom*: "nobody has taken the book seriously. It has been glanced at and pushed to one side... It may well be true...that by collecting in one volume my more theoretical essays I have exposed the fact that I am not a serious thinker but a political journalist who takes himself a bit too seriously... Anyway, I couldn't care less about the fate of the book."[14] The task remains therefore to ask what, if anything, Crossman's conception of socialism actually amounted to. It will become apparent to any reader of his work that it is much easier to define Crossman by what he was opposed to than to state clearly what he actually believed socialism to be. The following section will therefore begin by dealing with Crossman's critical positions in the 1950s.

Crossman on Socialism in the 1950s

Reading Crossman's published work covering the 1950s it is possible to find criticisms of the most common forms of socialism present in political discussion on the left at this time – Labour Party empiricism, Marxism and Revisionism. Crossman directed much of his criticism at the Labour Party's adherence to empiricism, which he characterised as a pragmatic rather than ideological approach to politics. This owed much to the Fabian tradition of technocratic and gradualist reform, which "concentrated on wringing out of the existing ruling class not control, but concessions through the social services: its aim was a high standard of living, not freedom and power."[15] The limitations of the Labour Government after 1945 were due to its reliance on this same empirical approach, lacking ideological direction: "my contention is that this absence of a theoretical basis for practical programmes of action, is the main reason why the post-war Labour Government marked the end of a century of social reform and not, as its socialist supporters had hoped, the beginning of a new epoch."[16] In this, Crossman was consistent with the Labour left who argued that the 1945 manifesto had been a radical document, calling for the introduction of socialism in Britain. The initial phase of the Government was indeed radical, with the effect that the majority of its manifesto commitments had been implemented by 1947-48. This period amounted to a turning-point in the Labour Government for it faced economic problems mostly relating to the convertability of sterling and also since the initial unity of the Labour Party around the 1945 manifesto gave way to increasingly hostile debate between the left and right of the Party over its future direction.

The argument of those on the right, most clearly articulated by Herbert Morrison was for a period of 'consolidation' allowing the reforms to become embedded. The left, in contrast, wanted a further phase of radical reform including more public ownership, industrial democracy and a policy of neutralism[17] in international affairs.[18] The left-wing position was most clearly set out in two documents published during the Attlee Government, *Keep Left* and *Keeping Left*, with Crossman being a major contributor to both.[19] The essence of Crossman's critique was that the Labour Government lacked a clear socialist ideology, so that once the manifesto had been implemented it became difficult to determine the future direction of policy and also to find arguments to resist the pressure of the capitalist economy and USA in the ensuing economic crisis of 1947-8. The consequence of this was that the Government lost direction and ultimately failed to introduce socialism: "what was achieved by the first Labour Government, was, in fact, the climax of a long process, in the course of which capitalism has been civilised and, to a large extent, reconciled with the principles of democracy. This is a historic achievement, but the fact remains that, in achieving it, the Labour Party is in danger of becoming not the party of change, but the defender of the status quo."[20]

Hence, Crossman sought to reject the empirical tradition within the Labour Party, but as this final quotation suggests he also rejected the two leading alternatives to it – Marxism and Revisionism. According to Crossman, Marxists had failed to predict the ability of democracy to 'civilise' capitalism. In this his ideas differed little from those of Strachey who, as we have already seen, began to distance himself from Marxism from the late-1930s on these same grounds. For this, Strachey received Crossman's praise.[21] Crossman also sought to defend Keynesian economics against its Marxist critics: "in his *General Theory*, John Maynard Keynes provided the theoretical demonstration that the collapse of capitalism was neither inevitable nor a precondition of the social justice and full employment which the working-class demanded."[22] Although the Marxists had predicted a fundamental clash between a democratic government seeking to introduce economic and social reform and capitalists, in the end the Attlee Government had been able to implement its reforms with considerable ease.[23] However, a crucial difference is that Crossman had never entertained Marxist ideas in the first place, something which distinguished him not just from Strachey, but also from many others on the Labour left in the 1930s. Crossman's intense anti-communism was the subject of a set of essays entitled *The God that Failed*, consisting of six contributions from former Marxists, for which Crossman contributed an introduction to explain as to why he was never attracted to communism, which he did in terms of his earlier religious influences: "the Protestant is, at least in origin, a conscientious objector against spiritual subjection to any hierarchy. He claims to know what is right or wrong by the inner light, and democracy for him is not merely a convenient or just form of government, but a necessity of human dignity... Then why did I feel no inner response to the Communist appeal? The answer, I am pretty sure, was sheer non-conformist cussedness, or if you prefer it, pride. No Pope for me, whether spiritual or secular."[24] Hence, Crossman is of interest because he was a Labour left figure, who had never held a serious commitment to Marxism.[25]

However, if Crossman had no faith in Marxism he was also critical of much of the revisionist output in the 1950s as well. Crossman's scepticism of the quality of revisionist thought was apparent from the early 1950s when he edited the *New Fabian Essays*. Although he wrote positively of the essays in his introductory remarks in the privacy of his diary he was more critical and wrote of "how bankrupt most of the writers are."[26] He was critical in particular of the over-emphasis on economics made by revisionist writers and argued that socialism should remain an essentially moral argument against capitalist power: "Labour's real dynamic has always been a moral protest against social injustice, not an intellectual demonstration that capitalism is bound to collapse; a challenge to capitalist privilege, not a proof that those privileges must inevitably be replaced by a classless society. Keynesianism may have undermined the old-fashioned economic case for socialism, but it has left the political and moral case for it completely unaffected."[27] Hence, Crossman was arguing that whereas the revisionists had been correct to reject the Marxist, scientific analysis of capitalism they had gone too far and were offering no more than an acceptance of post-war welfare capitalism. Instead, it was necessary not just to manage the economy in a fairer and more efficient way through Keynesian economics but to continue to protest against the undemocratic nature of capitalism. As a critique of Revisionism this is rather odd and misses the point since Crosland, Jay and others were placing emphasis on socialist values in their distinction between ends and means and the values they had in mind were social justice and equality.[28] It does however, allow us to begin to attempt a comprehension of Crossman's thought since if he was neither a Marxist nor a revisionist what was he?

Crossman's Socialist Position

It is not difficult to see why Crossman should be regarded as a dilettante when examining his political development in the 1950s. He is rightly associated as being on the left of the Party in the late-1940s with his major contribution to the *Keep Left* pamphlet (May, 1947) criticising some policy developments under the Attlee Government.[29] However it is worth making two points here. The first is that the *Keep Left* pamphlet was not an attempt to form a left-wing faction within the Parliamentary Labour Party, although its authors did not do themselves any favours in stating that the document emerged from discussions held in the rooms of the main authors, which gave the appearance of a conspiracy of critical Labour MPs. The second point is that re-reading the two *Keep Left* pamphlets reveals that they do not appear to be radically left-wing, certainly *Keep Left* which raised a number of likely problems which the Government went on to face, and simply suggested that in a number of respects what was needed was what was being done already but that it needed doing more quickly. *Keeping Left*[30] marked a more concerted effort to set out an alternative policy developing a number of themes including the need for extensions of state planning and industrial democracy. However, the main focus of *Keeping Left* was on foreign and defence issues, where the distinction between the right and the left of the Party was often clearer at this time.

With the departure of Aneurin Bevan from the Cabinet in 1951 following the introduction of prescription charges and the decisions to send military support to the U.S. in Korea and to develop an independent nuclear weapon, the *Keep Left* group gradually became the 'Bevanite' group. There is some

evidence that Crossman was concerned by such a
development.[31] No doubt this was in part due for personal
reasons since Crossman went from being a key intellectual
influence in the *Keep Left* group to being subsumed within a
new group under the dominant personality of Bevan.
However, there is a more deep-seated reason why Crossman
should be concerned by the development of the Bevanite
grouping within the Parliamentary Labour Party, namely that
the group became over-dependent on Bevan who proved
not to be a particularly effective leader of the group.
Crossman privately expressed his concerns from an early
stage: "so far from being a great strategist and organiser of
cabals, Nye is an individualist."[32]   As Anthony Howard
comments, the meetings of the Bevanite group were often
held in Bevan's absence. Bevan failed to provide leadership
to the group and indeed, may not even have shared the
passion they held on several issues.[33]   The famous
intervention of Bevan at the Labour Party Conference in
1957, reversing his earlier support for unilateral nuclear
disarmament, marked the effective end of the Bevanite
position.[34]

Crossman had distanced himself from Bevan from an
earlier stage, moving away from the Bevanite group from
1954.[35] One reason for this was that Crossman realised that
internal Party divisions had made the Party unpopular,
culminating in the 1955 General Election defeat. He also,
surprisingly, found it easier to work with Hugh Gaitskell
after he became Leader in 1955 than he had with Clement
Attlee.   Indeed, as Howard shows, he became close to
Gaitskell, who seemed to value his input as both a candid
friend and also as someone who was effective in his dealings
with the media, and Crossman was asked to develop policy
proposals on pension reform.[36] However, Crossman never
accepted the more radical revisionist arguments and
launched a strong critique of them after the 1959 General
Election defeat, which produced a Conservative majority of

over 100 seats. This heavier election defeat led some Gaitskellites to propose radical changes to the Labour Party, notably the public call from Douglas Jay to scrap Clause IV of the Labour Party's constitution[37], which had been drawn up by Sidney Webb in 1918 and committed the Party to public or 'common' ownership of the means of production, distribution and exchange. Although the Party had never taken this statement seriously when in power it was felt by Jay that it put floating voters off voting Labour since there was always the risk of a future Labour government introducing extensive public ownership. Crossman was alarmed by this partly because he thought it was a bad tactic that would only divide the Labour Party and lead to defeat, which, since this is what happened, proved to be good advice. However, this disagreement soured the relationship between Crossman and Gaitskell with Crossman saying that he was hurt by Gaitskell's hostile response to his advice and Gaitskell saying that he had expected his loyalty.[38] In the late-1950s Crossman served as Deputy Chairman and then Chairman of the Labour Party and regarded his role as defending the grass-roots of the Party against the parliamentary leadership thus moving from being a close associate of Gaitskell to being a leading critic.[39]

Crossman's closest political relationship by the end of the 1950s was with Harold Wilson, whose position in the Labour Party was rising at this time. This may well give the appearance that Crossman was inconsistent and sought to find favour with whoever was gaining importance in the Party. However, this view is mistaken since Crossman, throughout all his political meandering, appears to have held to some consistent attitudes. Indeed, the first key point to make in understanding Crossman's socialism is that in Labour Party terms he was a 'centrist'. The centre ground of political parties is often neglected in favour of the left and the right positions.[40] However, Crossman's position in the Labour Party can be understood better by describing him as a centrist, at least from the mid-1950s onwards. One reason why Crossman and Bevan moved apart is that Crossman was one of the few Bevanite MPs to publicly endorse Wilson's decision to replace Bevan in the Shadow Cabinet following his resignation in 1954.[41] Following the 1959 General Election defeat and the attempts to modernise the Party by replacing Clause IV, Crossman again associated himself with Wilson. What Wilson offered was an emphasis on party unity and a greater affinity with the grass-roots members of the Labour Party. Hence, Crossman endorsed Wilson's candidacy in the 1960 Leadership contest. The aim, at least as far as Crossman was concerned, was to restore Party unity, which had been broken by the revisionists. However, the 1960 result reinforced Gaitskell's position since he won by 166 votes to 81.[42] Crossman continued to associate himself with Wilson, who he helped to become Leader following Gaitskell's early death in 1963 and could be said to have had some influence on policy, or at least the rhetoric of 'planning'. Although, in Government from 1964, Crossman consistently argued in favour of devaluation, thus opposing Wilson's attempts to maintain the parity of sterling.[43] His ministerial record was mixed. He attempted to introduce a number of reforms such as the extension of the House of Commons committee system and supported others including the televising of Commons debates designed to re-strengthen Parliament, but he failed to implement any of these measures. The same can be said of his plans for the reform of state pensions including the linking of pensions to earnings.[44]

Hence, in terms of political strategy Crossman can be described as a centrist and this position was also expressed in his writing, notably a much neglected article in *Encounter* written in 1954 in which he argued that supporters of political parties held to an irrational, or anti-rational, ideological commitment in which they felt a sense of loyalty to the 'myths' of that particular political party.[45] In so doing, a rationalist approach to politics would ultimately be limited since the non-rational elements of political behaviour were more important to the success or failure of political parties. This argument was to be vitally important when considering his opposition to the attempts to revise Clause IV after 1959. It was not that Crossman was committed to a large-scale nationalisation policy, unlike many of Gaitskell's left-wing critics, but rather that the attempt to revise Clause IV was an attack on one of the central myths of the Labour Party.[46] He did however continue to hold that public ownership was important in order to increase efficiency and argued in one of his most famous essays at this time that the revisionists were parochial and had failed to see that while the mixed economy continued in Britain the Soviet Union was developing technologically at a much faster rate.[47] Public ownership therefore continued to be a necessary means to improve economic efficiency, and also for greater equality and democracy. Hence, Crossman argued that "we can predict with mathematical certainty that, as long as the public sector of industry remains the minority sector throughout the Western world, we are bound to be defeated in every kind of peaceful competition which we undertake with the Russians and the Eastern bloc."[48] Crossman's case here is similar to that of John Strachey, as examined in the previous chapter and so does not need to be analysed further here, except to say that Crossman's strictures on nationalisation and political economy more generally were limited. Crossman realised that a new political economy was required given that the Attlee Government had shown the Marxist theory that democracy could do little to transform capitalism to be of limited use. However, he lacked the inclination to work through a more detailed economic programme, unlike Strachey. He did suggest that while the revisionist position was misguided since it amounted to an acceptance of post-war welfare capitalism[49], there was a basis for a more satisfactory programme emerging in the 1950s

from a number of individuals including Thomas Balogh and
J.K. Galbraith, who both placed greater emphasis on the
economic planning role of the state.[50]

However, Crossman's alternative to Revisionism outlined
in the late-1950s in 'The Spectre of Revisionism' and
'Labour in the Affluent Society' – was deeply problematic.[51]
Crossman argued that the role of the Labour Party was to
provide a voice of opposition rather than to seek to provide
an alternative government. The revisionist case rested on
the 'swing of the pendulum' theory, which stated that there
would be frequent changes of the governing party. This
was, according to Crossman, a flawed theory since there was
no evidence for it. Instead, there tended to be long periods
of one-party government, in which a left-wing party could
only be elected if there was a period of economic crisis
during which time the Opposition party would win the
respect of the electorate by opposing the government and
providing a radical, alternative programme. Crossman
argued that, "the prime function of the Labour Party, as of
the Liberal Party before it, is to provide an ideology for
nonconformist critics of the Establishment. A Labour Party
of this kind is likely to be out of office for much longer
periods than the Tories."[52] The limited nature of economic
planning under the previous Labour Government led to
short-termism, which by the end the 1950s was resulting in
ever more severe economic problems. "It is I believe for
this creeping crisis of the 1960s and the 1970s that the
leadership of the Labour Party should hold itself in reserve,
refusing in any way to come to terms with the Affluent
Society."[53] This thesis was problematic for a number of
reasons, not least that what it amounted to was a call to
remain in Opposition until an economic crisis would allow
the Labour Party to return to power. What, critics asked,
was the Party to do in the meantime; and not surprisingly
the call to stay in Opposition was treated with derision.
Crosland in particular regarded this as an immoral position

drawing on Max Weber's distinction between the ethic of
ultimate ends and the ethic of responsibility and argued that
the Labour Party had a moral responsibility to accommodate
with social change in order to regain power so as to
represent the interests of the poor.[54]

One further issue requires attention in any understanding
of Crossman's socialism, namely his attitude to democracy,
which shows at the same time both the consistency and the
ultimate limitations of his thought. Crossman argued that
post-war Britain was marked by the growth of oligarchies
and that, "the first task of socialism, therefore, must be to
expose this growth of irresponsible power; to challenge this
new managerial oligarchy; to show that its monopolistic – or
oligopolistic – privileges are a threat to democracy and to
demand that it should become not the master but the
servant of the nation."[55] This argument was a consistent one
in Crossman's writing from at least the early 1950s when he
argued in his contribution to the *New Fabian Essays* that the
Attlee Government had not introduced socialism since there
remained concentrated power in capitalist enterprises and
public sector bureaucracies.[56] In this drift to oligarchy,
Crossman identified with the work of J.K. Galbraith who
had stressed the concentration of power in the economy as
the main feature of the new managerial society.[57] Similarly,
Crossman's thesis coincided with, and was influenced by,
Strachey's argument that there were strong counter-
pressures to democratisation in the economy.

Crossman identified several areas where there was
growing concentration of power including the office of
Prime Minister, the civil service, public and private sector
corporations, the trade unions and even the Labour Party.
He argued in his 'Introduction' to the new edition of
Bagehot's *The English Constitution* and again in a series of
lectures – which formed his book *The Myths of Cabinet
Government* – in the early 1970s reflecting on his time as a
Cabinet Minister, that there had been much more

centralisation in the political system, in which the power of
the Prime Minister had increased at the expense of the
Cabinet and the power of the bureaucracy had increased at
the expense of Parliament.[58] Crossman stated that, "as early
as 1870 Bagehot pointed to the contrast between the
semblance and the reality of power in British politics. Since
his epoch, parliamentary government has been replaced by
what can be described as alternating party dictatorship."[59]
His answer, reflecting a number of his concerns as a
Minister after 1964, was to defend the traditional role of
Cabinet: to increase the role of political advisors; to reform
the House of Commons including an extension of the
Standing Committee system; to reduce the powers of the
House of Lords and to reform of the judiciary in order to
enforce human rights.[60]

   A major threat to democracy came from the growth of
oligarchic power in the public and private sector
corporations. Here there was a need to increase the level of
industrial democracy not only in the private sector but in the
public sector also. Moreover, the Morrisonian model of the
public corporation, whereby nationalised industries were run
by corporate boards in much the same way as private sector
companies, had failed to introduce high-level industrial
democracy. It was therefore necessary for future socialist
advance that public and private corporations were reformed.
However, a further dilemma related to how this should be
achieved since an additional area in which there had been
concentration of power was in the trade unions.[61] The
attempts that had been made to introduce participation in
public corporations had led to trade union leaders
dominating the labour interest, with little or no
accountability to their own members. Crossman was
therefore sceptical of socialist advance coming from the
trade unions: "we must not expect the initiative for the next
stage of socialism to come…from the leadership of the trade
unions."[62] This criticism of trade union leaders led to

conflict with Gaitskell who urged him with some success to remove some of the more controversial statements.[63] One further institution where a concentration of power could be identified was in the Labour Party itself, where despite the chimera of democracy and the division of responsibilities between the parliamentary and extra-parliamentary elements, the two had become separated and the Leader had increased his power over the rest of the Party. Although Attlee had claimed that the Party was a democratic institution[64], this centralisation of power had been occurring since at least 1945.

The tension arose from the question of how socialism was to be achieved. Many of the thinkers discussed in this book placed the main emphasis on the state, whereas others such as G.D.H. Cole placed the greatest emphasis on the trade unions. The difficulty for Crossman was that he had questioned the commitment to socialism held by the central state, the trade unions leaders and Labour Party leadership since they all held on to concentrated power. Crossman's most consistent view was that socialism could best be achieved by greater state planning, needed in order to make people free.[65] However, the inherent tension within this argument is obvious – planning required more not less state power and required the compliance of other institutions in order to be effective. Planning required more order rather than more freedom.[66] Moreover, planning would require a fact-finding bureau under the power of the Prime Minister in order to counter the power of the Treasury, thus contradicting his 'solution' to prime ministerial government.[67]

Conclusion

By way of conclusion, several points can be made. The chapter has hopefully demonstrated that critics have tended to exaggerate Crossman's inconsistency and that there are several key themes that can be identified in Crossman's writing. Firstly, it has been argued that Crossman can be characterised as a Labour Party centrist, seeking to maintain – particularly at vital stages of internal conflict – the unity of the Labour Party, not just within Parliament but between MPs and the grass-roots of the Party. For this reason, he associated himself with Gaitskell rather than Bevan when it appeared that the Bevanite faction was creating division and then with Wilson when the revisionists produced internal division over Clause IV at the end of the decade. Secondly, despite this, he maintained his earlier radicalism in political thought which had led him to become one of the most open critics of the Attlee Government from 1947 with the publication of *Keep Left*. This radicalism led him to consistently argue that Revisionism was intellectually and morally deficient, and that socialism should maintain a radical commitment to democratisation and empowerment, which meant that intellectually he was closer to Bevan[68] and to Strachey than to the revisionists even when he was supportive of Gaistkell between 1955-59.

However, although it is possible to offer a more positive perspective on Crossman than is usually given, it is difficult to escape the ultimate conclusion that Crossman's thought was deficient. This is so for several reasons. Firstly, the two elements of Crossman's thought identified – his Labour Party centrism and his radical commitment to democracy – are, if not incompatible, certainly difficult to synthesise so that his actions and his arguments frequently appeared inconsistent. Moreover, he failed to provide a major contribution to British socialism, indeed it can be argued that despite some interesting rhetorical flourishes his output is the least impressive of any thinker in this book.[69] He failed, as may well have been expected given his lack of expertise, to provide a work of political economy; but he also failed to provide a significant work of socialist philosophy, which he could have done much more effectively than many other individuals featured in this book given his previous role as an academic political philosopher. He failed to produce a book on socialism, limiting himself to shorter pieces. A problem with this approach is that it lacked the sustained focus of Strachey or Crosland for example. He therefore raised concerns with Revisionism and what he regarded as the concentration of power and also pointed to the irrelevance of Marxism in the post-1951 era, but failed, in the final analysis, to provide a clear alternative.

[1] R.H.S. Crossman, 'Towards a Philosophy of Socialism' in R.H.S. Crossman (ed.) *New Fabian Essays* (Dent, London, 1970, 2nd edition), p.2.

[2] R.H.S. Crossman, 'John Strachey and the Left Book Club' (1956) in R.H.S. Crossman (ed.) *The Charm of Politics and Other Essays in Political Criticism* (Hamilton, London, 1958), pp.139-140.

[3] See R.H.S. Crossman, 'Introduction' in R.H.S. Crossman (ed.) *The God that Failed: Six Studies in Communism* (Hamilton, London, 1950); R.H.S. Crossman, *Socialist Values in a Changing Civilisation*, Fabian Tract 286 (Fabian Society, London, 1951); Crossman, *The Charm of Politics*; R.H.S. Crossman (ed.) *Planning for Freedom: Essays in Socialism* (Hamilton, London, 1965); J. Morgan (ed.) *The Backbench Diaries of Richard Crossman* (Hamilton and Cape, London, 1981); T. Dalyell, *Dick Crossman: A Portrait* (Weidenfeld and Nicolson, London, 1989) and A. Howard, *Crossman: the Pursuit of Power* (Cape, London, 1990). The Crossman papers are located at the Modern Records Centre, University of Warwick.

[4] See principally, S. Haseler, *The Gaitskellites: Revisionism in the British Labour Party 1951-64* (Macmillan, London, 1969), pp.112-137 and 178-208. See also D. Howell, *British Social Democracy* (Croom Helm, London, 1976) and T. Jones, *Remaking the Labour Party: from Gaitskell to Blair* (Routledge, London, 1996) for further discussions of these issues.

[5] Of which one of the more interesting is R. Cooney, S. Fielding and N. Tiratsoo (eds.) *The Wilson Government 1964-70* (Pinter, London, 1993).

[6] Tam Dalyell was of course, a politician and Tony Howard a journalist. Both of these studies are useful and Howard in particular makes use of the Crossman archive. A recent academic reflection on Crossman's ideas has at last been provided by Victoria Honeyman, 'A Study of the Life of Richard Crossman, MP for Coventry East from 1945 to 1974', unpublished PhD thesis, University of Leeds, 2005.

[7] J. Braddock and B. Braddock, *The Braddocks* (Macdonald, London, 1963), p.209.

[8] Morgan (ed.) *The Backbench Diaries of Richard Crossman*, 19 January 1956, p.467.

[9] D. Marquand, *The Progressive Dilemma: from Lloyd George to Blair* (2nd edition, Phoenix, London, 1999), pp.137-146.

[10] D. Healey, *The Time of My Life* (Penguin, London, 1990), pp.107-108

[11] G. Foote, *The Labour Party's Political Thought: A History* (Palgrave, Basingstoke, 1997, 3rd edition), p.278.

[12] R. Plant, M. Beech and K. Hickson *The Struggle for Labour's Soul: Understanding Labour's Political Thought since 1945* (Routledge, London, 2004).

[13] Howard, *Crossman: the Pursuit of Power*, p.3.

14 A. Howard (ed.) *The Crossman Diaries: Selections from Dairies of a Cabinet Minister, 1964-70* (Hamilton and Cape, London, 1979), 21 March 1965, p.80.

15 R.H.S. Crossman, 'The Theory and Practice of British Freedom' (1938) in Crossman (ed.) *Planning for Freedom*, p.30.

16 R.H.S. Crossman 'Towards a New Philosophy of Socialism' (1951) in Crossman (ed.) *Planning for Freedom*, p.39.

17 This issue became one of the most sensitive in the debates of the 1950s. Broadly speaking, the left wanted to find common cause with France as a neutral zone between the two superpowers, whereas the right wanted to maintain the alliance with USA against the Soviet threat.

18 The best discussion of the Labour Government 1945-51, at least as far as this author is concerned, remains K.O. Morgan, *Labour in Power 1945-51* (Oxford University Press, Oxford, 1984).

19 *Keep Left* (New Statesman, London, 1947) and *Keeping Left* (New Statesman, London, 1950). *Keep Left* was written by Crossman together with Michael Foot and Ian Mikardo and was also signed by G. Bing, D. Bruce, H. Davies, L. Hale, F. Lee, B.W. Levy, R.W.G. Mackay, E.L. Mallalieu, E.R. Millington, S. Swingler, G. Wigg and W. Wyatt. Signatories to *Keeping Left* were, R. Acland, D. Bruce, B. Castle, R. Crossman, H. Davies, L. Hale, T. Horabin, M. Lipton, I. Mikardo, S. Swingler, G. Wigg and T. Williams. See S. Haseler, *The Gaitskellites* (Macmillan, London, 1969) pp.19-21 for a discussion.

20 Crossman 'Towards a New Philosophy of Socialism', p.40.

21 See R.H.S. Crossman, 'John Strachey and the Left Book Club'.

22 Ibid. p.142.

23 See R.H.S. Crossman, *What do we mean by Socialism?* (1948) Crossman papers, University of Warwick, MSS154/3/KL/1/1A-H and Crossman, *Socialist Values in a Changing Civilisation*.

24 Crossman, 'Introduction', in Crossman (ed.) *The God that Failed*, pp.12-13. This use of language was rather odd given his agnosticism.

25 In attempting to explain this, Crossman identified himself with R.H. Tawney's *Acquisitive Society* (Bell, London, 1961). See Crossman, 'John Strachey and the Left Book Club' in Crossman (ed.) *The Charm of Politics*, p.140.

26 Morgan (ed.) *The Backbench Diaries of Richard Crossman*, 20 May 1952, p.107.

27 Crossman, 'Planning for Freedom' in Crossman (ed.) *Planning for Freedom* pp.62-63.

28 See C.A.R. Crosland, *The Future of Socialism* (Cape, London, 1956) and D. Jay, *Socialism in the New Society* (Longmans, London, 1962).

29 Crossman et.al., *Keep Left*.

[30] Acland et.al. *Keeping Left*.

[31] Howard, *Crossman*, p.155-163.

[32] Morgan, *The Backbench Diaries of Richard Crossman*, 17 December 1951, p.51.

[33] Howard, *Crossman*, p.172.

[34] Bevan died in 1960.

[35] Howard, *Crossman*, pp.176-182.

[36] Ibid., pp.183-218.

[37] This suggestion was made by Jay in *Forward* 16 October 1959. See also Howard, *Crossman* pp.222-230 and also Jones, *Remaking the Labour Party*, pp.41-64.

[38] Howard, *Crossman*, p.219-242.

[39] Ibid., pp.231-232.

[40] See the chapters on the 'Centre' by Noel Thompson and Mark Garnett respectively in Plant et.al., *The Struggle for Labour's Soul* and K. Hickson (ed.) *The Political Thought of the Conservative Party since 1945* (Palgrave, Basingstoke, 2005) in an attempt to improve understanding of these issues.

[41] Howard, *Crossman*, pp.178-179.

[42] Ibid., p.233.

[43] Ibid., pp.262-298.

[44] Ibid.

[45] R.H.S. Crossman, 'On Political Neuroses' *Encounter* May 1954, pp.65-67. A similar view had been expressed earlier in an article he wrote on Attlee in 1948, see 'Mr Attlee as Prime Minister' in Crossman (ed.) *The Charm of Politics*. The role of nationalisation as 'myth' is the central theme of Jones, *Remaking the Labour Party*.

[46] R.H.S. Crossman, 'The Spectre of Revisionism' *Encounter*, April 1960, republished as 'The Clause IV Controversy' in Crossman (ed.) *Planning for Freedom*, pp.113-122. This was a response to Crosland's *Encounter* article of March 1960 republished as 'The Future of the Left' in C.A.R. Crosland (ed.) *The Conservative Enemy: A Programme of Radical Reform for the 1960s* (Cape, London, 1962).

[47] R.H.S. Crossman, *Labour in the Affluent Society*, Fabian Tract 325 (Fabian Society, London, 1960) republished as 'The Affluent Society' in Crossman (ed.) *Planning for Freedom*, pp.86-112.

[48] Crossman 'The Affluent Society' p.110.

[49] Not so – see the following chapter.

[50] See Crossman, 'The Affluent Society' pp.102-103. Balogh wrote on economic issues for the *Keep Left* Group, see his paper 'Economic Points for a Programme' 17 February 1953, Crossman papers, University of Warwick, MSS154/3/KL/4/4.

[51] See Howard, *Crossman*, pp.228-230 for a discussion.

[52] Crossman 'The Affluent Society', p.91.

[53] Ibid. p.101.

[54] C.A.R. Crosland, *Can Labour Win?* Fabian Tract 324 (Fabian Society, London, 1960) republished as 'Can Labour Win?' in C.A.R. Crosland (ed.) *The Conservative Enemy*, pp.143-163. See also his 'Radical Reform and the Left' *Encounter* October 1960 and republished in *The Conservative Enemy*, pp.127-142.

[55] Crossman, 'Planning for Freedom', p.63.

[56] Crossman, 'Towards a New Philosophy of Socialism' in Crossman (ed.) *New Fabian Essays*, pp.56-57.

[57] J.K. Galbraith, *The Affluent Society* (Hamish Hamilton, London, 1958).

[58] R.H.S. Crossman, *The Myths of Cabinet Government* (Harvard University Press, Harvard, 1972) and 'Introduction' to W. Bagehot, *The English Constitution* (Collins/Fontana, London, 1963), although note his initial impression on entering Cabinet in 1964 when he felt that it was "a much more genuine forum of opinion than I had been led to expect." Howard (ed.) *The Crossman Diaries*, 22 October 1965, p.29. This proved not to be the case given the difficulties those who favoured early devaluation had in raising the issue in Cabinet from 1964.

[59] Crossman, 'Preface' to *The Charm of Politics*, pp.ix-x.

[60] Crossman, 'Planning for Freedom', pp.75-81.

[61] Ibid., pp.66-70. See also, Crossman 'What do we mean by socialism?' and 'A Socialist Plan for Fair Shares under Rearmament' Keep Left Group paper 81, Crossman papers, University of Warwick, MSS154/3/KL/2/56-61 where it is argued that trade unions need to be controlled as part of a wider planning framework.

[62] Crossman, 'Planning for Freedom', pp.70-71.

[63] See Morgan (ed.) *The Backbench Diaries of Richard Crossman*, 19 January 1956, p.467 and Howard, *Crossman*, pp.200-201.

[64] See, C. Attlee, *The Labour Party in Perspective* (Gollancz, London, 1937).

[65] Hence the title of his major work on socialism, *Planning for Freedom*.

[66] For example, Crossman argued at several stages for incomes policy, which would limit the capacity of trade unions to enter into free collective bargaining so as to allow for the planned expansion of wages. See, for example, *Keeping Left* p.39 and also Crossman, 'Towards a New Philosophy of Socialism' pp.57-58.

[67] Crossman, 'Planning for Freedom', pp.74-75.

[68] See A. Bevan, *In Place of Fear* (Heinemann, London, 1952).

[69] Including Gordon Brown, who has also failed to produce a detailed exposition of his version of socialism, but has provided more sustained focus on economic and welfare policies.

8

C.A.R. CROSLAND

'The conclusion must be that in Britain equality of opportunity and social mobility…are not enough. The limited goal (equality of opportunity) is not, from a socialist point of view, sufficient.'[1]

Tony Crosland's statement about the limits of equality of opportunity as a socialist objective highlights the central concerns of this chapter, namely what did Crosland mean by equality, how did he come to such a position and how did he think his objective should be realised. The chapter aims first to provide an analysis of Crosland's thesis as outlined in his major work *The Future of Socialism*[2] and defended subsequently in *The Conservative Enemy*[3] and *Socialism Now*[4] together with a substantial number of articles in the quality press and specialist journals. Crosland argued that the economy had undergone radical change, partly as a result of what the Labour Government of 1945-51 had done but also as a result of longer-term economic trends. These changes required socialists to rethink their doctrines. For Crosland this meant a concern primarily with equality. In turn this required specific reforms to the school and higher education systems and the tax structure. Hence, we see the three elements of Crosland's thesis, which this chapter discusses: the nature of economic change, the redefinition of socialist objectives and finally the identification of appropriate policies.

Moreover, it is argued that Crosland maintained a commitment to public ownership, which he thought had a role to play in increasing the efficiency of the British economy. This is against the view that Crosland rejected the extension of public ownership in any form. This allows for a more accurate comparison with John Strachey and Richard Crossman when examining the development of British socialism in the 1950s and with Stuart Holland when discussing later developments in socialist political economy. Finally, it is the opinion of this author that Crosland's arguments continue to be of relevance for contemporary social democracy and it will be suggested at the end of the chapter what form this may take.

The Transformation of Capitalism

In the immediate pre-war period Crosland had assumed a Marxist position. This has been documented by his biographers.[5] At Oxford, he had made explicit his Marxist views. In the post-war period he was to reject his earlier Marxist beliefs as insufficient in the new conditions of the 1950s. The catalyst for change had been the Second World War. There exists in the Crosland archive a lengthy correspondence with Philip Williams, in which he sates his wish to write a major work of revisionist socialism and become the new Bernstein.[6] Crosland appears to have read Bernstein around 1940. The reforms of the Attlee Government between 1945-51 were seen to have demonstrated the capacity of the state to reform the economy and society in a way in which Marx had not predicted. The third development which Crosland was to argue would require a new, revised socialism was the transformation of the economy, in particular the growth of large firms and the separation of ownership and control of industry. This was encouraged by the war and by the policies of the Labour Government but was occurring independently prior to 1939. These three factors, he argued, necessarily required a re-definition of socialism.

Crosland's starting point was to outline in greater detail the changes to capitalism. This was first done in the *New Fabian Essays* published in 1952.[7] The essays included contributions from both the revisionists and the traditional left, and were edited by a representative of the left (at least at that point in time), Richard Crossman. However, the balance was in favour of the revisionists and it can be argued that Crosland's essay was the most original contribution in the book. His essay outlined what he regarded as the 'transformation of capitalism'. This was elaborated in the early chapters of *The Future of Socialism*. He argued that Marxist analysis had been made redundant by the transformation of capitalism. At the time Marx wrote owners of capital also had control of industry, recent changes had reduced irrevocably the power of the owners.

Specifically, the power of owners had been lost in three directions.[8] The first major transformation was in the increased power of the state. Marx had argued that the power of state was limited and in some accounts was little more than the agent of the dominant class. Attempts at increased state control of the economy or of welfare reform would be curtailed by the interests of capital. Crosland argued that recent developments had falsified this claim. First, the Attlee Government had nationalised approximately 20 per cent of industry. Although this had been, with the exception of iron and steel, the loss-making industries and had been enacted on grounds of efficiency rather than socialist ideology they were the basic industries upon which the remainder of the private sector depended. This gave the state significant power - if it chose to exercise it[9] - in the planning and investment decisions of the private sector firm. In addition, the use of Keynesian techniques, in particular the use of fiscal policy, gave the state substantial powers over the private sector, which it could choose to utilise.

The second broad development that had occurred in the economy was the transfer of power from the owners of industry to managers. In effect, the ownership of industry had become separated from its control. Ownership had fragmented into a large number of shareholders who were excluded from effective decision-making and who held shares in different companies so that they had little interest in the specific decisions of individual firms. Managers had taken control and worked in the wider interests of the company and often with beneficial social impact: "the talk, and part of it is at least genuine, is now of the social responsibilities of industry... Aggressive individualism is giving way to a suave and sophisticated sociability."[10] Here Crosland had been influenced by the work of Berle and Means about the separation of ownership and control with the large number of shareholders and the idea of the 'managerial revolution' promoted by James Burnham.[11] In addition, these trends had been identified by pre-war Labour thinkers such as Douglas Jay and Evan Durbin, although they formed only a minor part of their arguments.[12] This was a controversial thesis involving both a quantitative assessment of the ownership patterns of industry and a qualitative assertion of the social responsibility of management. Not surprisingly, both aspects of this argument were questioned.[13]

Third, there had been a transfer of power from owners to workers. This was largely in the form of organised labour, which had become more powerful partly as a result of legislation enacted by the Attlee Government but mainly due to the increase in trade union membership after the war. This had increased the collective bargaining power of labour, particularly in the full employment conditions of the 1950s.

A final development noted by Crosland was the transformation in British politics, particularly in the

Conservative Party.[14] The Conservatives had rejected the
earlier free market stance in favour of the welfare state and
mixed economy. Although this was largely due to the
pressures of electoral competition and the shock of losing in
1945, Crosland thought that a future Conservative
government was unlikely to undo the social and economic
reforms of the Attlee Administration.

These changes were fundamental and irreversible and
Crosland questioned the extent to which the contemporary
economy was still capitalist. He suggested in 1952 that the
new form of economic relations was 'statist'[15] but in *The
Future of Socialism* rejected this term: "I once rashly joined in
the search for a suitable name, and in *New Fabian Essays*
called the new society 'statism'. But it was, on reflection, a
bad choice... Having had no better idea since then, I have
no intention of trying again. Nevertheless, I believe that our
present society is sufficiently defined, and distinct from
classical capitalism, to require a different name."[16] This may
appear to be a semantic argument but the point is crucial.
Crosland was stating that British society in the 1950s was
post-capitalist. His critics, and Strachey can here be used as
a prime example[17], were arguing that society was still
capitalist.

It is easy to criticise these arguments with the benefit of
hindsight and Crosland was probably caught up in the
euphoria of Labour politics in the post-war period. As
discussed already in this book, Strachey among others
suggested that Crosland had been too sanguine and that the
reforms of 1945-51 had not gone as far as he had thought.
By the 1970s Crosland himself came to admit to having been
over-optimistic.[18] However, the failure of the Wilson
Government to raise growth to the levels specified in the
National Plan owed less, Crosland argued, to the persistence
of capitalist power but rather to the failures of the
Government, especially in refusing to devalue the pound
earlier than 1967.

Nevertheless, on a range of specific points Crosland did counter the arguments of his critics, largely in his book *The Conservative Enemy*, which was addressed not just to Conservatives but also to 'conservative' critics on the left and pragmatic right of the Labour Party who both failed in his opinion to formulate a radical ideological politics in the new conditions.[19] It was the attachment to 'ends' that Crosland felt distinguished his brand of radical revisionism from the pragmatists on the Labour right and to which we must now turn.

Identification of 'Ends'

Crosland made a distinction between 'ends' and 'means'. The former are the value positions held by social democrats, whereas the latter are the policies used to achieve them. It was Crosland's assertion that the two could be clearly distinguished and that a variety of possible means existed to realise the stated objectives. Both of these assumptions were accepted by revisionists in the Labour Party and formed a key part of the arguments made by Hugh Gaitskell and Douglas Jay.[20] Indeed, such a distinction was central to the strategy of reducing the importance of public ownership in the programme offered by the Labour Party in the 1950s. Public ownership had since the 1918 Constitution been seen as central to a socialist programme – that the transfer of ownership from the private to the public sector was in itself socialist. Now, ownership was to be reduced to be a means: "ownership, while it can influence, does not determine the character of the society."[21] However, it is worth noting that criticisms of Crosland and the revisionist position more generally by those on the left tended not to focus on the ends-means distinction. That is not to say that the left conceded to the revisionists that public ownership was not a central part of socialism but that the defence of public ownership often did not take an explicitly ends-means formulation. There was no specific rebuttal of the ends-means distinction posed by the revisionists. The distinction was then raised by New Labour in its reformulation of social democracy in the 1990s. The claim often made by modernised social democrats is that the ends of socialism have remained constant but that the means have changed to take account of contemporary conditions. I will return to this issue at the end of the chapter.

Following the discussion on the transformation of capitalism, Crosland continued by outlining what he thought constituted the essence of socialism. This was a difficult task as he emphasised – there was no past socialist society that acted as a guide and there was a wide range of socialist approaches so that talk of a 'true' form of socialism was incorrect.[22] What was needed was to outline what the socialist traditions were and what common themes emerged from these differing approaches. Crosland identified ten traditions – briefly stated these are a natural law tradition, the Owenite influence on self-governing communities, the labour theory of value stressing that the production of wealth was made by the working-class, Christian socialism, Marxism, the theory of rent as unearned income that stressed the need for public control of land, the cultural approach of William Morris, Fabian gradualism, the Independent Labour Party tradition and the welfare state tradition.[23] These approaches suggested a wide range of means and also divergence over the form of socialist society that was idealised. However, according to Crosland, there were five ends common to these approaches: the elimination of material poverty, the promotion of social welfare, equality, fraternity and the pursuit and maintenance of full employment.[24]

As noted Crosland thought that changes to the capitalist system were permanent and that several of the ends of socialism stated in pre-war accounts had become irrelevant in the new conditions. Material poverty, common in the 1930s, had been largely eliminated by the creation of the welfare state between 1945-51. There was a need to raise benefit levels and target specific groups left out of the reforms after 1945. Similarly, the fifth objective of full employment had been largely achieved. The three remaining objectives were welfare, equality and fraternity. Of these, Crosland declared that he was unsure of how the fraternal commitment could be extended – not because he was opposed to it but "simply because I find it impossible to reach a definite conclusion about its relevance in contemporary conditions."[25] It was still necessary to increase welfare expenditure in order to eliminate remaining poverty on humanitarian grounds. Above all importance should be attached to equality, defined in terms of altering the basic hierarchical pattern of society: "this belief in social equality, which has been the strongest ethical inspiration of virtually every socialist doctrine, still remains the most characteristic feature of socialist thought today."[26]

The question remains of what this form of equality should take. In particular, left-wing critics argued that Crosland advocated merely equality of opportunity. This was reflected in academic studies of revisionist thought. Bernard Crick claimed that Crosland was committed to equality of opportunity.[27] Similarly, David Howell states that "considerable emphasis was placed on 'equality', by which was generally meant equality of opportunity, plus whatever safeguards were required to prevent the emergence of a meritocratic elite."[28] However, it was these 'safeguards' that were crucial to a full understanding of Crosland's equality.

The most detailed discussion of this issue is made in several places by Raymond Plant.[29] Plant distinguishes three forms of equality. The first is equality of opportunity which in its minimal format concerns the removal of barriers to access, especially in access to paid employment, through to more positive action to help people realise their opportunities. It is this fuller conception of equality of opportunity to which Crick and Howell presumably refer. The second form of equality is equality of outcome. In practice, complete equality of outcome was only explicitly argued by Bernard Shaw[30] although a number of left-wing critics have argued that the need for financial incentives is much less than often assumed and that human nature will be less self-interested outside of a capitalist society.[31]

The final form of equality is what can be termed, following Rawls[32], as 'democratic equality' which is a concern with both opportunities and a narrowing of outcomes. Crosland himself commented in his last major work *Socialism Now* that he had meant something similar to democratic equality: "by equality we meant more than a meritocratic society of equal opportunities in which the greatest rewards would go to those with the most fortunate genetic endowment and family background; we adopted a 'strong' definition of equality – what Rawls has subsequently called the 'democratic' as opposed to the 'liberal' conception."[33] In fact this is a complex issue, Crosland had not sought to provide a theoretical account of how people would choose equality in a position of ignorance as theorised by Rawls. It is not clear therefore that Crosland had meant the same thing as Rawls despite stating that he did, or at least that he came to a similar position from a very different angle. The significance of Plant's distinction is that there is something between equality of opportunity and equality of outcome. The task still remains to distinguish what Crosland did mean in his complex notion of equality.

First, Crosland did state his support for equality of opportunity.[34] He rejected arguments that a competitive society would cause psychological problems and welcomed the greater opportunities that he believed existed in the United States. In looking for alternative societies that Britain could seek to emulate, he emphasised the United States and Sweden. The former was controversial since many on the left regarded the U.S. as the leading capitalist state. However, what he liked about the US was the absence, as he saw it, of an upper class and the increased social mobility that was not hampered by social class, accent, manners and so forth that existed in Britain: "from the point of view of social justice, an aristocracy of talent is an obvious improvement on a hereditary aristocracy, since no one is in fact denied an equal chance."[35] Equality of opportunity was preferable to a traditional elitist society since the most able would rise rather than the senior positions being allocated on the basis of nepotism. Hence, Crosland rejected the arguments made by critics of equality of opportunity about the deleterious consequences of competition: "I conclude that the case often made against the mobile equal-opportunity society both exaggerates the evils and underestimates the compensating gains."[36]

However, in echoing Michael Young[37], there were clear limits of an equal opportunity framework since the traditional ruling class would be replaced by a meritocratic one in which senior positions and an above average share of income and wealth would pass to those best able to compete: "I do not believe, as a personal value judgement, that it can be described as a 'just' society. It implies that very unequal rewards and privileges are distributed solely on the basis of, if not one, at any rate a particular group of traits of human personality."[38] Although Crick, Howell and others say that Crosland meant by equality an equality of opportunity he did in fact mean much more than this. The additional features of Crosland's conception of equality meant much more than additional safeguards. The equality that Crosland had in mind was of a morally distinct kind to equality of opportunity. There were two main problems with equality of opportunity. The first is that with widespread economic and social inequality he believed that there were unequal starting points. What may be presented as theoretical equality of opportunity did in fact mean that those who were already in a privileged position would have the best prospects. The second problem is that the distribution of wealth and income, even assuming equality of opportunity, would still be decided by the market. This prioritised certain distributive principles above others in an arbitrary way. Those most able to compete in the marketplace would get the greatest rewards. However, the abilities and attributes needed to compete in the marketplace were not necessarily the responsibility of the individual who possessed them. Conversely, those who were not able to compete in the marketplace due to factors beyond their control would be penalised. Market outcomes would not therefore be fully deserved due to factors such as family background, educational ability, genetic inheritance and so forth. This is in fact a moral critique of markets and means that Crosland had in mind much more than equality of opportunity and did indeed bring his argument closer to that developed by Rawls in his 'difference principle'.

We are therefore in a position to outline what Crosland meant by equality. First, an equality of opportunity in which all positions would be open to competition and where people would not be barred from that competition. Secondly, greater equality of income and wealth to be achieved, as will be discussed below, through the fiscal redistribution of economic growth. This was to both allow for genuine equality of opportunity and to redress market outcomes deemed to be unjust. Finally, a thoroughgoing social equality in which the main features of the British class structure would be removed – not just income and wealth inequalities but also accent, manners, family background, the elitist school system and so forth. This can be distinguished from both equality of opportunity and equality of outcome as outlined above. It was distinct from equality of opportunity since it was concerned with tackling unjust market outcomes. The main way that this position was distinguished from equality of outcome was the recognition that income and wealth differentials were needed as a form of 'rent of ability' to allow for incentives to work and undertake tasks that would benefit the worse off.

The case for such a notion of equality had three justifications.[39] The first was the promotion of social contentment. It was noted that Britain faced a significant degree of class antagonism despite the creation of the welfare state and full employment. This was due to the existence of widespread inequality and a feeling that the existing distribution was unfair. Secondly, for reasons already pointed out, it was argued that there existed with the current distribution a social injustice that would be rectified by redistribution. Finally, in an economy which had a combination of relative poverty and nepotism there was a significant degree of social and economic waste – individuals were unable to realise their potential and this also undermined British economic performance.

The final part of Crosland's case for equality was to counter three criticisms of the pursuit of greater equality.[40] The first criticism was that greater equality was a threat to economic efficiency. The argument went that inequalities were needed to allow for incentives. The second argument was that the pursuit of greater equality was a threat to personal liberty, largely since it required the state to impose certain ends on society – in this case the higher tax revenue needed to raise the position of the poorest. The final argument was that the pursuit of equality was a threat to culture since large concentrations of individual wealth were needed to purchase cultural artefacts such as paintings. These three arguments were rejected. Crosland argued for a 'levelling-up' approach by which the absolute position of the rich would be maintained while the absolute position of the poor would be increased, thus raising the relative position of the poor. This would reduce neither incentives nor the spending power of the rich. It would increase economic efficiency by reducing the barriers to economic opportunities and increase the effective liberty of most individuals. Furthermore, it was debated how far the rich had aided cultural activity and the way pointed to non-economic aspects of life and the role of central government and municipal activity in the promotion of recreational, sporting and cultural activities.

The Relevance of Means

By themselves 'ends' are abstract conceptualisations, which for their realisation require appropriate policies. It was this link between values and policies which was significant for Crosland. It led him to argue that his politics was more than mere pragmatism and that he did have a different social organisation in mind when he wrote about socialism. As we have seen this social objective was a more equal society. Socialism could be distinguished from Conservatism with its emphasis on equality and despite the achievements of the Labour Government of 1945-51, there was still too much inequality in society. This also led him to question the programmes not only of the Labour left with its emphasis on public ownership but also the traditional, pragmatic Labour right, personified in the 1950s by Herbert Morrison's call for 'consolidation', that lacked ideological direction.[41] It was also this emphasis on equality that led Crosland to place greatest priority on educational and tax reforms and to reach certain novel positions on trade unions and industrial relations and also the role of public ownership. In the space available it is only possible to make brief statements on what Crosland thought Labour policy should look like. The important point is that underlying these policy prescriptions was an ideological commitment to greater equality.

Crosland argued that despite the reforms of the Attlee Government there was still too much inequality in society.[42] He asked why this was so and argued that the education system was primarily responsible for the persistence of *social* inequality: "the school system remains the most divisive, unjust, and wasteful of all the aspects of social inequality."[43] Two particular aspects of the school system were singled out for criticism.[44] The first was the grammar schools, which despite the reforms of the Attlee Government, still favoured the middle classes, whose children tended to pass the '11+' examination with relative ease, a result that evidence had suggested owed more to social background than academic ability. Those who failed would receive a more technical education in a secondary school while those who passed would go to a grammar school and receive an academic education. Since selection was more socially based this selection would reinforce social stratification. More criticism was directed at the public schools: "this is much the most flagrant inequality of opportunity as it is cause of class inequality generally."[45] Crosland, however, did not advocate the abolition of public schools but did argue that they needed to be integrated into the state system by allocating free places – as advocated by the Fleming Committee (1944) – starting with 25% of state-aided places increasing to 100%.[46] The argument went further however since the removal of grammar schools and the integration of public schools would create a school system based on equality of opportunity only. In order to develop a school system capable of fostering wider social equality there was a need for a comprehensive school structure in which children from all social backgrounds would mix in a single school environment. The comprehensive school system, Crosland argued, should be encouraged by a future Labour government. This was in fact to be the policy pursued by Crosland when he served as Secretary of State for Education in the 1960s.

In terms of fiscal policy, Crosland's broad position was that it would be difficult to achieve greater income equality by tax increases but that there was substantial room for further equalisation of wealth. The higher rate of income tax stood at 70%, which he believed could erode incentives if raised further. This point is significant in the contemporary context and I return to it at the end. In contrast, Crosland asserted that the Labour Government had done little to redistribute wealth after 1945 and that a major difference between what he initially called statism and socialism was the extent of the inequality of wealth. Following the pioneering work of Douglas Jay and Hugh Dalton in the pre-war period and also in line with other revisionists in the 1950s he argued that the most effective way to redistribute wealth was through taxation.[47] This argument was theoretically significant since it assumed first that the state had the capacity to redistribute wealth thus challenging Marxist assumptions that the state was structurally dependent upon the capitalists and represented their interests and that further public ownership was irrelevant in the redistribution of wealth (a point which is discussed further in the following chapter).

In terms of specific measures, Crosland advocated a gifts tax since the burden of inheritance tax was being avoided by the transfer of wealth before death. The aim would be to tax the transfer of substantial wealth in this way. In addition, it was argued that higher death duties would allow for the further equalisation of inherited wealth. Since wealth could also count as part of individual's income it was suggested that a property tax and a capital gains tax should also be introduced. Together these constituted a radical set of fiscal measures designed to redistribute wealth in addition to the continuing redistribution of income.

The third broad area of reform proposed in *The Future of Socialism* concerned trade unions and industrial relations.[48] Crosland's position was one deeply sceptical of measures to increase industrial democracy that involved workers, either individually or collectively through trade unions, in the direct management or control of industry. This was against the

general position of the Labour left at this time, which
wanted to see greater 'democratisation' in the workplace.
However, it was in keeping with the trade union tradition of
seeing management and labour as separate and in opposition
to one another with fundamentally distinct objectives which
although in conflict could be reached through gradual
reform of the workplace. It was also in tune with the main
findings of the Clegg Report.[49]   Given his general thesis
about social equality, Crosland placed emphasis on the
extent of social difference in the workplace as the root cause
of industrial discontent.   He therefore argued for the
reduction of non-pecuniary benefits in the workplace and
argued that Britain had much to learn here from the United
States: "this point is particularly important. Non-pecuniary
status privileges are exceptionally widespread in British
industry; and their persistence acts as a constant irritant.
They can hardly all be justified on grounds of discipline or
incentives, since they are so much less conspicuous in
American firms whose efficiency is beyond dispute."[50] The
creation of more harmonious industrial relations in the
1950s therefore, Crosland asserted, required three things:
greater social equality, higher wages and 'better' management
and trade union practices, which legislation alone could not
achieve. Although he continued to place emphasis on this
aspect of industrial relations, Crosland did come to accept
the relevance of participation in the 1970s with increased
trade union action.

The final area addressed by Crosland was the role of
nationalisation and economic planning.[51]   It is often
assumed, as noted above, that public ownership was seen by
Crosland specifically and by the revisionists more generally
as being irrelevant. Certainly, it was moved from being an
'end' of socialism to being a 'means' and that equality, the
true objective of socialism, could be achieved without large
increases in public ownership. However, this is different
from saying that public ownership was seen as irrelevant to

socialism, at least as perceived by Crosland. First, it was argued, as stated above, that the transfer of power away from the owners of wealth that was seen as central to the progress of socialism was in a large part due to the increased power of the state and the nationalisation programme of the Attlee Government had done much to bring this about. This programme may well have been carried out largely for reasons of efficiency in the immediate post-war context but there had been some reform of working and management procedures and also the state had gained a major source of power when dealing with the private sector. The role of planning and public ownership was therefore to be seen in this context. Planning should be used to regulate macroeconomic activity and supplement fiscal policy. Public ownership should be used where existing government policy tools proved insufficient to meet social objectives.

Public ownership, he argued, should be extended in two forms.[52] The first was to gain control of the development land through municipal and central government acquisition. The other idea developed at this time and increasingly part of Labour Party policy as seen in the 1957 document *Industry and Society* was an emphasis on public ownership of firms as distinct from whole industries.[53] This would allow the government to gain control of new economic sectors without the creation of state-owned monopolies and also encourage competition and efficiency: "avoiding as it does the problems of vast scale and centralised monopoly, the competing public firm is an attractive notion."[54] This was to be of central relevance in the debate between Crosland and Stuart Holland in the 1970s, when the latter advocated the competitive public enterprise as the most effective means of countering the growth of large-scale private sector corporate organisation - the mesoeconomy (this will be addressed in a later chapter). What should be emphasised here, finally, is that Crosland, despite the widespread conception to the contrary, continued to advocate public ownership, albeit in a different form and as a last resort when other measures failed.

Conclusion

By way of conclusion, the discussion will focus first on criticisms of Crosland's thesis and then suggest the contemporary relevance of his ideas. It will be argued, in contrast to 'modernised' social democrats[55], that there is still much in Crosland's thesis that is relevant to contemporary centre-left politics in Britain.

The Crosland archives reveal the extent to which his thesis was met with critical reaction. Criticism was directed at almost all the arguments outlined above. Some questioned the specific policy commitments such as educational reform either by arguing that public schools should be left unreformed (as was argued by many on the right) or that they should be abolished altogether (as argued by many on the radical left). Some questioned whether local authorities should actually be forced to introduce comprehensive schools rather than merely be 'encouraged', an issue that was to resurface when Crosland served as Education Secretary in the mid-1960s. Others criticised the tax reforms suggested by Crosland, either those on the right who thought they interfered with the rights of property owners to pass on their estates or those on the left who wanted higher rates on taxation and in particular higher taxes on personal income.

However, two broad criticisms are worth emphasising here. The first is the argument made regarding the transfer of power and the role of ownership. As was expected this attracted widespread criticism from those on the left who argued that there had not been a transformation of capitalism and that those who owned corporate wealth still held power so that socialism could not be advanced without the further extension of public ownership. Such an argument was to be expected since Crosland's contribution was part of the wider development of revisionist thought that was seeking to downplay the significance of public ownership which was deemed to be electorally unpopular and irrelevant to the development of socialist policy in the changed conditions of the 1950s. This argument has already been addressed at greater length in relation to John Strachey and will be discussed further in the following chapter on Stuart Holland and so will not be discussed further at this stage.

One other broad criticism that raises interesting aspects of Crosland's thinking and how his ideas were received at the time is the issue of 'community'. As Stephen Haseler noted in his detailed study of *The Gaitskellites*, there were two broad movements that shared a commitment to modernisation.[56] One was the *New Fabian Essays* and subsequent work from within the parliamentary party, of which Crosland was of course one, and the Socialist Union and its offshoot the journal *Socialist Commentary*. Despite both supporting modernisation under Gaistkell, the two groups continued to hold different positions, which although minor on some issues had as its ideological underpinning a different conception of the value of community. This can be seen in the review of *The Future of Socialism* by Rita Hinden[57], the editor of *Socialist Commentary*, in which she criticised Crosland's limited commitment to the notion of 'community'. This point was furthered in subsequent developments in British social democracy, in particular the era of 'neo-revisionism' in the 1970s and analysed recently in an article by the author.[58] This grouping, since it was formed around Roy Jenkins, appeared to be concerned mainly with the promotion of the EEC within the parliamentary party but did seek a reformulation of socialism in the 1970s, which some thought Crosland had failed to do in his last major essay *Socialism Now*. The ideas of this group, developed most by the Labour MP and academic John Mackintosh,[59] tended to place emphasis on the notion of 'community' and a number of arguments were made in favour of the decentralisation of decision-making to the local level.[60] The notion of community was also given increased emphasis by New Labour both in terms of constitutional reform (Scottish and Welsh devolution, English regional government and increased powers for local authorities[61]) and also in the emphasis on individual 'responsibilities'. What many of those associated with both 'neo-revisionism' and New Labour argued was that the concept of community was neglected by Crosland.

It has already been noted that Crosland was sceptical of the notion of community, in particular of the idea of 'participation'. Indeed, in *The Future of Socialism* he had said that, "it is not easy to avoid a certain irritation when one hears the word 'participation'... It (has become) a catch-phrase, bandied about as though it were a nostrum for every social evil."[62] Crosland goes on to assert that the attitude of the Socialist Union was incorrect. They had argued that: "man cannot find his fulfilment in selfish isolation... He may limit his creative activities to his home and his garden, but in so doing he denies his responsibilities within his own community."[63] In contrast, Crosland argued that creative activities can be found in private activity, that being herded in to groups stunts human creativity and that if the aim of socialism is to pursue greater equality in order to promote individual freedom then people should be allowed to pursue private interests if they so choose.[64] Finally, Crosland argues that there will be a need to place more emphasis on cultural resources than economic policy in the future and calls for the reform of laws on censorship in the arts: "most of these are intolerable, and should be highly offensive to socialists, in whose blood there should always run a trace of the anarchist and the libertarian, and not too much of the prig and the prude."[65] It is not my intention to evaluate the relative merits of the communitarian and libertarian arguments of British social democracy here but simply to make two points. First, Crosland was a libertarian and there is a strong connection between equality and liberty in his work, which was to resurface in the 1980s.[66] Secondly, often those who have advocated a stronger emphasis on community – especially the 'neo-revisionists' in the 1970s and New Labour from the 1990s – have also sought to downplay the significance of inequality; almost that 'community' becomes an alternative core principle to 'equality'. This is not to say that these ideas are necessarily in conflict, indeed it may be argued that inequality undermines a sense of shared community, but nevertheless that those who have made the strongest arguments in favour of 'community' have tended to reduce the emphasis placed on 'equality'.

In asking what relevance Crosland has in the contemporary context it is worth emphasising once again that his ideas have been rejected explicitly by a number of contemporary social democrats. It has been argued that the changed context, in particular 'globalisation' and working-class fragmentation have created a need to emphasise new conceptions of socialism and that Crosland's socialism is largely irrelevant to the new situation.[67] Moreover, it is argued that he failed to see the limitations of public expenditure, and equated social and economic equality with high levels of public spending.[68] In contrast, it can be argued that social democrats should not be so quick as to reject the main parts of Crosland's thesis. There are three specific points to be made here.

First, it should be emphasised that the relationship between means and ends is more complex than is thought by some contemporary social democrats. It has been the tendency of modernised social democrats to argue that while policies have been revised to take account of changing circumstances this has been done without changing the underlying values. This position is usually expressed in terms of 'traditional values in a modern context' and Blair has stressed that: "the Third Way is not an attempt to split the difference between right and left. It is about traditional values in a changed world.... What of policy? Our view is 'permanent revisionism', a continual search for better means to meet our goals, based on a closer view of the changes taking place in advanced industrialised countries."[69] While the Third Way will be discussed in greater detail in relation to the thought of Anthony Giddens, it will be argued here that this notion of changed means and fixed principles is an oversimplification of the means-ends relationship.[70] If social democracy is to have realisable aims then it is necessary to do two things. First, it is necessary to define what specific conceptualisation of core values such as equality, liberty or community is held since these concepts are capable of different meanings. It is then necessary to identify what policies will be used to realise these objectives. It can be shown that there has indeed been a revision of means with New Labour as Blair states, but also a revision of ends.

Secondly, it can be argued that there is as much if not greater need to place emphasis on equality in contemporary conditions. The core objective of Crosland's socialism was, as we have seen, a complex notion of equality. This involved redistribution of income and wealth in order to reduce relative poverty and to tackle the *social* causes of inequality as a way of realising a genuine equality of opportunity and fairness of outcome. Inequality in income and wealth was narrower when Crosland wrote in the 1950s than today and yet New Labour has failed to reduce the gap between rich and poor since coming to power in 1997. Inequality increased substantially as a result of Thatcherite policy between 1979 and 1990. It flattened between 1990-97 and then rose as a result of New Labour's decision to maintain Conservative spending limits until 1999. Subsequent redistribution has been substantial but has only succeeded in returning to 1997 levels in broad terms.[71] However, New Labour states a commitment to equality of opportunity, but this is compromised from a Croslandite perspective by the level of income and wealth inequality. Given that such inequality is greater now than in the immediate post-war period it seems that a concern with relative poverty is more pressing now than it was even in the 1950s and there is scope to raise income tax (which, at 40% is lower than for most of the time Thatcher was in power) and to seek to redistribute wealth.

Finally, the revisionist case for public ownership, limited and in the form of competitive public enterprise, is still relevant. New Labour's approach to public ownership has been mixed, often claiming that 'what works is what counts.' This has involved increased use of the private sector in health and education and the privatisation of key services from air traffic control to examination boards. On the other hand the role of the state has been increased in terms of regulation and even in a more direct form in the effective re-nationalisation of the rail infrastructure when Railtrack was replaced by a non-profit organisation. However, the logic of the revisionist argument for competitive public enterprises is that if regulation fails then direct ownership should be considered for the realisation of wider policy objectives. As a recent Catalyst pamphlet has suggested the increased regulation of rail operators has had little public benefit, either in terms of increased efficiency or control of public investment.[72] Such a case would allow for the greater use of state ownership. This in turn would require a changed attitude on public ownership from the government and Gerald Holtham has argued that in certain situations, "the case for public ownership can be strong. This needs to be asserted at the present time when the intellectual climate, reinforced by political calculation, leads any public ownership to be regarded as an embarrassing hangover from the past or an opportunity to raise quick funds via the sale of assets."[73] Holtham's detailed treatment of this issue shows that public ownership can be defended in current conditions in several ways[74]: first in terms of the generation of funds for health and education through a 'community fund' financed from public ownership of profitable economic activity. Moreover, the ability of publicly-owned companies to borrow on the open market at lower rates of interest when underwritten by the state challenges a central justification of privatisation that private firms can borrow more efficiently on the finance markets. Finally, the role of non-profit activity is central to the wider promotion of citizenship values. This case brings us back to the Croslandite position on public ownership in the form of core industries and competitive public enterprise.

¹ C.A.R. Crosland, *The Future of Socialism* (Cape, London, 1956; all references are to the second edition, Schocken, London, 1963), p.169.

² Ibid. The Crosland archive contains comments made on the initial drafts of the book from a number of individuals and reviews and correspondence following its publication. Crosland papers, British Library of Political and Economic Science (BLPES), London, 13/8-13/10.

³ C.A.R. Crosland, *The Conservative Enemy* (Cape, London, 1962). See also, Crosland papers, BLPES, London, 13/11-13/12 for comments on drafts and reviews.

⁴ D. Leonard (ed.) *Socialism Now and Other Essays* (Cape, London, 1974). See also, Crosland papers, BLPES, London, 13/15-13/18 for comments on drafts and reviews.

⁵ S. Crosland, *Tony Crosland* (Cape, London, 1982) and K. Jefferys, *Anthony Crosland* (Cohen, London, 1999).

⁶ See Crosland papers, BLPES, London, 3/26.

⁷ C.A.R. Crosland, 'The Transition from Capitalism' in R.H.S Crossman (ed.) *New Fabian Essays* (Turnstile, London, 1952).

⁸ See Crosland, 'The Transition from Capitalism' and *The Future of Socialism*, pp.1-22.

⁹ The argument that government had sufficient power to bring about greater equality but often failed to do so was a consistent theme in Crosland's work. See the comparison between his approach and that of Stuart Holland later in this volume.

¹⁰ Crosland, *The Future of Socialism* p.18.

¹¹ A. Berle and G. Means, *The Modern Corporation and Private Property* (Macmillan, New York, 1932). J. Burnham, *The Managerial Revolution* (Putnam, London, 1942). Crosland wrote a full chapter on Burnham's thesis but decided to cut it from the final version of *The Future of Socialism*. The 'missing chapter' can be located in the Crosland papers, BLPES, London, 13/7.

¹² D. Jay, *The Socialist Case* (Faber, London, 1937) and E. Durbin, *The Politics of Democratic Socialism* (Routledge, London, 1940).

¹³ See M. Barratt Brown, 'The Insiders' *Universities and Left Review*, Winter, 1958 and 'The Controllers' *Universities and Left Review*, 4, 1959. See J. Tomlinson, *The Unequal Struggle? British Socialism and the Capitalist Enterprise* (Methuen, London, 1982), pp.80-98 for a further critical discussion of these ideas.

¹⁴ Crosland, *The Future of Socialism*, pp.27-29.

¹⁵ Crosland, 'The Transition from Capitalism'.

¹⁶ Crosland, *The Future of Socialism* p.34.

[17] See the earlier discussion of Strachey's post-war position.

[18] Crosland, 'Socialism Now' in D. Leonard (ed.) *Socialism Now and Other Essays*.

[19] See the Preface to Crosland, *The Conservative Enemy*.

[20] D. Jay, *Socialism and the New Society* (Longmans, London, 1962) and H. Gaitskell, 'Public Ownership and Equality' *Socialist Commentary* (1955) and *Socialism and Nationalisation* (Fabian Society, London, 1956).

[21] Crosland, *The Conservative Enemy* p.49.

[22] Crosland, *The Future of Socialism* p.44.

[23] Ibid. pp.45-60.

[24] Ibid. pp.67-69.

[25] Ibid. p.69.

[26] Ibid. p.77.

[27] B. Crick 'Socialist Literature in the Fifties' *Political Quarterly* (1960).

[28] D. Howell, *British Social Democracy* (Croom Helm, London, 1976), p.193.

[29] See for example R. Plant, 'Democratic Socialism and Equality' in D. Lipsey and D. Leonard (eds.) *The Socialist Agenda: Crosland's Legacy* (Cape, London, 1981).

[30] G. B. Shaw, *The Intelligent Woman's Guide to Socialism and Capitalism* (Constable, London, 1928).

[31] See for example S. Lukes, 'Socialism and Equality' in his *Essays in Social Theory* (Macmillan, London, 1977).

[32] J. Rawls, *A Theory of Justice* (Oxford University Press, Oxford, 1999, 1st edition 1971).

[33] Crosland, 'Socialism Now' p.15.

[34] Crosland, *The Future of Socialism* pp.159-164.

[35] Ibid. p.167.

[36] Ibid. p.163.

[37] M. Young, *The Rise of the Meritocracy* (Thames and Hudson, London, 1958). Although this book appeared two years later than *The Future of Socialism*, Young had been developing his ideas for some time and influenced Crosland. See *The Future of Socialism*, p.167, footnote.

[38] Crosland, *The Future of Socialism* p.167.

[39] Ibid. pp.135-147.

[40] Ibid. pp.170-178 .

[41] Preface to Crosland, *The Conservative Enemy*.

[42] Crosland, *The Future of Socialism* Part One.

[43] Ibid. p.188.

[44] Ibid. pp.188-198.

[45] Ibid. p.191.

[46] *The Public Schools and the General Education System* (HMSO, London, 1944).

[47] Crosland, *The Future of Socialism* pp.224-246; Jay, *The Socialist Case* and H. Dalton, *Practical Socialism for Britain* (Routledge, London, 1935).

[48] Crosland, *The Future of Socialism* pp.248-264.

[49] See H. Clegg, *A New Approach to Industrial Democracy* (Blackwell, Oxford, 1960) for Clegg's views on industrial relations.

[50] Crosland, *The Future of Socialism* p.250.

[51] Ibid. pp.312-352.

[52] Ibid. pp.322-327 and pp.332-340.

[53] Labour Party, *Industry and Society* (Labour Party, London, 1957).

[54] Crosland, *The Conservative Enemy* pp.42-43.

[55] See for example, T. Wright, 'New Labour, Old Crosland?' in D. Leonard (ed.) *Crosland and New Labour* (Macmillan, Basingstoke, 1999) who argues that Crosland's ideas are of only limited relevance for contemporary social democrats.

[56] S. Haseler, *The Gaitskellites: Revisionism in the Labour Party 1951-64* (Macmillan, London, 1969).

[57] R. Hinden, 'The New Socialism' *Socialist Commentary* November 1956.

[58] K. Hickson, 'Revisionism Revisited: From Crosland to New Labour' *Imprints* vol. 8, no. 3 (2005).

[59] D. Marquand (ed.) *John P. Mackintosh on Parliament and Social Democracy* (Longman, London, 1982).

[60] David Owen can be taken as representative of this position.

[61] Although it can be fairly pointed out that reform of local government has been limited in terms of decentralising power and the attempts to introduce regional government in England failed to win much popular support as seen in the North East regional assembly referendum.

[62] Crosland, *The Future of Socialism* p.254.

[63] *Socialism: A New Statement of Principles* (Socialist Union, London, 1952) Quoted in Crosland, *The Future of Socialism*, p.255.

[64] Crosland, *The Future of Socialism*, pp.255-256.

[65] Ibid. p.355.

[66] See the discussion of Roy Hattersley's thinking on this issue later in this volume.

[67] See, for example, Wright, 'New Labour, Old Crosland?'.

[68] This charge is made by Peter Mandelson and Roger Liddle in their book *The Blair Revolution* (Faber and Faber, London, 1996).

[69] T. Blair, *The Third Way* (Fabian Society, London, 1998).

[70] This argument is largely drawn from R. Plant, 'Ends, Means and Political Identity' in R. Plant, M. Beech and K. Hickson (eds.) *The Struggle*

for Labour's Soul: Understanding Labour's Political Thought since 1945 (Routledge, London, 2004).

[71] These trends are drawn from frequent reports in the 'Households Below Average Income' surveys conducted and published by the Department of Work and Pensions.

[72] 'The Railway in a Third Term' Catalyst Pre-election Briefing Paper, March 2005.

[73] G. Holtham, 'Ownership and Social Democracy' in A. Gamble and T. Wright (eds.) *The New Social Democracy* (Blackwell, Oxford, 1999) p.67.

[74] Ibid. pp.59-67.

9

STUART HOLLAND[1]

'What is the socialist challenge? Essentially, it is the claim that we can transform the injustice, inequality and inefficiency of modern capitalism. In Britain in the early 1970s the Labour Party shaped a radical new strategy for the beginnings of such transformation. This programme for extended public ownership, strategic planning and workers' democracy opened the feasibility of a genuine transition to socialism in a democratic society.'[2]

In the 1970s with the development of a radical left alternative to the dominant Labour revisionist paradigm the significance of Stuart Holland's contribution to British socialism reached its zenith. Following the 1983 defeat, the Labour Party began its move back to the centre ground of British politics. By the late 1980s, Stuart Holland had left the House of Commons for a post at the European Commission. His thought has received considerably less attention than many thinkers on the left in British politics. This chapter seeks to redress the balance by providing a detailed analysis of his ideas.

The chapter will first outline the thesis he developed in the 1970s through several books, articles and Labour Party policy documents but most significantly in *The Socialist Challenge* (1975). The central argument was that the trend to increased industrial concentration with the emergence of a 'meso-economy' and transnational corporations questioned the continuing feasibility of Labour Party revisionism. The chapter will then relate Holland's ideas to the wider Alternative Economic Strategy developed at this time by the Labour left and beyond. Next, Holland's thesis will be compared to Tony Crosland's revisionist position. It is readily apparent from a reading of *The Socialist Challenge* that Holland intended his thesis to be a rejection of Crosland's socialism. The chapter will examine the response from revisionists, notably Crosland, and ask if an adequate critique of Holland's thesis was formulated. By way of conclusion, the chapter will relate these debates to the subsequent development both of Holland's thought and of Labour Party political economy.

Holland's Thesis[3]

Stuart Holland's thesis can therefore be seen as an attempt to build a new political economy for the Labour Party that was capable of acting as a new paradigm replacing the Keynesian policy of the post-war period. To be precise it was less an attempt to *replace* Keynesian economics as to *supplement* it and to provide a new framework in which effective demand management could be maintained. What this amounted to was a much more active state, involving more extensive planning of the private sector and public ownership. What Holland did was to argue that the domestic and international economy that was present when Keynesianism was first formulated had been replaced by one marked more by the concentration of industrial ownership.

The theoretical core of Holland's analysis was the *meso* economy. In order to fully understand this concept it is necessary to contrast it with the Keynesian framework. The essence of Keynes' critique of classical economics was that the national economy worked in a different way from that of specific markets. The classical approach had been to assume that the national economy would operate in the same way as the microeconomy and that consequently markets would clear to full employment if left to their own devices. The point made by Keynes was that the macro economy worked in a different way from the micro economy and that state intervention would be required, largely in the form of counter-cyclical fiscal policy, if full employment were to be realised. This distinction between the macro and micro sectors of economic activity presupposed a competitive economy since the price mechanism was a way of allowing consumers to express their choices. Keynes argued that state intervention was only required in the macro sector, once full employment was achieved there would be no need to intervene in the micro economy and consumer sovereignty would be unaffected. This distinction between a macro sector requiring state intervention to achieve full employment and a competitive micro sector in which the state should only intervene to realise macro objectives was the basis for post-war political economy in the Labour Party.

However, Holland argued that such a distinction was made invalid by subsequent economic developments.[4] These can be briefly summarised as the inter-related developments of the concentration of domestic corporate ownership and the growth of transnational corporations. This led to the development of a meso-economy (from the Greek *mesos* meaning intermediate) that lay between the micro sector and the macro sector: "the trend to monopoly and mulitnational capital has set a new mode of production *in between* the Keynesian macroeconomic and microeconomic categories. This is the new *mesoeconomic* sector which controls the commanding heights of big business in the national and international economy."[5] The micro sector of small competitive firms was unable to compete with the new large firms in the meso sector. The new large firms did not have competitors and were able to determine prices in order to maintain if not increase profits.[6] This effectively meant that consumer sovereignty in the market had been lost.[7] The state was also unable to manipulate economic activity since the range of policies available were designed to alter the behaviour of competitive firms. The large companies could simply ignore such policies, nullifying their impact and could make demands on the state. Holland claimed that in 1950, 20% of domestic output was controlled by large firms, but by 1980 this would increase to 66%.[8] Power had been taken away from the state by the large corporations. There was a need for new policies designed to achieve traditional objectives.

In a similar way, the growth of multinational corporations undermined the capacity for national governments to control the economy. There had been a growth in both multinational trade, which undermined the capacity of nation states since firms could offer to relocate or avoid domestic taxation by transfer pricing where declared profits were reduced by transferring profit from one sector of a corporation to another in a different country. Moreover, there had been a growth in transnational financial activity, especially in the form of the Eurodollar market where dollars were held in overseas accounts and could be transferred to avoid the effects of domestic economic policies. It was the growth of the Eurodollar markets that finally undermined the Bretton Woods system of fixed exchange rates designed to defend domestic economies from international financial instability. These processes of multinational corporations and finance were identified by Holland, and formed the basis of much of the controversy between himself and those such as Crosland who sought to defend established (Keynesian) policy. The lasting significance of Holland's thesis is the identification of these trends now commonly termed 'globalisation', especially in terms of the impact of multinational corporations on domestic economic policies.

Holland had been an economic advisor to Harold Wilson
in the 1960s and his evolving thesis after 1970 can be seen as
a response to the economic difficulties faced by the 1964-70
Government.[9] As we shall see, the Crosland position was
that the failures of the Wilson Government were largely due
to an absence of political will to achieve high growth.
However, for Holland the cause of economic failure ran
deeper.   The development of the meso-economy
undermined the policies that were attempted by the Wilson
Government. Attempts to reach planning agreements with
the private sector were limited since large firms had
sufficient power to reject such plans.[10] Moreover, the failure
of regional policy could be explained in the same way, since
large firms simply refused to relocate and large state
subsidies were simply swallowed up by the large firms. Such
firms were in a position to declare whatever profits they
wished since the state lacked power to scrutinise corporate
accounts. The perceived decline in profits in the British
economy were explained by Holland as inaccurate since as
there was no accurate data about profits and it was likely
that, since large firms could charge whatever level of prices
they wished without the threat of competition, profits were
increasing.[11] The multinationals could avoid the impact of
interest rate changes by borrowing from elsewhere, could
relocate more easily to avoid the impact of devaluation,
evade taxes by transferring profits to other sectors of the
corporation and so forth.

Initially, it appears that it was elements of the Labour right
who were interested in Holland's thesis. There were broadly
three perspectives within the Labour Party to economic
policy in the early 1970s.[12] The first group argued that there
was no need to revise fundamentally the broad framework
of economic policy since the failures of the 1964-70
administration could be explained in terms of the lack of
political will at the top of government and the obsession
with the parity of sterling which reduced the capacity for

economic growth. This position was advocated most clearly by Crosland. The second position was to argue that the experiences of 1964-70 showed the need for new forms of state planning on similar lines to a number of European countries. This position was advocated, at least initially, by Roy Jenkins[13] among others. The final position was to argue that the policy failures of the 1964-70 government showed the intellectual limitations of revisionist social democracy and the continuing relevance of capitalist structures, which would need to be tackled by a future Labour government. At first, Holland's arguments had appeal to the pro-European Labour right for several reasons. First, the more radical connotations of Holland's argument were not apparent in his earlier work. His approach was essentially technocratic, seeking to find pragmatic solutions to the planning failures of 1964-70.[14] Secondly, his theory made much use of European models, notably the Italian IRI, which was subjected to a detailed study in his book *The State as Entrepreneur*[15], and so was seen as a 'pro-European' solution to Britain's industrial problems.

However, it was clear by the mid-1970s that his thesis had developed explicitly a more radical solution to industrial policy that appealed to the Labour left. In *The Socialist Challenge* Holland declared his support for *Labour's Programme 1973*.[16] He associated much more with those on the Labour Party's New left[17] and sat on the key policy subcommittees of the National Executive Committee of the Labour Party that formulated the 1973 Programme. His subsequent work focused on the contrast between his ideas and those of the moderate Labour right, who were seen as upholding capitalism. His radicalism can be seen in a chapter he contributed to a book that constituted the left-wing response to the failure of the Labour Government of 1974-79, *What Went Wrong*.[18] He made frequent use of Marxist academic literature on the post-war economy in a way which Labour left figures in the 1950s had not[19] and argued that the development of the meso-economy had validated Marxist analysis: "this trend to national and mulitnational monopoly clearly corroborates the main emphasis in Marx's analysis of the location of power in the organisation of production. It supports the traditional socialist argument that without public ownership and control of the dominant means of production, distribution and exchange, the state will never manage the strategic features of the economy in the public interest."[20]   This is clearly relevant to the later discussion comparing Holland's ideas with revisionism since he clearly felt that Crosland had failed to realise the continuing relevance of ownership in his over-reaction against Marxism.[21]

It is therefore worth comparing his thesis with the wider Alternative Economic Strategy and then to contrast it with the revisionist thesis as it stood in the 1970s.

The Alternative Economic Strategy (AES)

Mark Wickham-Jones, in the most comprehensive analysis of the AES, argued that, "the most complete account of its theoretical underpinnings is Stuart Holland's *The Socialist Challenge*."[22]   It is therefore worth examining more closely Holland's precise contribution to the development of the AES. First, it is necessary to outline what the AES was. In fact there was no single AES position, but rather a broad framework of discussion on a spectrum from those in the Labour Party who wished to supplement the Keynesian framework by moderate protection and/or further state intervention in the domestic economy, through to a radical Labour left that regarded the AES as a mechanism for socialist transformation broadly in line with the conception of the AES held by the Communist Party. Hence, Peter Shore favoured limited, temporary protectionary measures at the time of the 1976 IMF Crisis in order to aid economic expansion but without the radical rhetoric of Tony Benn, with whom he is often associated at this time.[23] Following the Labour Party programmes of 1973 and 1975 (formulated against the wishes of the Party leadership) and the discussion of the AES by Wickham-Jones we can identify the following aspects of the AES.[24]

- Reflation. Although this had been the central aspect of the economic policy of 1950s revisionists it was seen as insufficient by itself largely because of the changed economic circumstances that would undermine the impact of reflation without wider state intervention.

- Public ownership. The extension of public ownership was seen as central to the development of socialism. In so doing it reflected earlier left-wing concerns with the power of the owners of capital in the mixed economy. However, there were differences from the Labour left in the 1950s both in the sense that specific proposals were given and a justification for such transfer of ownership and also because emphasis was placed on public ownership of firms rather than whole industries.

- Finance. Further to plans in the 1973 document to extend the public ownership of industry, specific proposals were outlined in later documents for the transfer of banking and insurance companies to the state.

- Planning agreements. Compulsory planning agreements were devised that would be binding on private firms. This was seen as necessary for the extension of state control over the remaining private sector and to avoid the negative impact of the National

Plan in the 1960s that failed to win the consent of private sector companies.

- Industrial democracy. Attached to the above proposals was a commitment to expand radically industrial democracy. Trade unions would participate in the discussion of planning agreements and workers would hold executive positions within companies. A clear emphasis was placed by supporters of the AES on the reform of the supply-side of the economy. Reflationary measures acting on the demand-side of the economy would be insufficient without reforms to the supply-side. In this, the AES reflected the increased emphasis on supply-side measures of the economy from advocates of free market economics. However, what was considered as the 'supply-side' differed fundamentally. For AES advocates the emphasis should be placed on radical industrial democracy bringing workers in to corporate decision-making processes and allowing them a greater stake in their place of employment thus fostering a greater commitment to work. For laissez-faire advocates, the barriers to a free labour market created by powerful trade unions, minimum wage legislation and high social security payments reduced incentives to work and over-priced labour making it harder for employers to expand their labour base.[25]

- Price controls. Inflation had been caused not by excess wage demands but by monopolistic pricing policies. It was therefore wrong to impose incomes policies on trade unionists and instead the control of inflation should be done through the government control of prices directly. Hence the scope for a 'Social Contract' with the trade unions whereby they would limit industrial action in return for social policies designed to redistribute income and improve the material and working conditions of the working classes.

- Import controls. The domestic economy at a time of crisis was being further undermined by the inflow of cheap foreign imports. There would be a mixture of measures designed to control the level of imports, at least during the time needed to restructure British industry.

- Opposition to the European Economic Community (EEC). The EEC represented a further constraint on the capacity of a Labour government to introduce socialism in Britain and represented the interests of capitalism. Proponents of the AES broadly supported the campaign for Britain's withdrawal from the EEC in the 1975 referendum and subsequent calls for withdrawal or comprehensive renegotiation of Britain's terms of entry.

What is clear is that the AES was a radical basis for a new political economy, which sought directly to challenge the existing Keynesian framework. With this, Holland was in agreement. The failures of the National Plan in the 1960s could not be explained fully by a lack of political will, but instead were due to the failure to recognise the tensions between government intervention and the objectives of a capitalist economy. The National Plan was a failure because it was essentially technocratic and did not grasp the fundamental clash between capital and labour within a capitalist framework.[26] Rather than seeking to alter the basis of capitalism, the National Plan sought only to raise output in specific sectors of a pre-existing capitalist economy. As Holland argued: "it failed to appreciate that, without a transformation of the dominant mode of capitalist production in the economy, state power could only be used to attempt to make the prevailing system work against a tide of internal contradictions in that system."[27] The design of the National Plan had been influenced by the French planning structure, but there a tradition of extensive state intervention already existed. Also, under low growth conditions the ambitious objectives of the National Plan seemed unrealistic to employers, who were seeking to avoid a further loss of profits rather than intending to plan for high growth. The National Plan had been based on Keynesian notions of economic activity and such a framework was unrealistic in the changed capitalist conditions.

The new conditions required a far more substantial role for the state. Holland was clear on what form this should take: "*Labour Programme 1973*, and its two manifestoes of 1974, embody a strategy which makes possible a democratic transition to socialism in this country."[28] The summary of the AES position above shows the significance of Holland's thesis. The argument that reflation could not be achieved without further public ownership is apparent in Holland's work and in a number of policy documents produced by the Labour Party and its various committees, which placed emphasis on the meso-economy. In *The Socialist Challenge*, Holland was explicit on the need for further public ownership, and provided the intellectual basis for the increased demand for public ownership in the 1970s. First, public ownership on traditional lines of the transfer of whole industries from the private to the public sector was deemed unnecessary. Instead there should be a new form of public ownership consisting of individual firms that would create a genuinely mixed economy and allow the state to exercise a decisive influence and provide a lead in key sectors of the economy without public monopoly.[29] The idea was raised by Crosland in the 1950s and 1960s and this issue became one of debate between the two. Secondly, Holland provided a basis for the selection and extent of such public enterprises. Industrial activity could be divided in to roughly 25 sectors and each had a single or small number of leading firms (together constituting the *meso* sector): "what we need is to transform the private dominances of the mesoeconomic leaders who at present command the rest of the economy. In the case of the top 100 hundred manufacturing companies, this is the case for twenty to twenty-five new public enterprise leaders."[30] There was a clear rationale for the extension of public ownership to 25 of the leading companies: "no transformation will be possible unless a critical minimum of leading firms in the meso-sector is brought into public ownership and control."[31] This would cover the leading sectors of industry and would be supplemented by municipal and worker-owned industry and the public ownership of investment, banking and insurance companies.

A key emphasis in Holland's writing is the role of planning agreements, although here the emphasis was on voluntary agreements with mechanisms designed to encourage their acceptance by private firms rather than on compulsion.[32] As already noted, Holland was very interested in the planning systems used in France and in Italy. The Department of Economic Affairs faced serious limitations. The new system would be optional, with firms being encouraged to reach agreements with the government. Plans would be published and therefore would only contain relevant information for the expansion of economic activity. The government would have increased leverage by the existence of the competitive public enterprises and would be able to use sanctions in the last resort such as the withholding of investment funds or even nationalisation.[33] The scope for industrial democracy would be increased by planning agreements since the trade unions would participate in negotiation of such agreements.[34] Holland rejected the 'oppositionist' thesis of

Hugh Clegg, where trade unions were seen as having fundamentally different objectives to managers and thus ruled out the possibility for high-level industrial partnerships, and instead argued that the powers of workers could only be extended by radical industrial democracy leading to workers' representatives forming the majority on company boards. Without such an extension of industrial democracy planning would amount to state capitalism, not socialism.[35]

On the international aspects of the AES, Holland was more ambivalent. His position on the EEC shifted over time.[36] In *The Socialist Challenge* Holland stated: "it is arguable that the EEC is neither European, Economic or a Community."[37] In the early 1970s, he appeared undecided as to whether Britain's membership of the EEC would have economic benefits.[38] He later argued that the EEC worked in the interests of capitalism and was dominated by the French national interest and that it had neglected key aspects of economic expansion and instead favoured monetary union that would add to deflationary pressures.[39] At times he seemed to think that it was sufficient to reform the EEC, while at other times he argued for withdrawal. For a significant time from the mid-1970s through to the early-1980s, Holland was more critical of the EEC. In *The Socialist Challenge* he argued that the nation-state could restore economic sovereignty if it withdrew from the EEC and introduced planning agreements and public ownership as outlined above.[40] His argument in the early-1980s was sceptical of the EEC, notably in his book *The Uncommon Market*.[41] Following this he became more sympathetic to European integration and I return to this at the end of the chapter. It is on the role of import controls that he is most distinct from the AES. Holland did not ascribe any role to import controls in *The Socialist Challenge* and he thought that the scope for their effective use was limited by the growth of multinational corporations, which led him to be sceptical of proposals for import restraint.[42]   The main impetus for import controls came not from Holland but from the Cambridge Economic Policy Group (CEPG), which included Wynne Godley and Francis Cripps.[43] It was argued that import controls were needed to improve the balance of payments position and allow for industrial reconstruction. Holland instead placed emphasis on public ownership and planning agreements.   This distinction marked a central tension within the AES concerning the relative openness of the British economy and also where emphasis should be placed on AES policy priorities.

Holland *contra* Crosland

Having outlined Holland's thesis and gone on to compare it with the AES, it is now possible to offer some evaluations. This is most appropriately done when comparing his thesis with Crosland's.   It is clear that Holland sought to provide a clear alternative to Croslandite revisionism. He argued that: "the rise of the mesoeconomic power has fundamentally undermined the Crosland analysis."[44] The power of owners had not diminished in the way that Crosland had asserted. Instead, Crosland had failed to predict the increased concentration of ownership. This failure to recognise the continuing power of the capitalists had led to the failure of the economic policies of the Wilson Government 1964-70. The National Plan "failed to appreciate that, without a transformation of the dominant mode of production in the economy, state power could only be used to attempt to make the prevailing system work against a tide of internal contradictions in that system."[45] Holland further argued that the Wilson Government's policy position was based on ideas developed by Crosland in the pre-1964 period: "the fact is that Labour lost the 1970 election on the Croslandite social democratic policies it had attempted in 1964."[46]   Hence,

Crosland's influence is not underestimated by Holland, indeed when examining the policies of the 1964-70 Government we could say it was exaggerated. Crosland was the leading revisionist thinker in the 1950s, he argued that capitalism had been replaced and that the state had sufficient power to achieve high growth and realise its social policy objectives, and finally that his ideas were the intellectual underpinning of the Wilson Government (1964-70). Crosland had failed to see the emergence of the meso-economy. This had undermined most of his analysis and also explained the failures of the Wilson Administration. Hence, Holland did not question the underlying political values emphasised by Crosland or the importance of economic growth for their realisation, but instead argued that he was wrong to reject traditional socialist concerns with public ownership. The new economic organisation required an extension of public ownership to realise Croslandite values: "thus, ironically enough, socialist means have become a necessary condition for the ends of conventional social democratic policies."[47]

Holland's thesis did not go unchallenged with the clearest response coming from Crosland, with others making contributions to the revisionist counter-argument.[48] Crosland argued in *Socialism Now* that the failures of the Wilson Government were due largely to the concern of the most senior ministers to maintain the value of sterling and therefore not to the existing pattern of ownership: "the reason why the economy did not grow up to the limit of this higher productive potential was that the final *demand* was not there. This had nothing to do with too much or too little socialism; it was due to the deflationary policies which stemmed inexorably from the Labour Government's obsession with a particular parity for sterling."[49] This would seem a fair judgement. The failure to sustain sufficient economic growth to realise social objectives was largely due to the decision made in private between Wilson, James

Callaghan and George Brown to defend the parity of sterling immediately after coming to power in 1964. Several rounds of spending cuts were implemented before the Government was forced to devalue in 1967. In addition, the Treasury opposed the separation of responsibility for economic policy with the Department of Economic Affairs and sought to obstruct it.

Crosland argued that the trend towards concentration had itself been encouraged by the Labour Government's commitment to industrial reorganisation and could be reversed by a more effective competition policy.[50] Moreover, according to Crosland the trend towards concentration in the domestic economy was in conflict with the trend towards multinational corporate activity since the latter would increase competition within the British economy.[51] He then summarised the relevance of public ownership to power, equality and economic performance. In each area he argued that public ownership continued to be of only minor importance.[52] Power remained concentrated whether ownership was in public or private hands so that the advocates of further public ownership would need to show how it would disperse power. Equality of income and wealth would be more directly affected by tax reform rather than public ownership, which with fair compensation had little impact on the distribution of wealth. The relative economic performance of public industries had improved in the 1960s but this was unlikely to continue in the 1970s. However, Crosland did accept that public ownership of profitable firms would both create a 'community fund' for social investment and may in cases of private sector failure raise economic performance.[53] Both Holland and Crosland advocated competitive public enterprise. Holland argued that, "while new public enterprise at the level of leading firms shares features with first generation nationalisation, its focus in firms with profitable sectors gives it genuinely new potential for

promoting the public interest."[54]   Crosland stated that "this
is a fresher and more attractive notion than the old one.   It
moves away from monolithic industry nationalisation
towards nationalisation by *company*."[55]   However, despite
sounding similar to Holland here, Crosland had in mind
something much smaller in scope.   Competitive public
enterprise would be used as a last resort when existing
policies designed to alter the behaviour of private firms
failed to work.   Crosland still believed in the validity of the
competitive model of the economy and consequently that
fiscal, monetary and other policies could be used to
determine the behaviour of firms.   Competitive public
enterprises could be used in cases when the existing policies
failed to work.   In contrast, Holland believed that the
competitive model of the economy had been invalidated by
the increased concentration of ownership and that
consequently extensive public ownership was needed to
realise socialist objectives.

Assessment

In making an assessment of Holland's contribution to
British socialism it is apparent that there is a key weakness in
his analysis, which can be summarised in terms of an
unresolved tension between structure and agency.   Holland
was critical of Crosland as we have seen.   Crosland placed
emphasis on the role of agency in his socialism.   He believed
that major changes had taken place in the economy when he
wrote in the 1950s that amounted to a substantial transfer of
power from owners to the state, organised labour and
corporate managers in the private and public sectors.   He
defended this thesis in *Socialism Now*.   The failure of the
Wilson Government to achieve high economic growth and
social policy objectives was due to the absence of sufficient
political will.   That the Government had enough power to

achieve its objectives was not questioned. There is a clear, some would say simplistic, approach here. Since the 1950s Crosland had believed that "a determined, reforming government can now generally get its way without a change in ownership."[56]

Holland was influenced by the writing of Robin Murray, who argued that changes within capitalism were placing increased strain on the policy roles of the state.[57] According to Murray the state had several roles under capitalism. These included the guaranteeing of property rights, the promotion of economic liberalisation, demand orchestration, the assurance of supply including provision of subsidies, social intervention in order to maintain order and provide welfare and the maintenance of favourable external economic relations.[58] These were coming increasingly in to conflict. In particular, the nation state was losing power to transnational corporations. The conclusion made by Murray was that this process of globalisation was inevitable and that the nation state must alter its policies in accordance with the demands of multinational capital. There was a clear position taken here on structure and agency. The nation state is, *contra* Crosland, structurally constrained by multinational capitalism.

However, despite being influenced by Murray's thesis, Holland reached different conclusions. He argued that the power of national and multinational corporations had increased substantially yet also that the nation state could reclaim this power with the correct policies – planning agreements and public ownership: "if a massively extended public sector is used with the kind of planning controls outlined...the state can recover sufficient power to reintroduce responsiveness to exchange rate changes in the mesoeconomic sector. It can thereby restore the main part of that sovereignty already lost to multinational capital."[59] However, there is a tension here between structure and agency, which was arguably left unresolved within Holland's

contribution to British socialism in the 1970s. Either the
nation-state retained sufficient power to manage the
economy so as to achieve higher growth and social
democratic objectives in social policy in which case such
radical reform was unnecessary as Crosland argued; or
alternatively that the power of the nation state had been lost
to multinational corporations and finance markets, in which
case it could not introduce radical reforms needed to restore
power to the state. This tension was at the heart of
Holland's thesis and also at the centre of the AES. The AES
could therefore be said to have failed not just because of
power realities within the Labour Party and the need to
attract centrist voters within the majoritarian electoral system
but also because of its own internal divisions and intellectual
limitations.

Holland's subsequent development can be seen as a way
of trying to resolve this tension between structure and
agency. After the economic crisis in France following the
attempt to reflate the economy, Holland advocated
multinational responses. In 1984 he argued for a combined
left-wing response to the recession: "if even some like-
minded left governments can jointly face this global
challenge on the lines of the recovery programme spelled
out in the 1984 manifesto of the Confederation of Socialist
Parties, then not only Europe but also the world would have
a chance of surmounting the current crisis."[60] Holland then
worked closely with Jacques Delors leading to a 'Euro-
Keynesian' policy, justified in his book *The European
Imperative*.[61] This reflected a development in the Labour
Party's political economy dating around the late-1980s and
early-1990s, advocating a more pro-European stance. The
EEC could act with sufficient power to counteract global
economic actors and could also provide an institutional
mechanism for the pursuit of social democracy in Britain
against the increasingly radical reforms of the New Right.
Europe offered an alternative economic model to the Anglo-

Saxon model. Moreover, with the Labour Party seeking to modernise and attract centrist voters a pro-European stance would also show that the Party had moved from its isolationist position of the early 1980s. The development of a 'New Labour' political economy from the mid-1990s, despite a pro-European rhetoric, was increasingly sympathetic to the competitive U.S. model, with Gordon Brown particularly interested in U.S. economic policy ideas. This shift in Holland's thinking does show an attempt to reach a more satisfactory position on the relationship between structure and agency in matters of political economy.

---

[1] This chapter benefits from discussions with Stuart Holland in London and by email. I am grateful for his input. In addition, I have made extensive use of his published work and the Labour History archive located in Manchester, which contains the internal reports listed below. I am also grateful to Noel Thompson for commenting on an earlier draft of this chapter.

[2] S. Holland, *The Socialist Challenge* (Quartet, London, 1975), p.12.

[3] The most detailed discussion of Holland's thesis is M. Wickham-Jones, *Economic Strategy and the Labour Party: Politics and Policy-making 1970-83* (Macmillan, London, 1996). This chapter takes a more critical view of Holland's views.

[4] Holland, *The Socialist Challenge*, pp.44-95. Holland's argument was presented in a number of internal Labour Party papers, most notably 'Planning Strategy, Tactics and Techniques' RD442 (October 1972) and 'The New Economic Imperatives' RD473 (November 1972).

[5] Holland, *The Socialist Challenge*, p.15.

[6] S. Holland, 'Planning Strategy, Tactics and Techniques'.

[7] Holland, *The Socialist Challenge*, pp.58-61.

[8] Ibid. pp.48-50.

[9] See S. Holland, 'Ownership, Planning and Markets' in R. Plant, M. Beech and K. Hickson (eds.) *The Struggle for Labour's Soul: Understanding Labour's Political Thought since 1945* (Routledge, London, 2004) and discussions with Stuart Holland.

[10] Holland, *The Socialist Challenge*, pp.95-103.

[11] The most well known account of declining profit was A. Glyn and B. Sutcliffe, *British Capitalism, Workers and the Profits Squeeze* (Penguin, Harmondsworth, 1972). Holland, *The Socialist Challenge* p. 55: "mesoeconomic companies are largely in a position to declare what profits they want to declare."

[12] S. Holland (ed.) *Beyond Capitalist Planning* (Blackwell, Oxford, 1978), pp.137-150 and Holland 'Ownership, Planning and Markets'.

[13] See R. Jenkins, *What Happens Now* (Fontana, London, 1972).

[14] See 'Planning and Policy Co-ordination' RD 315 (March 1972).

[15] S. Holland (ed.) *The State as Entrepreneur: the IRI State-holding Formula* (Weidenfeld and Nicolson, London, 1972).

[16] Holland, *Socialist Challenge*, pp.9-10, 29-30.

[17] For a discussion of the New left of the Labour Party and its association with other ideological positions in the Party since 1945 see R. Plant, M. Beech and K. Hickson (eds.) *The Struggle for Labour's Soul: Understanding Labour's Political Thought since 1945* (Routledge, London, 2004).

[18] S. Holland, 'Capital, Labour and the State' in K. Coates (ed.) *What Went Wrong* (Spokesman, Nottingham, 1979).

[19] For example Holland made frequent use of the arguments of Paul Sweezy in *The Socialist Challenge*, who was subjected to criticism by John Strachey in his *Contemporary Capitalism* - D. Reisman (ed.) *Theories of the Mixed Economy*, Volume VIII (Pickering and Chatto, London, 1994) pp.236-9.

[20] Holland, *The Socialist Challenge* p.15.

[21] Ibid., pp.26-27.

[22] Wickham-Jones, *Economic Strategy and the Labour Party*, p.54.

[23] See K. Hickson, *The IMF Crisis of 1976 and British Politics* (Tauris, London, 2005) for a detailed discussion of the views of Cabinet ministers at this time.

[24] Wickham-Jones, *Economic Strategy and the Labour Party*, pp.61-76.

[25] See Hickson, *The IMF Crisis of 1976 and British Politics*, Chapter 6.

[26] Holland, *The Socialist Challenge*, pp.120-134.

[27] Ibid. p.121.

[28] Ibid. pp.9-10.

[29] Ibid. pp.154-160.

[30] Ibid. p.179.

[31] Ibid. p.160.

[32] Ibid. pp.223-254.

[33] This was argued in Holland, 'Planning Strategy, Tactics and Techniques'.

[34] Ibid. pp.270-293. See also, 'Industrial Democracy' RD930 (November 1973).

[35] See Holland, 'Introduction' in Holland (ed.) *Beyond Capitalist Planning*, p.3 "without a socialisation of control, with new forms of industrial and economic democracy, and new negotiation of changed ends for the use of resources, the institutions of state ownership and planning would tend to mean corporatism or state capitalism, rather than a transition to socialist planning and socialised development." Here Holland can be said to have been influenced by the work of Ken Coates and Michael Barratt Brown. See, for example, K. Coates and T. Topham, *The New Unionism: The Case for Workers' Control* (Owen, London, 1972) and Michael Barratt Brown, *From Labourism to Socialism: The Political Economy of Labour in the 1970s* (Spokesman, Nottingham, 1972).

[36] For example, he was critical of the EEC in 'The EEC and UK Industrial Policy' RE961 (January 1977) but more favourable in 'Socialism, Europe and the Community' RE1114 (April 1977).

[37] Holland, *The Socialist Challenge* p.316.

[38] S. Holland 'State Entrepreneurship and State Intervention' in S. Holland (ed.) *The State as Entrepreneur* (Weidenfeld and Nicolson, London, 1972), p.16.

[39] See in particular, *The Socialist Challenge*, pp.316-336.

[40] Holland, *The Socialist Challenge*, pp.336-362.

[41] S. Holland, *Uncommon Market* (Macmillan, Basingstoke, 1980).

[42] See S. Holland, 'An Alternative Economic Strategy' in M. Barratt Brown, K. Coates, K. Fleet and J. Hughes (eds.) *Full Employment: Priority* (Nottingham, Spokesman, 1978).

[43] See Wickham-Jones, *Economic Strategy and the Labour Party* and Hickson, *The IMF Crisis of 1976 and British Politics*, Chapter Six for discussions of the ideas of the CEPG.

[44] Holland, *The Socialist Challenge*, p.70.

[45] Ibid., p.121.

[46] Ibid., p.26.

[47] Ibid., p.154.

[48] Crosland, 'Socialism Now' in D. Leonard (ed.) *Socialism Now and Other Essays* (Cape, London, 1974).   See notably, W. Beckerman 'Labour's Plans for Industry' *New Statesman* (8 June 1973). Wickham-Jones, *Economic Strategy and the Labour Party*, pp.86-93 offers a discussion of the revisionist response.

[49] Crosland, Ibid., p.37.

[50] Ibid., p.28, p.34.

[51] Ibid., pp.30-32.

[52] Ibid., pp.28-38.

[53] Ibid., pp.38-39.

[54] Holland, *The Socialist Challenge*, p.198.

[55] Crosland, 'Socialism Now', p.39.

[56] C.A.R. Crosland, 'The Role of Public Ownership' in C.A.R. Crosland, *The Conservative Enemy* (Cape, London, 1962), p.42.

[57] R. Murray, *Multinational Companies and Nation States* (Spokesman, Nottingham, 1975).

[58] See Holland, *The Socialist Challenge*, pp.134-138.

[59] Ibid., pp.336-337.

[60] S. Holland, 'Out of Crisis: International Economic Recovery' in J. Curran (ed.) *The Future of the Left* (Polity and New Socialist, Cambridge, 1984), pp.263-264.

[61] S. Holland, *The European Imperative: Economic and Social Cohesion in the 1990s* (Spokesman, Nottingham, 1993).   Delors had contributed to Holland's 1978 publication, *Beyond Capitalist Planning*.

10

DAVID OWEN

'For my part I was a Social Democrat when I joined the party Hugh Gaitskell led in 1959, I was a Social Democrat when I helped found the Social Democratic Party in 1981 and I intend to remain a Social Democrat.'[1]

This chapter [2] charts the intellectual trajectory of David Owen from 'Old right', Labour social democrat to member of the Social Democratic Party (SDP) 1981-1987, to leader of the 'continuing' SDP 1987-1990, to being created a life peer by John Major in 1992 and sitting as a crossbencher to this day. The chapter argues that some on the left have erroneously classified Owen as a neo-liberal when the evidence suggests he is a social democrat. In addition, it is argued that Owen's intellectual development pre-empted much of New Labour's modernised social democracy. Owen's ideas in *Face the Future*, *A Future that will Work: Competitiveness and Compassion*, *A United Kingdom*, and *The Time Has Come* can be understood up to a point as proto-New Labour or taken chronologically New Labour ideas owe an intellectual debt to Owen and his tenure as leader of the SDP.

Owen's Political Trajectory

Ian Bradley made a summary of David Owen in his 1981 book on the SDP entitled, *Breaking the Mould? : The Birth and Prospects of the Social Democratic Party*.

'David Owen is the most intriguing and, on the face of it, the most surprising person to find among the leaders of the SDP. At 43 he is the youngest by some years. He is also the most ambitious. He enjoyed a meteoric rise to power in Callaghan's Government, becoming the youngest Foreign Secretary this century...Owen already effectively leads the Party in parliament, chairing the weekly meetings of Social Democrat MPs which decide what line should be taken in debates...and his book, *Face the Future* gives him some claim to be regarded as a political thinker...His speeches are full of praise for the achievements of Scandinavian countries and the success of European social democracy. He insists that the SDP must be clearly to the left of centre, and of all the 'Gang' he has the least time for the Liberals.'[3]

What this chapter seeks to do is to chart Owen's political trajectory, then respond to the charge that Owen moved from social democracy to neo-liberalism and, finally to link his ideas to the politics of New Labour.

Owen, as Bradley notes in his book, did very well in Callaghan's Government rising to the position of Foreign Secretary due to the sudden death of Tony Crosland in February 1977. There is something strangely ironic about this. Before breaking with the Labour Party Owen was a fairly traditional right-wing Labour MP, one could even call him a social democrat in the revisionist tradition because on entering parliament in 1966 he was soon nominated to be a member of the 1963 Club which was a Gaitskellite dining club that succeeded the Campaign for Democratic

Socialism.[4] It comprised a group of right-wing Labour MPs attempting to recover Gaitskellite social democracy during the Wilson Administration and especially intent on wrestling power from the hands of the left on the National Executive Committee (NEC). Owen was from his early days in parliament a supporter of European social democracy but it is wrong to see him as a pro-European in the sense of being a Jenkinsite. He was a supporter of Britain's membership of the Common Market and resigned from the shadow cabinet in 1972 over the Labour Party's refusal to support British entry to the European Economic Community (EEC). As Foreign Secretary he was involved in the British presidency of the European Community and the formulation of a coherent European policy for Labour. Yet he has never advocated that the European project should be a federal project.

By 1980 the right of the Labour Party was in a state of turmoil. This was due to three main reasons. Firstly, because of the sudden death of Tony Crosland, the intellectual driving force behind revisionist social democracy in the Labour Party. Crosland died in January 1977 and his death could not have come at a more difficult time for those who believed in the validity of his revisionist thesis. Secondly, the revisionist thesis itself was being fiercely criticised by the New left and by the neo-liberals in the Conservative Party.[5] Both the New left and the neo-liberals pointed to Crosland's over-optimism about the ability of economic growth to maintain full employment and deliver the conditions so that a more equal society could be constructed. Obviously, the New left and neo-liberal conclusions were contradictory but their observations were similar and equally damning. This forced the Labour right into a period of reflection whereby they questioned the appropriateness of Crosland's revisionist thesis to the economic and social problems facing Britain in the 1980s. Thirdly and most crucially, several notable Labour right-wingers and supporters of Crosland were becoming impatient with the direction that the Labour Party was moving under the influence of the New left. Bernard Crick notes in his 1984 Fabian pamphlet, *Socialist Values and Time*[6] that some of the social democratic right-wing Labour MPs who joined the Social Democratic Party could have stayed in the Labour Party because theirs was not a difference in doctrine but as he notes: ' …a political misjudgement and a failure of nerve at the crucial moment.'[7]

This can explain the departure of some of the social democratic right-wing Labour MPs because more right-wing MPs stayed in the Labour Party than left and joined the SDP. Nevertheless, by 1980 Williams, Owen and Rodgers were considering leaving the Labour Party and setting up a new social democratic party as the Labour Party in their opinion had become extremely left-wing and no longer represented their views. As David Kogan and Maurice Kogan assert: 'On 1 August 1980 David Owen, Shirley Williams and William Rodgers published a letter in the Guardian declaring their beliefs in policies almost wholly contradictory to the general trend of constituency opinion, though perhaps not the views of Labour voters at large.'[8]

Owen, perhaps more than Shirley Williams, Roy Jenkins and Bill Rodgers had a relatively coherent political philosophy that was clearly social democratic but in certain ways distinct from traditional Labour right thought, and it was written down and published by 1981 in the form of a book, entitled *Face the Future*. [9] Owen's book attempts two main things. The first is to outline his brand of social democracy and one can assume the brand that the SDP or at least the Gang of Three[10] would be arguing for, because it is accurate to say that Roy Jenkins was by that time a liberal and a critic of the social democratic principle of greater equality. [11] The second task that Owen undertakes is to provide historical evidence to support the values of his brand of social democracy. The main tenets within Owen's social democracy are decentralisation of power, fellowship, greater equality and freedom. On co-founding the Council for Social Democracy in 1981 his core political principles do not appear to be radically different than when in the Labour Party. Moreover, his politics he still described as socialist/social democratic interchangeably [12] and *Face the Future* is not incommensurable with moderate social democracy. In fact it would not seem too out of place if penned by the Chancellor or another New Labour politician today. What can be said is that Owen did highlight other issues and policy preferences that did not hold widespread appeal on the traditional Labour right. For example, decentralisation figured prominently in his book, along with constitutional reform and the principle of community understood as fellowship that was out of fashion in Labour circles in much of the post-war era. The 26th March 1981 marked the official launch of the Social Democratic Party and by June of that year the SDP and the Liberal Party issued a statement, *A fresh start for Britain* which outlined areas of common policy between the two parties. [13] In July 1982 eighteen months after the SDP was formally launched they held their first leadership election and Jenkins defeated Owen. Owen took up the role of Deputy Leader in October of that year. The General election of June 1983 was a disappointing result for the SDP as they were reduced to six seats and Jenkins resigned as Leader and Owen was elected in an uncontested ballot. [14]

The next phase in Owen's career was the post-1983 period where he worked with David Steel to contest the 1987 election under the banner of the SDP-Liberal Alliance. It is worth noting that some SDP members - Jenkins being the most obvious - had wanted a merger between the two parties since the formation of the SDP. Jenkins' *raison d'etre* for returning to frontline British politics was to establish a party of 'the radical centre' in British politics as he set out in his 1979 Dimbleby Lecture. It is also worth noting as

Bradley infers in the opening quotation of this chapter that of all the leading figures in the SDP, Owen was the most reticent about merging with the Liberals. This point is also noticed by Ivor Crewe and Anthony King:

'He [Owen] was passionately devoted to the SDP, and he held the Liberal Party in considerable contempt. He admired the Liberals for their fortitude in managing to keep a minority party alive for a period of many decades, and he was sympathetic towards their emphasis on pluralism and decentralisation; but at the same time he thought the Liberals were soft on issues like defence, nuclear power and the environment.'[15]

Akin to his reticence of merging with the Liberal Party Owen sought to reform aspects of the SDP's approach and thus stamping more of his own *imprimatur* on their policy prescriptions, in the words of Crewe and King: 'David Owen... responded following the 1983 general election defeat by substantially reorientating the SDP's ideology and propaganda. Electoral considerations apart, he was also persuaded that many of the ideas he and others had inherited from the Labour Party – ideas about Keynesian fine-tuning, public ownership, state planning of the economy and co-operation between government and the trade unions - were no longer intellectually sustainable and so should be abandoned.'[16] Patricia Lee Sykes argues that Owen's thought moved to the right after the 1983 general election defeat[17] and this can be seen in his tough line on national defence [18] (including the Falklands War and the nuclear deterrent) and his more market friendly economic ideas.[19] However, it is argued here that giving support to positions on the necessity of the nuclear deterrent[20], the Falklands war[21] and a greater acceptance of markets does not preclude Owen from being regarded as a social democrat; as such views were also held by Denis Healey. The General

Election of 1987 was held on 11 June and the SDP-Alliance polled 23% of the popular vote but only returned with five MPs. Three days later David Steel issued a memo calling for a merger of the two parties.[22] In August 1987, Owen resigned as SDP Leader and Robert Maclennan was elected. At its 7th Annual Conference in late August the SDP voted to create a new party of the SDP and the Liberals.[23] A name was agreed upon in January 1988 - Social and Liberal Democrats. The SDP was re-established in March 1988 (the continuing SDP) and Owen was re-elected Leader. At that time the SDP comprised a small rump of the former party and it folded in June 1990.

David Marquand suggests a reason why Owen did not want a merger with the Liberals: 'The reason he did not want merger was that he knew that a merged party would be less malleable: that even if he led it, it would not be an extension of his personality in the way he hoped the SDP would be.'[24] Owen fought on as Leader of the 'continuing SDP' until April 1992 when he retired from the House of Commons and was given a peerage later that year by John Major. However, the issue of Major and Owen's cordial relationship provides another reason why the British left doubt Owen's social democratic credentials especially when coupled with Major's offer to Owen of a seat in his Cabinet. In November 1990 shortly after Major became Prime Minister discussions were held with Owen about him joining the Government as a Social Democrat MP.[25] The outcome was negative, but nevertheless it is sufficient evidence for some to argue that by 1990, after the continuing SDP had disbanded, Owen was obviously no longer a social democrat and had common cause with the Conservatives. Therefore when charting Owen's political trajectory such a view would suggest that by 1990 he was not a social democrat but actually a type of liberal, most probably a neo-liberal.

Social Democrat or Neo-Liberal?

Roy Jenkins was a notable political figure and former colleague of Owen's who was firm in his depiction of Owen's political position. Jenkins implies in his autobiography *A Life at the Centre* that Owen was to the right of him. This is significant because Jenkins describes himself as a liberal. Perhaps more accurately one could label Jenkins a left-leaning or social liberal not a neo-liberal in the Conservative mould which was the designation that he was applying to Owen:

'...I had given up describing myself as a socialist for several years before I left the Labour Party. Yet I see myself as being somewhat to the left of James Callaghan, maybe Denis Healey and certainly of David Owen....I do not share his [Owen] nuclear fixation, his free-market enthusiasm or his respect for Mrs. Thatcher's style of government.'[26]

Others have shared this viewpoint including Lee Sykes: 'Owen has shifted to the right since the 1983 general election. To explain this, many point to the fact that Tory seats now offer the best prospects for future Alliance gains.'[27] In addition, Lee Sykes holds up Jenkins's view and quotes him in an interview conducted in 1984 shortly after he resigned the SDP leadership and Owen succeeded him: 'In the beginning David Owen considered himself more radical. That's ridiculous and obviously not true now. He's much more pro-Thatcher than I am. He's more Conservative in economic matters and perhaps foreign affairs. I've always been quite sceptical about Owen's radicalism.'[28] But she does also note why Jenkins would want to portray Owen as an errant former centrist: 'The rivalry between Owen and Jenkins that began before the formation of the SDP continued until Jenkins resigned

following the 1983 General Election. Throughout this
period Owen promoted the SDP as a "radical left-of-centre"
party, and Jenkins emphasized moderation and continuity
with Britain's collectivist tradition. At no time did these two
men disagree on crucial matters.' [29]   In terms of policy
prescriptions in this period Owen emphasised the need to
maintain Britain's nuclear deterrent[30]; the need to encourage
market economics (in other words to emphasize
competition, the abolition of public and private monopolies
and have an open mind to privatisation where beneficial)[31];
he was consistent with his view of the importance of striving
for a more classless and equal society[32]; and he retained his
penchant for constitutional reform (proportional
representation and decentralisation of power and decision-
making). [33] Commenting on the task of explaining and
understanding ideological principles Anthony Arblaster
suggests that: '...what distinguishes one political creed from
another is often not so much the values to which they
officially subscribe, which may very well be substantially the
same, but the hierarchy of those values'[34] Thus it is a difficult
but necessary task to investigate the ordering of political
values in Owen's thought to see whether, as this chapter
argues, he is a social democrat or whether as some claim he
became a neo-liberal.[35]

Regarding his view of the market in particular Owen is
deemed by some including Peter Mandelson and Roger
Liddle to have wandered away from social democracy. [36]
This is partly to do with the fact that he was an early social
democratic advocate for a more positive view of markets[37]
and partly as he stated that the mixed economy that was part
of the consensus years was no longer sufficient and that a
dynamic private sector was needed to create wealth: 'We
needed to drop the term mixed economy and endorse
markets.'[38] During the Thatcher years with the dominance
of free-market ideas in the form of neo-liberalism Owen was
often characterised as a psuedo-Thatcherite by some on the

left.[39] Also his thoughts on the term 'social market' added
further confusion to his political beliefs, as the social market
was something outlined by Sir Keith Joseph when he
established the neo-liberal think-tank Centre for Policy
Studies in 1974. Owen recounts his own reluctance in
acknowledging that Joseph had associated himself with the
term several years before.[40] The Centre for Policy Studies
Memoranda of Association states that its purpose is: 'to
engage in research into methods available for improving the
standard of living, quality of life and freedom of choice of
the British people, with particular attention to social market
policies, and into all or any problems relating to government,
industry, business, the trade unions and economic and social
conditions in all or any countries.'[41] Though a fairly benign
statement, one can read the neo-liberal emphasis of free
markets leading to freedom for citizens. The Owenite
emphasis on the term social market did recognise the
economic benefits markets have and the need to accept
them in a more thorough way, but it also looked to the
German economic model often called the 'social market
economy' which it was argued, was successful at producing
economic growth and prosperity for its citizens as well as
mitigating against the social injustice caused by market
outcomes. As Owen states in his *Keith Joseph Memorial Lecture*
in 2000: 'The social market owes much to Germany. Alfred
Muller-Armack invented the phrase, Ludwig Erhard first
practised it and the SPD adopted it at Bad Godesberg in
1959.' Robert Skidelsky and Owen provide a pertinent
distinction between the different visions of the social
market. Skidelsky says that the social market is a break with
Crosland's view that: 'market capitalism was simply a
superior means of producing taxable wealth for
redistribution. Making the market economy a primary value
– by virtue of its association with liberty, self-reliance,
entrepreneurship, dynamism and efficiency - entails limiting
the claims of redistribution.'[42] In response to Skidelsky's

comments Owen stated, 'I agree but that does not exclude redistribution along the lines of John Rawls's principles of a 'just' or a 'fair' society.[43]

In *Face the Future* Owen argued that the debate surrounding equality in post-war Labour circles had subsumed any appreciation of other values like liberty and community.[44] Owen did not discard the principle of greater equality but he, like other members of the Gang of Four and later members of the SDP did suggest that the best economic model was a mixed economy[45] with a dynamic market sector. This in itself could produce higher rewards for some and at the same time produce income inequalities that some in the Labour Party would want to resist. Even New Labour acolytes such as Mandelson and Liddle interpret his ideas as being moderate conservatism:

'...Owen's concept of the social market went somewhat further and essentially put people in boxes. In their commercial lives they were to be aggressive entrepreneurs fighting to squeeze the last ounce of profit out of their business, but in their home lives they were to be concerned citizens prepared to back a stronger NHS and, if they were better off, pay higher taxes. This combination of individualism in people's economic lives with social concern outside them finds a parallel in the attitudes Kenneth Clarke and Conservatives like him would strike today.'[46]

However, such portrayals of his views are exaggerated and misunderstood. Discussing his belief in equality, he suggests that: 'Equality is a noble idea. We know it will not be achieved, but that of itself does not invalidate an aspiration - any more than the fact that wages and salaries will reflect different responsibilities and opportunities means that it is wrong to strive for a system which endeavours to make financial rewards fairer.'[47] An accusation that Owen like the other SDP social democrats had jettisoned equality is simply incorrect.[48] In many ways, Owen and the SDP were ahead of their time in accepting a greater role for the market in the economy as social democratic parties around the world were beginning to see the impact of globalisation. Social democracy began to accept that the market economy could generate significant goods and that they had to think afresh about how to mitigate the social evils that it also generated.

Owen's concept of freedom is less explicit in *Face the Future*. Owen classified his brand of social democracy as the: '...radical democratic libertarian tradition of decentralised socialism...'[49] This definition sheds little light on his view of freedom except that his emphasis on decentralisation of power coupled with a desire for greater participatory democracy increases personal freedom in theory. The greater choice involved by voting more at local level for local issues and to be given a greater say in how public services are to be organised and provided, would have the net effect of widening choice and in a sense would affect individual's political freedom to a greater extent. Furthermore, political accountability is transferred from the central state to local government or regional assembly in theory and the argument implies that therefore individuals as consumers and the local electorate at large have an increased say in the governing of their locality. Therefore, services are more responsive to the culture of accountability and in the process individuals are empowered. However, all of this is dependent on the accountability and responsiveness of devolved government to individual, the consumer and to the electoral demands at a regional level. In practice decentralisation of power from central government to local government does not preclude centralist and elitist tendencies. Local councils have long been accused of being too powerful and *étatiste*. The culture of organisations and bureaucracies that would be established at local level would provide the real test of accountability, responsiveness and empowerment for individuals. Furthermore, and on a slightly different note, one can only assume that Owen would support freedom defined in the positive as well as the negative conception of liberty which is typical for the social democratic tradition. This can be inferred from a section in his first chapter, which asserts that: 'Liberty-Equality-Fraternity the old radical cry still emphasizes an eternal truth: that none of these three can properly be fulfilled without being combined in some measure with the other two.'[50]

Part of Owen's idea of the need for a greater emphasis on freedom concerned the decentralisation of power.[51] In *Face the Future* he suggests that social democracy requires less central government control and further localised decision making. His argument is that social democratic thinkers have been consistently centrist and collectivist. He highlights the socialism of William Morris as an example of the decentralist democracy he believes to be necessary. As he says:

'For Social Democrats intent on reviving the decentralist strand of thinking and in advocating specific policies for the 1980s it is worth first re-examining the historical debate. The socialist societies of the 1880s and 1890s, with their mixed membership of socialists and anarchists, focused most of their attention on the issue of decentralised worker-control versus nationalisation. William Morris, although not an anarchist, criticised both the Fabian definition of socialism and the means by which the Fabians expected socialism to be realised.'[52]

Owen, obviously influenced by the decentralisation of nineteenth century socialists such as Morris and the twentieth century Guild socialism of G.D.H. Cole suggests that those principles of decentralisation and greater participatory democracy by workers and voters in various ways needs to be once again adopted by social democrats.[53] As a forgotten principle within the tradition of social

democracy, his advocacy of a decentralist brand of social
democracy to devolve power and re-engage the public
through greater participatory democracy was an interesting
concept for social democrats of the time. However, as a
'liberal' principle it appealed not only to Liberals but to
certain Conservatives as well. This does not reduce its
legitimacy as a counter measure against an increasingly
centralist state and against a significant build up of power in
the Government, however, one can appreciate the
ambivalence such a principle received in traditional quarters
of the Labour Party including the right-wing in the late
1970s and early 1980s. Moreover, the strongest counter
argument to the principle of decentralisation of power is that
greater devolution of power leads to different people
enacting a plurality of measures in various regions of the
country. Therefore, the goal of nation-wide equity in public
services is immediately called in to question.

A further principle that Owen elaborated was more widely
appealing to the Labour Movement and to social democrats
in the SDP. The emphasis on fellowship/fraternity or taken
synonymously, 'community' is one that many social
democrats today pay lip service to. What is interesting about
Owen's contribution is that he not only advocated the value
of community but he argued that for many decades it had
been overlooked and to a large extent forgotten by social
democrats.[54] This was remarkably accurate:

'For more than a century political thought has been
dominated by the interaction and balance between liberty
and equality, but surprisingly little attention has been given
to the other element of this historic triad, fraternity,
representing the sense of fellowship, cooperation,
neighbourliness, community and citizenship. This neglect of
fraternity, particularly by socialist thinkers, has meant that
the espousal of equality has lacked a unifying force to bridge
the gaps and contradictions between equality and liberty.'[55]

After the 1983 defeat Owen endorsed some of Thatcher's policies like her trade union reforms;[56] support for the Falklands war; support for Britain retaining its nuclear status;[57] and he was more overtly in favour of a dynamic market economy or as he described it the 'social market economy' which was driven by a large private sector but still remained a mixed economy and when operated by social democrats would emphasize education and skills and focus on supply side issues.[58] It was clearly not the free-market ideology of the New Right[59] and the confusion is heightened firstly by Owen using the term 'social market' that had been introduced into British politics in the 1970s by Keith Joseph and secondly by the fact that social democracy's economic approach and doctrine was undergoing reform. Keynesianism had been abandoned by some moderate social democrat Labour MPs and the Labour Party would finally endorse the need for a more market-led approach to economics by the 1992 manifesto. As Crewe and King correctly point out: 'Because Owen's views on the free market and defence aroused more controversy they were usually more widely reported, but he actually devoted considerably more space in his speeches and writings to matters of social concern.'[60] Therefore, for most Social Democrats and Liberals in the Alliance Owen's remarks were not too monetarist or even too Thatcherite. The division with Williams, Jenkins and Rodgers who were Owen's rivals thus interested in portraying him as a Thatcherite and also more ideologically tied to their Keynesian heritage: 'Among those who were most unhappy were the remainder of the Gang of Four. As so often, the tensions between Owen and them were partly political but also partly personal...All three deeply disliked Owen's constant belligerence, his free-market rhetoric and his scarcely concealed admiration for Margaret Thatcher.'[61] There were differences of opinion between Owen and the rest of the Gang of Four, but Owen's irascible personality, lust for control and his belief that the SDP had to mirror the decisive leadership of Thatcher ultimately led to the insurmountable problem of remaining a united political force in British politics. But that said, Owen's ideas can still be seen as commensurable with a version of social democracy; some evidence for this exists in the following passages from Owen and Steel's 1987 book *The Time Has Come*: 'Social Democrats believe that Government has a responsibility to rectify market deficiencies, working as far as possible with the grain of the market.'[62] 'Liberals and Social Democrats also believe that the state must redistribute the rewards which arise from the combination of inherited property rights and the market to ensure a fair distribution of wealth and income, and to help eliminate poverty. Free market mechanisms are also incapable of providing for many of society's most important needs.'[63] 'Our basic values, then, are personal freedom, opportunity, social justice, fair shares, community and participation.'[64]

Peter Zenter stated in his 1982 book, *Social Democracy in Britain: Must Labour Lose?* that:

'In a party where Michael Foot and Neil Kinnock are the moderates, where part of the right wing has left and more will follow into the SDP, and where the PLP the last bastion of the right, is to become predominantly of the left during the eighties, all the meaningful pressures are still left-wing. The Hattersleys and the Healeys, as long as they remain in the Party, will serve as a reminder of former times rather than have a significant role to play. For the Labour Party, the Social Democratic Mark II option is no longer on offer. Nor is the Broad Church party on offer.'[65]

For a time this observation was accurate. The gradual reform towards a more centrist social democratic perspective first under Kinnock, then Smith and fully under

Blair took Labour from being an unelected left-wing democratic socialist party to an electable moderate social democratic party. David Owen is indicative of that need to change and in a limited way helped to shape that change by joining the SDP and advocating more centrist ideas on issues such as markets, national defence, decentralisation and the role of trade unions.

Proto-New Labour?

There is a strong case to make that David Owen's ideas outlined in the 1980s especially the ones put forward in his books *Face the Future, A United Kingdom,* and *The Time Has Come* are similar to many New Labour perspectives and therefore he can be understood as a proto-New Labour politician. Most notably Owen's attitude to markets is a recurrent theme in the modernised social democracy of the Blair Governments, in the words of Mandelson and Liddle:

'New Labour welcomes the rigour of competitive markets as the most efficient means of anticipating and supplying consumer's wants, offering choice and stimulating innovation...But, unlike the New Right, New Labour recognises that free markets do not automatically serve the public interest. Especially where large investments are required, they may fail to deliver efficient outcomes; and left to themselves, markets tend to reinforce inequalities and may entrench privilege. Only in these circumstances should markets be regulated.'[66]

Also, Owen's emphasis on community is certainly an area of overlap with New Labour so much so that one could categorise his social philosophy as being in the communitarian mould as he stressed the importance of the rights and responsibilities of citizens which is a central plank of New Labour's modernised social democracy.[67] As for the principle of freedom it has been said that Owen did not adequately define what he meant and what he envisioned a social democratic concept of freedom to be. Similarly New Labour talks more about opportunity as the outworking of liberty, so they are similarly quiet and vague on this issue. What can be said is that Owen did partly view greater liberty as coming about through greater democratisation of British civic life in terms of increased referenda; reform of the electoral system; and above all, decentralisation of power to the regions and to local government.[68] In this sense New Labour has followed some of this logic but whether it truly does increase civic participation and thus grants more choice for citizens has yet to be seen. In addition, there is an argument to say that elements of New Labour including the Prime Minister are lukewarm about decentralisation of power and hold no overall theory of the state. Mandelson and Liddle doff their hats to the SDP and perhaps this can be seen as acknowledging an intellectual debt to the likes of Owen as they assert that:

'The founders of the Social Democratic Party wanted to create an electable left-of-centre alternative to the Conservatives which had some realistic hope of governing Britain with success at a time when it appeared to them that the Labour Party had deserted its traditional roots and values and was set on a course of self-destruction. The political programme they initially offered was familiar fare by the standards of most continental social-democratic parties and represented much of what Labour had traditionally stood for, shorn of its contemporary excesses and ambiguities.'[69]

However they also noted their view albeit a mistaken one of the difference between New Labour and the social democracy of David Owen: 'Unlike the Owenite SDP, New

Labour marries the social market with more traditional Labour values of community and responsibility.'[70]

Conclusion

If the revisionist right of the 1960s and 1970s are the progenitors of the SDP, then the SDP is a New Labour parent. Policy prescriptions aside, the SDP of 1981 provided New Labour with an intellectual inheritance of markets, national defence, decentralisation, pro-Europeanism and a scepticism for the inherent value of trade unions in the policy-making process. It is also worth noting the ambivalence of the SDP towards the principle of equality which is also a fair criticism of New Labour and the Blairites in particular. The genealogy does not cohere neatly because New Labour is a product of people who remained inside the Labour Party unlike the Gang of Four. Also, New Labour is a political organisation with at least two competing tendencies vying for power and possibly different versions of social democracy. Furthermore, New Labour is a government and has had to face different issues that have affected their politics unlike the SDP. With these considerations in place one can see how New Labour is part of an intellectual history within the Labour Party that reaches back as far as the Gaitskellite-Croslandite revisionist approach to democratic socialism in the 1950s and 1960s and is akin to the break away SDP from the Labour Party in 1981.

Overall it is fair to say that what was published by Owen appears to be modernised social democracy in a form that would be compatible with the majority of New Labour politics. The reason why Owen never rejoined the Labour Party on Blair's election to Party Leader or on New Labour's victory in 1997 is unknown. Much of it I imagine is down to his personality and temperament having led the SDP for so long. Also personal relationships are central to such an issue. Owen did not help himself by offending the sensibilities of the British left in the words of Crewe and King: 'Owen was said to be Margaret Thatcher's favourite opposition politician; she occasionally sounded like his favourite prime minister. Temperamentally, the two had much in common.'[71] In addition Owen further blotted his copybook with Labour and destroyed any possibility of returning to the fold by writing an article in the Mail on Sunday on the eve of the 1992 General Election endorsing John Major. The piece also criticised Neil Kinnock for his '...record of political misjudgements.'[72] For him Kinnock was not only incompetent but a figure of the Labour left. It is patently obvious that by 1992 Kinnock and Labour were as moderately social democratic as Owen and ideologically speaking, were a party he could have rejoined if he so desired. Moreover what is apparent when assessing Owen's political ideas is that the evidence suggests that he is a social democrat and not a neo-liberal. The bad feelings of many in the Labour Party who will always see Owen as a traitor to the cause and for many years an opponent of Shadow Labour administrations must have played their part. In terms of political thought, the gulf is not so wide as to preclude Owen from being regarded as a social democrat even if he is never regarded by the Labour Party as part of the Labour Movement and *ergo*, as 'one of us.'

[1] D. Owen, *Personally Speaking to Kenneth Harris* (Pan Books, London, 1987), p.239.

[2] This chapter originates from a conference paper I delivered to the Labour Movements Group at the PSA Annual Conference that was held at the University of Leeds in April 2005. Thanks go to my colleagues in the Labour Movements Group for their constructive comments.

[3] I. Bradley, *Breaking the Mould?: The Birth and Prospects of the Social Democratic Party* (Martin Robertson, Oxford, 1981), p.103.

[4] In addition, Owen's revisionist right credentials are evident in a 1967 pamphlet that he co-authored which set out his view of what the Wilson Government's priorities should be, which included '...the struggle for equality and social justice.' See, D. Owen, D. Marquand and J. Mackintosh, *Change Gear: Towards A Socialist Strategy* (Socialist Commentary, London, 1967), David Owen Papers, University of Liverpool, D709 2/10/1.

[5] For the New Left critique of Crosland's revisionist thesis see, S. Holland, *The Socialist Challenge* (Quartet Books, London, 1975). However, there has been no single work produced by a neo-liberal thinker specifically concerned with critiquing Crosland's brand of social democracy.

[6] B. Crick, *Socialist Values and Time* (Fabian Society Tract 495, London, 1984).

[7] Ibid. p.3.

[8] D. Kogan and M. Kogan, *The Battle for the Labour Party* (Kogan Page, London, 1983), p.69.

[9] D. Owen, *Face The Future* (Oxford University Press, Oxford, 1981).

[10] Shirley Williams published a book later that year; S. Williams, *Politics is for People* (Jonathan Cape, London, 1981). William Rodgers published a book the following year; W. Rodgers, *The Politics of Change* (Secker & Warburg, London, 1982). Owen's book is more philosophically linked to his vision of what British social democracy should strive to be than either of these publications.

[11] See R. Jenkins, 'Dimbleby Lecture: Home Thoughts From Abroad' in K. Wayland, (ed.) *The Rebirth of Britain* (Weidenfeld & Nicolson, London, 1982).

[12] This is a revealing point. In the first edition of *Face the Future* in 1981 the term 'democratic socialism' is used. The book was written before Owen left the Labour Party. By the second edition in 1983 it has been supplanted with the term 'social democracy'. I am grateful to Dr. Mark Wickham-Jones for this point. Owen was obviously making the point of

distinguishing the SDP from the Foot and Benn brand of democratic socialism that was dominant in the Labour Party at that time.

[13] Biographical notes, David Owen Papers, University of Liverpool.

[14] Ibid.

[15] I. Crewe and A. King, *SDP: The Birth, Life and Death of the Social Democratic Party* (Oxford University Press, Oxford, 1995), p.310.

[16] Ibid. p.332.

[17] See P. Lee Sykes, *Losing From the Inside: The Cost of Conflict in the British Social Democratic Party* (Transaction Books, New Brunswick, 1988) and I. Crewe and A. King, *SDP: The Birth, Life and Death of the Social Democratic Party*.

[18] D. Owen, *A United Kingdom* (Penguin Books, Harmondsworth, 1986), pp.57-79.

[19] D. Owen, 'Agenda for Competitiveness with Compassion' *Economic Affairs*, 4 (1983), 26-33 and D. Owen, *A Future that will Work: Competitiveness and Compassion* (Penguin Books, Harmondsworth, 1984).

[20] As a point of information it was the Attlee Government spearheaded in this regard by Ernest Bevin who instigated Britain's nuclear age and many Labour leaders including Attlee, Gaitskell, Wilson, Callaghan, Smith and Blair have supported retaining Britain's nuclear capabilities. Owen as SDP leader was in favour of the nuclear deterrent but was against replacing Polaris with Trident on the grounds of cost and wanted to explore the possibility of co-operating with France in terms of nuclear deterrence.

[21] It is worth noting for example that Michael Foot was in favour of the Falklands War and he was significantly more left-wing than Owen.

[22] Biographical notes, David Owen Papers, University of Liverpool.

[23] Ibid.

[24] D. Marquand, *The Progressive Dilemma* (Heinemann, London, 1991), p.185.

[25] Biographical notes, David Owen Papers, University of Liverpool.

[26] R. Jenkins, *A Life at the Centre* (Macmillan, London, 1991), p.617.

[27] P. Lee Sykes, *Losing From the Inside*, p.97.

[28] Ibid. p.99.

[29] Ibid.p.109.

[30] D. Owen, *A United Kingdom*, pp.68-79.

[31] Ibid. pp.99-116.

[32] David Owen, 'Social Market and Social Justice' *Tawney Society 5th Annual Lecture* (Tawney Society, London, 1987).

[33] D. Owen, *A United Kingdom*, pp. 42-56.

[34] A. Arblaster, 'Liberal and Socialist Values' *Socialist Register*, 1972, p.92.

[35] Other interesting publications which shed light on Owen's social democratic heritage are, D. Owen, *Personally Speaking: to Kenneth Harris* and D. Owen, *A Time To Declare* (Michael Joseph, London, 1991).

[36] P. Mandelson and R. Liddle, *The Blair Revolution: Can New Labour Deliver?* (Faber and Faber, London, 1996).

[37] See D. Owen, 'Agenda for Competitiveness with Compassion', D. Owen, *A Future that will Work*, D. Owen, 'Social Market and Social Justice' and R. Jenkins, *A Life at the Centre*, p.617.

[38] D. Owen, *The Fifth Keith Joseph Memorial Lecture* (Centre for Policy Studies, London, 2000), p.1.

[39] See R. Plant, *Equality, Markets and the State* (Fabian Society, London, 1984) and H. Young, 'Why David Owen might want to keep his options open', *The Guardian*, 24th July 1986.

[40] D. Owen, *The Fifth Keith Joseph Memorial Lecture*, p.1.

[41] Centre for Policy Studies, *Memoranda of Association* (Centre for Policy Studies, London, 1974).

[42] R. Skidelsky, *The Social Market Economy* (Social Market Foundation, London, 1989).

[43] D. Owen, *The Fifth Keith Joseph Memorial Lecture*, p.2.

[44] D. Owen, *Face the Future*, p.4.

[45] See, Letter to the Committee of the Parliamentary Labour Party, 21st November 1980, David Owen Papers, University of Liverpool, D709 2/17/1/3.

[46] P. Mandelson and R. Liddle, *The Blair Revolution*, p.29.

[47] D. Owen, *Face the Future*, p.4.

[48] See Letter to Rev. Scharf stating his social democratic beliefs, 11th December 1980, David Owen Papers, University of Liverpool, D709 2/17/1/3. Also see, D. Owen, 'Communism, Socialism, and Democracy' *The Washington Review of Strategic and International Studies*, Vol.1, No.2, April 1978, pp.4-15.

[49] D. Owen, *Face the Future*, p.1.

[50] Ibid. p.3.

[51] See, D. Owen, 'Labour's Co-operative Way Forward', 26th May 1980, *The Guardian*, David Owen Papers, University of Liverpool, D709 2/10/5.

[52] D. Owen, *Face the Future*, p.19.

[53] Ibid.p.27.

[54] See, D. Owen, 'This Serious Challenge Labour Must Fight', 30th January 1980, *The Times*, David Owen Papers, University of Liverpool, D709 2/10/5.

[55] D. Owen, *Face the Future*, pp.3-4.

[56] See, D. Owen, *A United Kingdom*, p. 118.

[57] Ibid. pp. 57-79. Owen's line on the nuclear deterrent is consistent throughout his career and commensurable with the traditions of moderate socialists in the Labour Party. In short, he advocated the need for a nuclear deterrent but was sceptical about replacing Polaris with Trident partly due to the huge cost and the impact that it would have on the defence budget for conventional armed services. In addition, Owen was sceptical of Trident because of the implications it may have on proliferating further nuclear weapons and on the global balance of power, namely how would the USSR interpret Britain's nuclear expansion if Trident was adopted? According to Owen's logic the adoption of Trident could reasonably be interpreted as an escalation of Britain's nuclear arsenal. I am grateful to Dr. Richard McGuire for discussions on this topic.

[58] Ibid. pp.99-116.

[59] For a critique of the New Right see, D. Owen, Letter to the Committee of the Parliamentary Labour Party, 21st November 1980, David Owen Papers, University of Liverpool, D709 2/17/1/3.

[60] I. Crewe and A. King, *SDP: The Birth, Life and Death of the Social Democratic Party*, p. 334.

[61] Ibid. p.335.

[62] D. Owen and D. Steel, *The Time Has Come: Partnership for Progress* (Weidenfeld and Nicholson, London, 1987), p.22.

[63] Ibid.p.39.

[64] Ibid.p.24.

[65] P. Zenter, *Social Democracy In Britain: Must Labour Lose?* (Hohn Martin Publishing, London, 1982), p.199.

[66] P. Mandelson and R. Liddle, *The Blair Revolution*, p.22.

[67] D. Owen, *A United Kingdom*, p. 174.

[68] Ibid. pp.198-208.

[69] P. Mandelson and R. Liddle, *The Blair Revolution*, p.28.

[70] Ibid.p.29.

[71] I. Crewe and A. King, *SDP: The Birth, Life and Death of the Social Democratic Party*, p. 335.

[72] Ibid. p.471.

11

ROY HATTERSLEY[1]

'The true object of socialism is the creation of a genuinely free society in which the protection and extension of individual liberty is the primary duty of the state... Socialism exists to provide – for the largest possible number of people – the ability to exercise effective liberty.'[2]

A chapter on Roy Hattersley in a book focusing on those who have most shaped the political thought of the Labour Party may seem rather odd. Hattersley has only written one book on socialist thought[3] and his impact was greatest when the Labour Party was in Opposition. Moreover, he is often interpreted as having been on the pragmatic right of the Labour Party for much of his career, so that his highly critical reaction to New Labour appears as resentment following his removal from the upper echelons of the Party after his retirement as Deputy Leader following the General Election defeat of 1992. It could further be assumed that his reaction against New Labour has been ill-tempered and non-constructive. A chapter on his ideas may be thought, therefore, to be based on very little substantive content.

Such a view would be mistaken. He frequently emphasises the importance of ideology in politics. His early influence in the Labour Party was Tony Crosland. Hattersley's importance in the Party reached its peak in Opposition to the Conservatives in the 1980s. Hattersley's contribution can be seen therefore as the most significant attempt by a senior

Labour Party politician after the 1983 General Election defeat to modernise democratic socialism/social democracy[4] in response to the intellectual challenge of the New Right.[5] His attempt to modernise the political thought of the Labour Party up to 1992 can then be contrasted with his critical reaction to New Labour.   Therefore Hattersley warrants attention in this volume as a 'thinking politician' at a crucial time in the Labour Party's history.

This chapter has two aims.   First, it will outline the neo-liberal theory and the social democratic response in the 1980s.   The second aim will be to examine the contribution made by Roy Hattersley to this process.   This will allow us to identify Hattersley's role as a thinker and to ask to what extent he has been consistent in his thinking, a necessary task if we are to understand the differences between the social democratic position as it stood in the 1980s and New Labour.   A central part of Hattersley's argument is the need to pursue greater equality of outcome, while he argues that this is not a clear commitment with New Labour.   The major work by Roy Hattersley is *Choose Freedom* and the title of this book, and the epigram for this chapter that is taken from it, highlight the importance given to 'freedom' at this time.   This was no accident since social democratic theorists were trying to reclaim the idea of freedom from the neo-liberals.   It is therefore worth examining neo-liberal arguments at some length before going on to discuss the social democratic response.

Neo-Liberalism and the Social Democratic Response

The New Right constituted a critique of social democratic theory in all its aspects.   This constituted both a neo-conservative strand that sought to restore social order and traditional morality against what was regarded as the permissiveness and welfarism of the post-war period.   In contrast, a neo-liberal strand sought to defend freedom against what was seen as an over-powerful state that threatened individual liberty in the pursuit of a misguided commitment to social justice. Although there was an obvious conflict between the promotion of individual freedom and the restoration of authority both elements were united, at least initially, around a commitment to free market economics.[6] The New Right was an attempt to unify these distinct elements in to a coherent programme.[7] Although this aim was never fully realised since ideological conflicts between freedom and authority remained and new challenges after 1979 strained the ideological coherence of the Thatcher Governments there was nevertheless a clear ideological purpose to Conservative politics pursued in the 1980s. The following discussion focuses on the neo-liberal element since it can be argued that as the 1980s progressed this strand of New Right thinking became dominant and consequently it was against this that social democrats sought to respond.

The theoretical case for neo-liberalism was provided by Friedrich von Hayek from the 1950s.[8] However, for much of the period Hayek was seen as a figure of only marginal importance. His ideas, promoted through the Institute of Economic Affairs and the Mont Pelerin Society, had only marginal importance initially but became more influential in the late-1960s when Conservative politicians sought to equip themselves with a theoretical case against the growth of the central state. The most prominent Conservative politicians who argued for the free market were Enoch Powell and then Keith Joseph and Geoffrey Howe. Joseph in particular was of major influence on Margaret Thatcher through the formation of the Centre for Policy Studies. The free market case received a significant boost in the 1970s from other think-tanks such as the Adam Smith Institute and the right-wing press including the *Times* and the *Financial Times*, which also presented to a British audience the arguments of free market economists such as the crowding-out theory of

Richard Bacon and Walter Eltis and Milton Friedman's monetarism. Increasingly, the tone of Conservative writers was sympathetic to a free market policy.

The neo-liberal thesis consisted of both a free market political economy and a critique of welfare.[9] Monetarists sought to question the Keynesian belief in budget deficits.[10] The emergence of the phenomenon of 'stagflation' (a simultaneous increase in unemployment and inflation) undermined the Keynesian argument that there could be a trade-off between the two and monetarists argued that there was no such trade-off so that the use of budget deficits would only raise inflation in the longer-term. This argument was presented more starkly by advocates of the rational expectations approach who stated that there would be an immediate inflationary impact of any use of budget deficits. The crowding-out theory stated that the growth of the central state had taken physical and financial resources away from the wealth-creating private sector.[11] Supply-side theorists such as Arthur Laffer[12] sought to demonstrate that increases in income tax rates undermined individual effort and reduced the total tax yield. This disincentive effect could be reduced by cutting rates of direct taxation. A common argument from neo-liberal economists is that barriers to the operation of free labour markets such as wages councils and trade unions increased the level of unemployment. What these various arguments amounted to was a rejection of state intervention in the economy. The role of the state would be reduced to a minimal role of maintaining order and the control of inflation. Indeed, even the monetary role of the state was questioned by Hayek who argued that there should be a denationalisation of money so that consumers could choose which currency they wished to use from a range on offer. Even currencies could become a tradable commodity.[13] In this sense even the monetary role of the state emphasised by monetarists was challenged by Hayek, although it was the former that had more impact on the

Conservative Governments who sought to control the money supply from 1979.

Turning to the neo-liberal critique of welfare we can identify several arguments here which can be listed as a philosophical critique of social democracy, a critique of state bureaucracies, a critical view of the role of pressure groups and a belief that welfare creates dependency.[14] The basis of the philosophical case made by neo-liberals is that it is possible to identify two notions of freedom in popular political usage. The first is a positive notion used by social democrats, social liberals and progressive conservatives, which discusses freedom in terms of the capacity to act and the consequent need for resources to act freely. The second is negative freedom defined as freedom from external constraint. The neo-liberal argument states that the first notion of freedom is theoretically incorrect and that consequently the increase in the size and functions of the state in the post-war period was founded on shaky moral ground. Freedom could only be undermined by intentional acts of coercion and since market outcomes are not intended but only the consequence of many individual transactions, they were not a diminution of individual freedom. Similarly, social justice is a false moral claim since an injustice can only take place through deliberate intentional acts and since the poverty of others is not intended by individual consumers then market transactions are not an injustice. Positive freedom and social justice are also dubious concepts since there is no way of deciding how to evaluate divergent claims on resources. Individuals will have different objectives that would require infinite resources if they are to be realised. Since there is an absence of a moral consensus in a pluralistic society on how these resources should be allocated there would be no objective means to distribute resources capable of gaining universal consent. This has an impact on both the way pressure groups campaign for resources and how they are allocated by state bureaucracies as will be demonstrated below. In a similar way since there is a lack of moral consensus as to what 'social justice' could mean, there is little objective purpose to a politics based on this false principle.[15]

Moreover, the social democratic conception of equality and rights is misguided. There is a categorical distinction that can be made between absolute and relative poverty. It is possible to defend a minimal welfare state, according to Hayek, that can protect people from absolute poverty (hunger, homelessness etc.) and would only require a minimal level of state expenditure free from the demands for greater spending by state bureaucracies and pressure groups. The concern with inequality as distinct from poverty leads to politics based on the principles of positive freedom and social justice, which for reasons outlined above, are intellectually dubious. Moreover, in the absence of a strong, objective ethical case for social justice and equality, demands for greater equality of outcome are based on envy, will require ever larger levels of state expenditure and the higher taxes needed to fund this will reduce incentives. The issue should then become one of how best to raise the absolute level of the poor, and neo-liberals because of the economic and philosophical arguments outlined favour the market, which is seen as a more efficient mechanism for the production of wealth. This wealth will then 'trickle down' to the poor through market mechanisms – increasing wages as profits increase and/or lowering prices as goods become more widely available. In a similar way a categorical distinction is made between positive and negative rights. Negative rights concern the protection of the individual from deliberate acts of coercion and are held to be absolute since they are not resource-dependent. In contrast, a positive right to welfare cannot exist since they are resource dependent. Since there will never be sufficient resources to meet all welfare needs there cannot be absolute rights to welfare. They will always be curtailed by limited resources.

What is clear is that neo-liberals such as Hayek offered a substantial critique of the ethical arguments of social democracy. The argument presented by neo-liberals contrasted each philosophical concept used by social democrats. For each concept used – freedom, social justice, rights, equality, poverty – neo-liberals formulated a different conception, one that they believed was intellectually superior. In place of positive freedom, social justice, welfare rights, economic equality and relative poverty; neo-liberals spoke of negative freedom, market justice, negative rights, inequality and absolute poverty. Since the values of social democracy turned out to be false ethical claims, the nature of politics was affected detrimentally. State bureaucracies instead of being the neutral administrators had clear self-interest in the expansion of the government activity from which they would gain more power and resources and could decide where and how resources were allocated in an arbitrary way. In a similar way the absence of a social consensus for the distribution of public expenditure allows pressure groups to make unlimited claims on resources. This process is fuelled by electoral competition between the parties, which consistently seek to raise expectations about what can be delivered in order to gain votes. The outcome of this process was the economic crisis of the 1970s, when the state became overloaded according to the neo-liberals. The neo-liberal conception of welfare, freedom, rights, justice and so forth would set clear constraints on the arbitrary actions of state bureaucracies and the allocation of resources. Finally, the drift to welfare dependency would be countered by the implementation of clear limits on welfare expenditure and the increased role for markets. Markets would be 'fairer' since they encouraged responsibility and moral pluralism in contrast to dependency and the arbitrary allocation of resources.

Space does not permit a full examination of the detailed response made by critics of neo-liberalism to each of these arguments. Instead, what will be attempted here is a presentation of the broad case made by social democrats in Britain to the challenge of neo-liberalism. In so doing, emphasis will be placed on the arguments of Raymond Plant.[16] This is so for two reasons. First, Plant attempted a clear and consistent rejection of neo-liberal arguments. Second, he had a demonstrable impact on the thought of many in the Labour Party including Hattersley.[17]

Plant and others argued that the neo-liberal critique of traditional social democratic conceptions of liberty, rights, equality and social justice could be rejected by stressing the philosophical validity of social democratic thought. A central focus of social democratic thought in the 1980s was on the concept of liberty, which is not surprising given that neo-liberals had sought to dominate the discourse on liberty. A social democratic defence of liberty had therefore to challenge the neo-liberal conception of liberty as freedom from external, intentionally imposed, constraint. Plant did this by asking the question, what is liberty for? The answer would presumably be that freedom is essential in order to do things. Negative freedom is desirable in order to act. This in turn implied possessing the capacity to act, which would require the means to do things. Hence Plant, following Gerald MacCallum[18], argued that there was no categorical distinction between negative and positive freedom – freedom *from* implied freedom *to*. Freedom therefore was resource dependent.

The next part of the social democratic response to the neo-liberal paradigm involved the defence of welfare rights. Again, Plant argued that the categorical distinction made between negative and positive rights was invalid. This was the case since both depended on the provision of resources, which were limited. For rights to become effective they needed to be enforced. The enforcement of rights was conditional on the availability of resources. In the case of negative rights, enforcement required funding for policing, prisons and so forth. Since resources were limited there could be no unlimited claim to the enforcement of negative rights. This meant that negative rights were in fact much closer to welfare rights than was assumed by the neo-liberals. Welfare rights were also resource dependent but whereas neo-liberals such as Hayek had argued that this meant that they were not proper 'rights', social democrats argued that they were rights in the same limited and resource-dependent way as negative rights.

A key part of the social democratic response in the 1980s was the defence of measures designed to reduce inequality and relative poverty. This was related to the conception of freedom outlined above. If freedom meant the capacity to act then such freedom would be limited by the absence of resources. The provision of resources was essential to freedom. Welfare was required therefore not just to remove absolute poverty (homelessness, hunger and so forth) but also in order to make effective choices. Since the range of choices could only be understood within particular social contexts then poverty was relative to the average levels of wealth in society at that given time. The assertion of Keith Joseph, following Hayek, that "poverty is not unfreedom,"[19] was rejected. The capacity to act was directly dependent on the availability of resources. In asking which inequalities are justified, social democrats set out two criteria for 'justifiable inequalities'. The first was the Rawlsian defence of inequalities required to provide incentives to fulfil duties that benefited the worse off.[20] Secondly, the argument derived from Fred Hirsch that certain forms of inequality were inevitable since certain goods – so-called 'positional goods' – could not be redistributed either through a 'trickle down' effect or through government redistribution.[21]

The final part of the philosophical defence of social democracy in the 1980s was the ethical justification for social justice. As noted above, Hayek rejected the concept of social justice on two grounds. The first was that justice and injustice could only take place in the intentional acts of human beings. If outcomes were unintended they may be unfortunate and require voluntary action but were not an injustice. This point was rejected by Plant. He argued that injustice resulted not only from intentional action, but also in situations in which outcomes are foreseeable but are not acted upon.[22] This was the case in law since manslaughter was an offence where the outcome (death) is a foreseeable but not an intended consequence of human action. Plant's argument was that injustice occurs not just from intentional action but also how we choose to respond to the unintended consequences of human action. The response of neo-liberals that market outcomes were not foreseeable was also rejected since a further neo-liberal argument was that markets were more effective in the production of wealth and through the trickle-down effect would raise the absolute level of the poor while increasing the level of inequality. If market outcomes were not foreseeable then such a claim for the trickle-down effect could not be made. Moreover, the trickle-down effect had not worked in that way since the absolute position of the poor had deteriorated over the course when this policy was used to fullest effect. The issue therefore became one concerning empirical claims that the trickle-down effect would raise the absolute position of the poor more effectively than fiscal redistribution, something which became increasingly implausible over the course of the 1980s. The other argument made by Hayek against the concept of social justice was that there was no objective way of determining how this concept was to be defined given that it was capable of a range of meanings. Within a morally pluralistic society this would result in competitive pressure on governments leading to fiscal crises. This point was partly accepted by social democrats who argued that the fostering of a social consensus was needed for the promotion of social justice given that no agreed definition of social justice existed.[23] However, rather than leading to the rejection of the concept of social justice, this required politicians to argue for a coherent notion of social justice as part of a citizenship approach incorporating positive liberty, welfare rights and equality.

Hattersley's Contribution to Social Democracy

The focus for the rest of this chapter is on Hattersley's contribution to British socialism.[24] It will be argued that Hattersley's views have remained remarkably consistent, rather than that he has re-created himself as a left-wing critic of New Labour since 1994 after being on the loyalist, pragmatic right of the Labour Party up to that point. It is demonstrated here that Hattersley's views are consistent and his ideological position that led him to be on the right of the Labour Party in the 1980s has also led him to be critical of New Labour.

In the 1960s, Hattersley served as a non-Cabinet minister with particular responsibility for defence issues. This close proximity to Denis Healey as Defence Secretary had significance in the internal Labour Party debates in the early 1980s, when Hattersley was a strong supporter of Healey's. However, the most important development that marked Hattersley's position was over Britain's membership of the EEC. Hattersley was one of the pro-EEC lobby within the Labour Party who voted with the Heath Government for entry into the EEC and then campaigned for a 'Yes' vote in the 1975 referendum. This led to his association with the pro-European Labour right. However, of more significance in defining Hattersley's ideological position was the 1976 IMF Crisis.[25] Hattersley was one of the supporters of Crosland's alternative proposal to the cuts in public expenditure at this time. Broadly there were three positions. The first, which was the view of Healey, with the support of Edmund Dell and Reginald Prentice, was that cuts were necessary both to restore international confidence, to secure the loan from the IMF to support sterling and to free resources for private sector investment. The two alternatives were to oppose IMF demands for cuts either by arguing for the economic benefits of high public spending as advocated by Crosland, or to adopt protectionist measures as advocated most forcefully by Tony Benn (see the discussion of the AES in this volume in relation to Stuart Holland). Initially, the Prime Minister, James Callaghan, sought to be neutral and allow the debate to run its full course eventually supporting Healey. The Benn position was defeated. Crosland initially had support from a number of Labour's social democrats within the Cabinet. However, his support dwindled as individuals such as Bill Rodgers questioned the feasibility of Crosland's proposals, others such as Shirley Williams thought his views were not sufficiently pro-European and Harold Lever was opposed to the moderately protectionist measures Crosland adopted at the end of the Cabinet debates. Only Hattersley remained a supporter of Crosland until the end, with both believing the cuts would undermine the Labour Party's commitment to equality. Crosland is reported to have said that Hattersley was a "genuine egalitararian," one of the few in the Cabinet.[26] This point is significant, Hatterlsey was a close associate of Crosland, who argued consistently in 1976 for an egalitarian, Keynesian response to the sterling crisis.

If Hattersley was opposed to the Labour Government's fiscal measures of 1976, he was also opposed to the Alternative Economic Strategy developing on the Labour left in the late-1970s and early-1980s. In addition to thinking that the measures were unpopular electorally he also continued to argue for a more internationalist outlook, which for Hattersley included a strong commitment to the EEC.[27] This can be seen in his stance after the 1979 General Election defeat. He supported Healey in the 1980 Leadership contest and the 1981 Deputy Leadership contest when challenged by Benn. He became a leading figure within the Labour right Solidarity Group and sought to resist the increasingly powerful left-wing. In his statement for the 1983 Leadership contest he argued for a pro-EEC stance but lost to Neil Kinnock. One interesting question is why did Hattersley stay in the Labour Party rather than joining the new Social Democratic Party (SDP). This reveals an interesting feature of Hattersley's political views. In the most comprehensive account of the SDP, Ivor Crewe and Anthony King[28] point to the sentimental attachment Hattersley felt for the Labour Party. They identify five reasons why some on the Labour right refused, despite significant pressure to do so, to leave Labour and join the SDP: an emotional attachment to Labour, a belief that Labour right could regain dominance within the Party, a belief that by joining and strengthening the SDP individuals would aid the electoral dominance of the Thatcher Government, a fear of de-selection by left-wing constituency parties or the personal costs of leaving. Although the reasons why individuals decided to stay in the Labour Party were multifaceted, one of these reasons would be more powerful than others in determining whether an individual would stay or leave the Party.[29] For Hattersley, the major factor why he did not even give any serious thought to leaving the Party was emotional: "I accept that part of my inability to contemplate leaving the Labour Party is emotional rather than rational – the product of upbringing and personal gratitude."[30] Hattersley was claiming that the experiences of his youth, growing up in a poor household in Sheffield and seeing the local impact of the reforms of the Attlee Government had conditioned his attitude to the Labour Party. However, it is also likely that Hattersley felt that some of those who formed the SDP had a limited commitment to equality. Of the 'Gang of Four', he felt that Shirley Williams had views closest to his own. Of the four, Owen held to a different conception of social democracy in which equality was limited to equality of opportunity, a meritocratic understanding which Hattersley did not share as will be shown below.[31]

In the 1983 Leadership/Deputy Leadership contest, Hattersley was essentially the right-wing candidate.[32] He placed emphasis on a value-based politics with equality at the centre. The key point was that the Labour Party needed to gain power: "that does not require us to abandon our ideals or reject our socialist philosophy. Indeed, if we are to become again a party of power rather than a party of protest we need to say more, not less, about both our idealism and our ideology. We cannot win as working-class Conservatives or shop-floor Liberals. Nor would we deserve to win if we abandoned our historic duty to evangelise for a more equal society."[33] Hattersley went on to outline his policy position including a national minimum wage, higher public spending on the poor, protection of minorities and the pursuit of greater equality through reductions in private health and education. He supported the retention of nuclear weapons and membership of the EEC, continued use of state planning and cooperation with the trade unions and also advocated one member one vote in Labour's internal elections.[34] However, it was equality that lay at the core of Hattersley's message: "it is our belief that 'socialism is about equality' which distinguishes us from the grim authoritarians of the far left and the social ameliorators of the soggy middle ground."[35]

The related questions then become what did Hattersley mean by equality and what did he do to promote his ideas as Deputy Leader? The main focus is inevitably his book *Choose Freedom* since this has been his only full-length exposition of his socialism and the *Statement of Democratic Socialist Aims and Values* which was an attempt to outline the core values upon which the Labour Party was based and was largely written by him.[36] Hattersley was critical of the empirical tradition within the Labour Party and argued explicitly for an ideological basis to politics. A doctrinal position was needed for the revival of the Labour Party in the 1980s for two reasons. First, there had been substantial economic and social change with the decline of manufacturing and the emergence of a more prosperous working class, which had changed Labour's traditional core vote. In addition, politics had become more ideological with the rise of the New Right. The Labour Party therefore needed to show why it was relevant both in changed social conditions and by winning the ideological debate with the New Right: "for all those reasons, a clear definition of our ideological position is now essential."[37] If explained properly, Labour's ideology could gain sufficient electoral support since: "democratic socialism, properly defined, is a philosophy with an immense natural appeal, for it is the gospel of personal emancipation."[38]

Hattersley's conception of democratic socialism is broadly similar in all its main points to the broader social democratic position outlined above. It sought to challenge the neo-liberal conception of liberty and to defend equality. Indeed, the former was dependent upon the latter: "socialists ought to support and advocate the extension of equality as a matter of principle, which if not an end in itself, is so closely related to the ultimate goal of freedom that...it needs no justification."[39] This involved a commitment to a positive conception of liberty, which Hattersley sought to defend explicitly: "to socialists, freedom is not the absence of restraint on the rich and the powerful, but the ability of the generality of men and women to exercise their inherent rights."[40] Hence for Hattersley, socialism was a concern with the interrelated values of equality and liberty: "I have no doubt at all that equality enhances the *sum* of liberty."[41] In advocating equality, Hattersley meant more than equality of opportunity and drew on arguments made by Tawney and Crosland in defence of greater equality of outcome. Hence, Hattersley argued that, "socialism is about the reorganisation of society with the specific object of creating a more equal distribution of power and wealth – not an equal chance to become one of the minority who are both powerful and wealthy."[42] Equality of opportunity was not an alternative to wider economic equality since the former was in fact dependent upon the latter. Differences in income and wealth create inequalities in opportunity. For example, educational attainment is often influenced by the social and economic background of children, so that not every child would be able to benefit in the same way from the educational opportunities provided. Educational reform can compensate for inequalities of wealth and income but only to a limited extent.

Hattersley went on to reject a number of the claims made by neo-liberals in defence of inequality, arguing that there was no automatic trickle-down effect in the market place, that inequality produces waste since not all talent is utilised in the market economy.[43] Indeed, Hattersley rejects a number of the claims usually made in support of the competitive market economy.[44] His case for markets is based largely on the role of tacit knowledge. This is the claim made most forcefully by Hayek that the state can only act upon 'propositional' knowledge (knowledge that) but that individuals will often act on 'tacit' knowledge (knowledge how). The relevance of tacit knowledge is the key argument Hattersley made for the defence of markets as the most effective mechanism to allow for individual choice, albeit markets regulated by the state, within a mixed economy and with protection for the vulnerable including trade unions and minimum wage legislation.[45] This limited argument in favour of markets is important both when examining how the Labour Party responded to Hattersley's socialism and also when comparing Hattersley with New Labour.

Hattersley feels that *Choose Freedom* had little impact, something which shows the Labour Party's lack of interest in ideology more generally: "although *Choose Freedom* was generally well reviewed it was forgotten within months of its publication."[46] Hattersley had encouraged Neil Kinnock to draw up a statement of Labour Party ideology following the 1987 General Election defeat. He had little success, until later when Kinnock asked him to write a document which became the *Labour Party's Statement of Democratic Socialist Aims and Values* published in 1988 and containing a similar message to *Choose Freedom*. The reasons for this change of attitude by Kinnock are significant since they show how ideology was used for strategic reasons in the internal politics of the Labour Party at this time.[47] First, Crick says that he had been asked by Kinnock two years earlier to write a statement of socialist principles but had then disagreed with Crick's draft. This document was later published as an alternative statement of aims and values written by Crick and David Blunkett and constituted the 'soft-left' alternative position.[48] It was, according to Crick, an attempt to unite the moderate left and the Party's right by using language that the majority of the Party could agree with, whereas Hattersley's was a 'hard-right' document that would only divide the Party.[49] There were two major areas of philosophical disagreement between the two versions. The Blunkett-Crick paper was critical of markets and had more emphasis on the value of community than on freedom. The Hattersley document was openly supportive of markets, without some of the conditions contained in *Choose Freedom*, and placed most emphasis on the social democratic notion of freedom outlined above. Kinnock had shown no interest in an ideological statement before but now wanted such a document in order to pre-empt publication of the Blunkett-Crick version, as Hattersley puts it: "the way to avoid accepting their view of socialism was to produce our own."[50] The second reason why Kinnock became supportive was because of the perceived need to provide some kind of statement of principle for the forthcoming Policy Review, which took place from 1989. Kinnock was aware of the potential harm that critics of the Review could do by saying that the Party was abandoning its principles in the run-up to the next General Election that finally took place in 1992, the last election under the Leadership of Kinnock as it proved to be.

Hattersley's statement met with widespread criticism when considered by the Shadow Cabinet, but this came not from the left-wingers but from those on the pragmatic Labour right, notably John Smith and Jack Cunningham, who thought that the document was far too sympathetic to the market and did little to outline the limitations of markets, something with which Hattersley agreed later when writing his memoirs.[51] The National Executive Committee passed the document by 22 votes to 4. The *Statement* then progressed to the Labour Party Conference where it received little discussion.[52] Hattersley has accepted in a recent interview that this was probably due to the limited scope for debate since there was an attempt to stop open discussion of Labour Party ideas but again also reflected the limited interest more generally in ideological discussion.[53] Within the academic literature two views are presented. The first is that the *Statement* marked a clear contribution to the modernisation of social democracy, the point at which the ideological direction of the Party was determined ahead of the Policy Review.[54] The other more critical position adopted by Heffernan and Marqusee is that the *Statement* marked an ideological acceptance of a further key element of the New Right, namely markets.[55] The former view is the more accurate since as Hattersley made clear in *Choose Freedom* markets were only accepted for particular reasons and would have clear limits and safeguards. The debate over the ideological future of the Labour Party also has significance for Hattersley's position in relation to Kinnock and also in relation to New Labour. Although Hattersley was loyal to Kinnock and supported much of the modernisation of the Labour Party, he was critical of the lack of ideological direction and the emphasis placed on media image. By 1992 it was possible that the Kinnockite reforms had moved the

Labour Party slightly to the right of where Hattersley wanted to be, in particular that there were efforts to reduce the egalitarian emphasis in the Party's ideology.[56] Further modernisation after 1992 was therefore going to be a move away from the egalitarian position Hattersley had stated in the 1980s.

Hattersley became a major and consistent critic of New Labour after the 1997 General Election. It is difficult to pinpoint the precise time that Hattersley became more critical. In 1995, he was supportive of the change to the Party's constitution, which involved the replacement of Clause IV that had previously committed the Labour Party, to public ownership, at least in theory. Hattersley regarded this as a symbolic statement of the reforms carried out within the Labour Party since 1983.[57] However, already by 1995 he was critical of the ideological direction the Party had taken. Comparing the discussions over the *Statement of Aims and Values* with statements made by Blair and others within New Labour he argued that: "the way in which my colleagues reacted to the Statement which I drafted is a vivid illustration of how much the Labour Party has changed between Neil Kinnock and Tony Blair. Nobody argued about the assertion that greater equality – with the redistribution of power and wealth which it required – was the bedrock of our philosophy."[58] By 1997 he had become particularly critical of Blair, who lacked any commitment to the Labour Party's ethos or key doctrines. He argued that Blair, "was the soldier who crossed a minefield in confident safety because he did not know that the mines were there."[59] Indeed, even before New Labour formed the Government, Hattersley argued that they constituted a successful entryist coup: "the prophets of New Labour succeeded where the Militant tendency had failed. They took over an established political party and re-created it in their own image."[60] Given Hattersley's emotional language, the fact that he had voted for Blair in the 1994 Leadership contest and the wide-ranging criticisms of policy that Hattersley mounted after 1997 it could seem that his argument was inconsistent.

However, there has been a consistent theme in the Hattersley critique of New Labour, based on his commitment to equality.[61] This can be seen most vividly in his response to Blair's statement that New Labour wanted a meritocratic society. In a significant article, Hattersley argued that, "after casting round to find himself a philosophy...Tony Blair discovered a big idea. His destiny is to create a meritocracy. Unfortunately meritocracy is not the form of society which social democrats want to see. Now my party not only pursues policies with which I disagree; its whole programme is based on a principle that I reject."[62] Hattersley rejects the New Labour commitment to equality of opportunity, not since it is wrong but that it is insufficient. In terms of specific policies, three examples will highlight this ideological distinction. First, Hattersley has been critical of the development of the City Academies that allow for partial selection of pupils and he believes evidence shows "takes a disproportionate percentage of their pupils from prosperous families. Education selection always works that way."[63] In addition, Hattersley has argued against the development of internal markets in health care developed under the name of the 'choice agenda' since it allows some to exercise more choice than others since they have more awareness and confidence in making choices, essentially the middle classes.[64] Finally, Hattersley has argued that the proposal of the Fabian Commission on Taxation and Citizenship (Chaired by Raymond Plant) for a 50% tax band on those earning over £100,000 per annum is fair as a first step in an egalitarian strategy.[65]

This brings us back to the arguments contained in *Choose Freedom* that the aim of social democrats is the pursuit of greater equality of outcome without which freedom for all – an extension of the 'sum of effective liberty' – cannot be realised. Moreover, Hattersley argues that, "it is inconceivable that we can end poverty without reducing inequality... You cannot possibly have one without the other."[66]   Hence, we can see that Hattersley presented a sophisticated democratic socialist case in the 1980s drawn in large part from the arguments made by Plant against the neo-liberals, which emphasised a positive conception of liberty, rights to welfare and the need to reduce inequalities in income and wealth.   However, the intellectual development of social democracy under New Labour has revised these positions, at least according to Hattersley.   The following chapter will develop some of the issues raised here by analysing the political thought of the Third Way through the work of Anthony Giddens, which offers a useful point of contrast from which we can identify contemporary debates in social democracy.

[1] I am grateful to Lord (Roy) Hattersley for agreeing to be interviewed for this chapter. In addition, the Hattersley archive at the University of Hull was consulted, although this contains little in relation to his political thought.

[2] R. Hattersley, *Choose Freedom: The Future for Democratic Socialism* (Michael Joseph, London, 1987) all references to the 1987 Penguin paperback edition, xv-xvi.

[3] Ibid.

[4] These terms can be used interchangeably for most of the history of the Labour Party but had more distinctive meanings in the 1980s. Social democrats were those who left the Labour Party to form the Social Democratic Party and those who remained in the Labour Party preferred to call themselves democratic socialists. For purposes of this chapter, the terms mean the same thing, namely those on the Labour right who sought to modernise the Labour Party in response to neo-liberalism.

[5] As will be argued below, the key intellectual input came from Raymond Plant, with a number of other politicians making contributions that are less significant than Hattersley's. See in particular B. Gould, *Socialism and Freedom* (Macmillan, Basingstoke, 1985) and *A Future for Socialism* (Cape, London, 1989); A. Mitchell, *Competitive Socialism* (Unwin, London, 1989) and G. Radice, *Revisionism: Labour's Path to Power* (Macmillan, Basingstoke, 1989).

[6] The neo-liberal argument has received both a far more detailed exposition and critical response. Arguably, the neo-conservative element has received too little attention. An attempt to remedy this is made by the author in M. Garnett and K. Hickson, *Conservative Thinkers* (Manchester University Press, Manchester, forthcoming).

[7] See A. Gamble, *The Free Economy and the Strong State: the Politics of Thatcherism* (Macmillan, Basingstoke, 1986) for a detailed examination of these issues.

[8] See especially F. A. Hayek, *The Constitution of Liberty* (Routledge, London, 1960).

[9] This discussion is based on K. Hoover and R. Plant, *Conservative Capitalism in Britain and the United States: A Critical Appraisal* (Routledge, London, 1989) with some important additions. For a recent overview of neo-liberal economics as it developed in Britain see K. Hickson, *The IMF Crisis of 1976 and British Politics* (IB Tauris, London, 2005).

[10] The main monetarist thinker was of course Milton Friedman. For a detailed account of his economic theory see M. Friedman, *Monetarist Economics* (Blackwell, Oxford, 1990).

[11] The financial crowding-out thesis was an extension of monetarist economics. For the physical crowding out argument see R. Bacon and W. Eltis, *Britain's Economic Problem: Too Few Producers* (Macmillan, London, 1976).

[12] See V. A. Canto, D. H. Joines, A. B. Laffer (eds.) *Foundations of Supply-side Economics: Theory and Evidence* (Academic, New York 1983).

[13] See F. A. Hayek, 'Denationalisation of Money' Hobart Paper 70, Institute of Economic Affairs, London, 1976.

[14] In addition to the philosophical critique of welfare provided by Hayek, the public choice school argued that bureaucracies were motivated by self-interest, the critique of pressure groups was developed by Samuel Brittan and key contributions to the argument on welfare dependency were made by Charles Murray and Lawrence Mead. See W. Niskanen, *Bureaucracy and Representative Government* (Aldine and Atherton, Chicago and New York, 1971); S. Brittan, *The Economic Consequences of Democracy* (London, Temple Smith, 1977); C. Murray, *Losing Ground: American Social Policy 1950-80* (Basic Books, New York, 1984) and L. Mead *Beyond Entitlement: The Social Obligations of Citizenship* (Free Press, New York, 1986).

[15] Indeed, Hayek even referred to 'market justice' in his book *Law Legislation and Liberty* volume 2, *The Mirage of Social Justice* (Routledge, London, 1976) since markets do not distribute on any arbitrary 'principle' of justice.

[16] See in particular, R. Plant, *Equality, Markets and the State* (Fabian Society, London, 1984) and *Citizenship, Rights and Socialism* (Fabian Society, London, 1988) and Hoover and Plant, *Conservative Capitalism*.

[17] See Hattersley, 'Afterword' in Hoover and Plant, *Conservative Capitalism*.

[18] G. MacCallum 'Negative and Positive Freedom' (1967) *Philosophical Review*.

[19] K. Joseph, *Equality* (Murray, London, 1979).

[20] J. Rawls, *A Theory of Justice* (Harvard University Press, Cambridge, 1971).

[21] F. Hirsch, *The Social Limits of Growth* (Routledge, London, 1977).

[22] Hoover and Plant, *Conservative Capitalism*, Chapter 10.

[23] Here Plant's argument reflected the need to build a 'progressive consensus' argued by David Marquand. See, D. Marquand, *The Progressive Dilemma: Lloyd-George to Blair* (Phoenix, London, 1999 2nd edition) for a more recent statement of his position on these issues.

[24] This discussion is based on interview material and Hattersley's books *Choose Freedom; Who Goes Home?* (Little, Brown and Company, London, 1995) and *Fifty Years On: A Prejudiced History of Post-war Britain* (Little,

Brown and Company, London, 1997) together with a survey of his regular contributions to *The Guardian* and *The Observer*.

[25] See K. Hickson, *The IMF Crisis of 1976 and British Politics*.

[26] See S. Crosland, *Tony Crosland* (Cape, London, 1982), p.357.

[27] This is clearly articulated in his contribution to *Labour's Choices* (Fabian Society, London, 1983) published for the 1983 Leadership and Deputy Leadership contests.

[28] I. Crewe and A. King, *The SDP* (Oxford University Press, Oxford, 1995).

[29] Ibid. pp.107-111.

[30] Ibid. p.535.

[31] Interview with Roy Hattersley (28 June 2005, London).

[32] See *Labour's Choices*. The candidates were Hattersley, Peter Shore who was on the right by this stage but remained strongly Euro-sceptic, Neil Kinnock from the soft-left and Eric Heffer who represented the hard left.

[33] *Labour's Choices*, p.3.

[34] Ibid., pp.4-5.

[35] Ibid., p.3.

[36] Hattersley, *Choose Freedom* and Labour Party, *Statement of Democratic Socialist Aims and Values* (Labour Party, London, 1988).

[37] *Choose Freedom*, p.21.

[38] Ibid., p.21.

[39] Ibid., p.62.

[40] Ibid., p.22.

[41] Interview with Roy Hattersley (28 June 2005).

[42] Ibid., p.26.

[43] Ibid., *passim*.

[44] Ibid., pp.148-171.

[45] Ibid., pp.148-171, where Hattersley makes the case for new forms of public ownership along the lines advocated by Crosland. See the discussion of Crosland's ideas regarding public ownership in this volume.

[46] Hattersley, *Who Goes Home?* and interview (28 June 2005).

[47] Hattersley, *Who Goes Home?* pp.289-293. Also, interview (28 June 2005), R. Heffernan and M. Marqusee, *Defeat from the Jaws of Victory: Inside Neil Kinnock's Labour Party* (Verso, London, 1992), C. Hughes and P. Wintour, *Labour Rebuilt* (Fourth Estate, London, 1990), Labour Party *Statement of Democratic Socialist Aims and Values* and D. Blunkett and B. Crick, *The Labour Party's Aims and Values: An Unofficial Statement* (Spokesman Press, Nottingham, 1988). I am grateful for discussions

here with Raymond Plant and for discussions and correspondence with Bernard Crick.

[48] Conversations with Bernard Crick.

[49] Conversations with Bernard Crick.

[50] Hattersley, *Who Goes Home?* p.292.

[51] Ibid.

[52] *Report of the Annual Conference of the Labour Party, 1988* (Labour Party, London, 1988), pp.12-15.

[53] Interview with Roy Hattersley (28 June 2005).

[54] See Hughes and Wintour, *Labour Rebuilt*, pp.64-75.

[55] Heffernan and Marqusee, *Defeat from the Jaws of Victory*, pp101-102.

[56] Ibid., p.138.

[57] R. Hattersley, 'Tone of the times' *The Guardian*, 27 April 1995.

[58] Hattersley, *Who Goes Home?* p.292.

[59] Hattersley, *Fifty Years On*, p.385.

[60] Ibid., p.385.

[61] Interview with Roy Hattersley (28 June 2005) when he stated that New Labour had made a "public disavowal of equality".

[62] R. Hattersley, 'It's no longer my party' *The Observer*, 24 June 2001

[63] Ibid.

[64] Interview with Roy Hattersley (28 June 2005). This develops an argument made in *Choose Freedom*, pp.111-120, that freedom must be organised so that it does not restrict the freedom of others. I am also grateful for discussions with Raymond Plant on this theoretical issue.

[65] Interview with Roy Hattersley (28 June 2005). For the Fabian Tax Commission see Fabian Society *Paying for Progress: A New Politics of Tax for Public Spending* (Fabian Society, London, 2000).

[66] Interview with Roy Hattersley (28 June 2005).

12

ANTHONY GIDDENS[1]

'The Third Way stands for a modernised social democracy, passionate in its commitment to social justice and the goals of the centre-left, but flexible, innovative and forward-looking in the means to achieve them.'[2] Tony Blair

'I believe social democracy can not only survive, but prosper, on an ideological as well as a practical level. It can only do so, however, if social democrats are prepared to revise their pre-existing views more thoroughly than most have done so far. They need to find a Third Way.'[3] Anthony Giddens

The idea of the 'Third Way' was most commonly articulated by New Labour between 1998-2000[4] but can be said to have had a longer influence on the thinking of New Labour, or at least the Prime Minister, while Anthony Giddens has been the leading academic exponent of the idea.[5] As the above statements by Blair and Giddens make clear the Third Way is defined as 'modernised' social democracy, which accepts traditional social democratic objectives but seeks to think afresh about the policies used to realise them. The argument goes that values are fixed but policies have been subject to radical revision. This is a necessary response to recent changes that have had a revolutionary affect on politics and society both in Britain and in a broader international context. These changes require social democrats to think anew about 'means' since established policy is outdated and does not meet the new expectations that societal changes have fostered. Previous social democrats had been unable or unwilling to be so radical in the formulation of new policies, either because they were concerned with a rejection of the New Right or were simply not prepared to be as radical as the Third Way approach required.[6]

This chapter will focus on the Third Way as the major contribution Anthony Giddens has made to British social democracy. Given that the term has generated much controversy the chapter will begin with a discussion of the Third Way idea. Commentators have argued that the Third Way stands for either modernised social democracy, or is a label for the modernisation of the Labour Party under Blair as it sought electoral revival, or is an empty concept, or marks the final capitulation to the New Right by social democrats.[7] Indeed, there was so much criticism of the original Third Way statements by Blair and Giddens that the latter felt the need to address such criticisms explicitly.[8] While some accounts on the Third Way have tended to focus on the policies of New Labour in government or have related Third Way debates in Britain to broader developments in European social democracy, this chapter will focus on the work of Giddens personally.[9]

The second aim of the chapter is to examine the claim that values have remained unchanged while only the means to achieve them have changed. This claim will be questioned through an examination of the Third Way approach to the idea of equality.[10] The focus on equality is useful since it allows us to identify how the Third Way has reconceptualised a core social democratic value. Moreover, for purposes of this volume, this will allow for direct comparison with preceding chapters on Tony Crosland and Roy Hattersley, who both placed equality at the centre of what they meant by social democracy/democratic socialism.

What is the Third Way?

The first attempts to provide a new basis for a radical social democratic politics along Third Way lines was outlined in two works published in 1994. The first was a collection of essays edited by a leading figure in the emergence of New Labour, David Miliband, entitled *Re-inventing the Left*.[11] The second book written by Giddens was *Beyond Left and Right*, relating changes in society and the economy in Britain and internationally to developments in British social democracy.[12] The phrase 'beyond left and right' led inevitably to the term the 'Third Way' and suggested a new form of politics transcending the old left-right divide. This was the tone of the key publications on the Third Way published in 1998 by Blair and Giddens.[13] As suggested above, it was argued that earlier social democratic revisionists had offered an insufficient conception of what the new politics – or Third Way – should be. However, this still left open the question of what the Third Way actually is.

Initially, the term 'Third Way' was offered as an electoral strategy[14] by New Labour modernisers to demonstrate that the Labour Party had changed and that New Labour offered something different from the two dominant approaches to politics in Britain since 1945, namely post-war social democracy with a commitment to a large, central state and Thatcherism with a commitment to individualism and the free market. The major symbolic statement that the Labour Party had changed was the new Clause IV adopted in 1995. The 'new' Labour Party would distance itself from the trade unions, accept the limits of state intervention and be more favourable to the market and wealth creation than 'Old Labour' had been.[15] This new approach marked a 'Third Way' – distinct from old-style social democracy and the New Right, both of which were subject to a debunking exercise in Giddens' *The Third Way*.[16] The New Right had been undermined by its internal contradictions, essentially a tension between conservatism, with its emphasis on tradition and social order, and free-market liberalism.[17]   Such a tension could be demonstrated between a commitment to the traditional family structure and to the demands of the market, which had been undermining the family. Old-style social democracy was rejected since Giddens claimed it was out-dated. It had been based on an economic structure in which national economies were isolated from international pressures, the workforce was largely male and employed in manufacturing and so forth.   The Third Way would therefore be a new politics transcending these out-dated and flawed approaches. This new approach was most marked in Britain where New Labour embarked on a Third Way, but Giddens also claimed that by 2001 there were similar developments elsewhere: "across the world left of centre governments are attempting to institute Third Way programmes – whether or not they favour the term itself."[18] Evidence of this could be found in the pamphlet produced jointly by Blair and Schroder *Europe: The Third Way* in 1999[19], although as time went on it became clearer that the two leaders had different ideas about what was intended by the Third Way and commentators argued that there were widely divergent positions on the Third Way that reflected national institutional and cultural contexts.[20]

The response to Giddens' book *The Third Way* was largely critical, to the extent that Giddens then wrote a defence of the Third Way against his critics, *The Third Way and Its Critics* published in 2000. Giddens identifies six central criticisms of the Third Way approach.[21] First, some argued that the term was vague, lacking any internal coherence. Secondly, critics, especially left-wing critics, argued that the Third Way was an acceptance of conservatism and marks a shift to the right.   An interesting contribution here is that made by Stuart Hall who argued that Thatcherism was best seen as an attempt to move public opinion to the right in the face of wider changes within capitalism. In contrast, the Third Way is an attempt to stand still and accepts the Thatcherite political settlement.[22] Others stated that in arguing that the world had changed and that these changes had to be accepted by the left, the Third Way was accepting the broad parameters of neo-liberalism. A different criticism from the continental commentators on the Third Way is that it was an Anglo-Saxon conception and had little relevance to continental approaches to social democracy. In addition, some argued that the Third Way was rhetorical and lacked policy, especially economic policy, so that it would have to accept the post-Thatcherite economic structures despite having genuine left-of-centre intentions. Finally, the Third Way lacks an environmental policy according to commentators interested in ecological issues.

In writing *The Third Way and Its Critics*, Giddens attempted to reply to these criticisms showing its commitment to left-wing values, its relevance to Europe and addressing itself to policy especially on welfare, the economy and the environment. In some ways this second book offers a more satisfactory approach to these issues than the first book. What is interesting here is Giddens' own use of the concept of the 'Third Way'. In *The Third Way* it was largely applied to Britain, in *The Third Way and Its Critics* it is applied to Britain but also, in an attempt to respond to continental critics, is developed to have a European dimension. By 2001 when Giddens edited *The Global Third Way Debate* there was a clear attempt to relate it to other areas of the world: "some speak of these developments (doctrinal change) as different 'Third Ways'. In my view, however, there is an overall political orientation and policy programme emerging, not just in Europe but also in other countries and continents, which can be described as the Third Way (or updated social democracy). It is still in the process of construction, rather than a fully rounded system."[23] However, in a recent interview, Giddens stated that the term 'the Third Way' does not actually matter and that what he had intended was a radical approach to 'rethinking'. It arguably mattered less what was being rethought (in terms of different national social democracies) or what the specifics of this new thinking are.[24] It was the tendency to think 'conservatively' that Giddens was opposed to, as he stated in his 2002 book *Where Now for New Labour*, in which he talked about the intellectual laziness of traditional social democrats – of which only Roy Hattersley is named – in failing to re-think their own social democratic beliefs in face of radical social and economic change.[25]

However, if the term 'the Third Way' is to have a more precise meaning it is necessary to think beyond what has so far been stated. There are three possible meanings that could be attached to the 'Third Way' at this stage. Briefly stated these are the idea that modern conditions are radically different from those that existed in the past; following on from this the idea that policy has to be radically rethought to take account of such changes and finally – an idea rejected explicitly by Giddens and Blair[26] – that the Third Way is concerned with revisionism of ends and not just means. Giddens argues that the Third Way "refers to a framework of thinking and policy-making that seeks to adapt social democracy to a world which has changed fundamentally over the past two or three decades."[27] The idea that social and economic reform has been revolutionary was contained in Giddens' book *Beyond Left and Right* when he talked of the new era of manufactured uncertainty in which the increase in the sum of knowledge had empowered individuals but had also increased risk and uncertainty. Three challenges in particular had increased such risk and uncertainty – globalisation of the economy and culture, the emergence of a post-traditional social order in which traditional values had been questioned and social reflexivity in which individuals would need to make decisions individually in a condition of moral uncertainty.[28] Within such a framework, the aims of social democracy were to repair damaged solidarities, promote individual emancipation, create a generative politics (which will be important later in the chapter when discussing inequalities), introduce radical constitutional reform so as to 'democratise democracy', rethink the welfare state in line with the increased focus on individuality and choice and find new ways to resolve world conflicts.[29] The idea that the world had changed was again emphasised in *The Third Way* when Giddens talked of five dilemmas that would need to be faced by social democrats: globalisation, individualism, the declining significance of the terms 'left' and 'right' with the emergence of new issues and problems, the role of political agency requiring alternatives to the state in response to new issues and the need to find ways to tackle ecological degradation.[30]

Several issues can be emphasised here. The first is that in setting out a new national and international context within which social democrats must find an adequate and equally radical response, there are parallels with the discourse of 'New Times' that cultural commentators such as Stuart Hall emphasised from the early 1980s onwards.[31] This is interesting given Hall's rejection of the 'Third Way' noted above. Hall argues that this is not what he had intended and that what he had called for was a radical form of socialism in response to Thatcherism that would capture the imagination of an electoral majority. However, it is worth emphasising that some of those associated with Hall at this time have become more sympathetic to modernised social democracy in its Third Way form. Indeed, more broadly many 'New Labour' ministers once occupied ground to the left of those once considered on the Labour right such as Roy Hattersley.[32] A second issue relates to the relationship between structure and agency. Although Giddens seeks to relate agency to structure the relationship is usually one of finding the adequate response to structural change which is accepted without question, such as globalisation, which in the Third Way is not contested. This view of globalisation has been challenged by a number of commentators who suggest that the extent to which nations have lost economic power has been exaggerated in the 'globalisation literature'.[33] A final point that can be made about the economic and social changes emphasised by Giddens is that there is a tension between seeing the Third Way as the framework to think radically and the Third Way as the only possible response to these changes. In other words there is, at times, a determinism in Third Way literature, which can be challenged.

The second possible meaning of the Third Way is the capacity to rethink radically the policies to be pursued by social democratic governments, as Giddens has recently stated, "for me you have to be pretty strongly revisionist. It doesn't make any sense not to be."[34]   Hence, Blair has frequently emphasised the need for new policies in light of radical social and economic change, which has both led to the making redundant many of the earlier policy positions held by social democrats and also generated new electoral demands which social democrats would have to respond to. Blair states that, "the Third Way is not an attempt to split the difference between right and left. It is about traditional values in a changed world… The Third Way is a serious reappraisal of social democracy, reaching deep into the values of the left to develop radical new policies."[35]   This raises a complex issue concerning the relationship between ends and means, or the values of social democracy and the policies used to realise them. Blair suggests the possibility of fixed ends with a large degree of pragmatism concerning means, which can be questioned and I return to this at the end of the chapter as the main point of criticism of the Third Way. In a similar way Giddens talks of the need to radically reformulate policies.   He sees the process of modernisation in the Labour Party starting with the Policy Review in the late-1980s. However, such a revision of policy was limited according to Giddens, due to the need to respond to the challenge of neo-liberalism at that time. The subsequent failures of neo-liberalism allow for a more radical revision of policy that earlier social democrats were not prepared to undertake.[36] Hence, Giddens states that: "Third Way politics, as I understand it at any rate, is an attempt to carry further the reform processes social democrats have already begun, and offers a framework within which these processes can be put... Social democracy has to transform itself to survive, but social democrats must be prepared to innovate even more if they are to prosper."[37]   This discussion brings us to the final issue relating to the definition of the Third Way, namely the Third Way position on ends. It is clear from the opening quotations from Blair and Giddens that they seek to revise policies, while regarding their values as the timeless values of social democracy, as Giddens states: "I always thought of it (the Third Way) as preserving most of the basic values of social democracy, but trying to apply those values in a context in which many of the traditional policies have lapsed because they refer to a different type of world."[38]   Hence, Blair lists Third Way values as equal worth, opportunity for all, responsibility and community.[39] The combination of the first two suggests a central commitment to equal opportunity. The emphasis on responsibility and community is significant for two reasons: first that Blair sees this as what distinguishes social democracy from the individualism of the neo-liberals. But also because he sees post-war social democrats as lacking a commitment to community and that his ideas are closer to the pre-war social democrats such as Tawney who emphasised the values of community and responsibility.[40] There is some truth here since as we have seen in this volume Crosland and Hattersley in particular had little to say about community but pre-war social democrats such as Tawney did. However, what Tawney meant by 'community' was a more egalitarian society[41] and so in order to understand whether the Third Way is a revision of means only or of both means and ends there is a need to focus on the Third Way conception of equality.

Giddens and Equality

A discussion of the Third Way approach to the issue of equality must deal with two issues. The first is the theoretical issue of what form of equality is intended by Giddens given that the term equality is a contested one. There are two questions here. First does Giddens' commitment to equality concern primarily inequality of opportunities or of outcomes? Secondly, given that Giddens places emphasis on the idea of 'empowerment', what implications does this have for the conception of equality? The second issue is what policies does Giddens advocate for the pursuit of equality? These issues are in fact interrelated since means and ends overlap, but for reasons of clarity I will examine each issue in turn.

Looking first at the meaning that Giddens attaches to equality, what we can say is that there appears to be some considerable confusion here. This confusion may well be due to the fact that the *Third Way* books were produced quickly and had in mind an audience beyond an academic one. It is still important, however, to highlight this conceptual tension within Giddens' discussion of equality. Giddens argues that: "the contemporary left needs to develop a dynamic, life-chances approach to equality, placing the prime stress upon equality of opportunity."[42] This is a clear statement in favour of limiting egalitarian concerns to equality of opportunity. Indeed, Giddens goes on to say that inequality is required for incentives. The market economy is now widely accepted, "yet many on the left have found it difficult to accept its correlates – that incentives are necessary to encourage those of talent to progress and that equality of opportunity typically creates higher rather than lower inequalities of outcome... Rather than seeking to suppress these consequences we should accept them."[43] However, Giddens then goes on to question the validity of a meritocratic structure since inequalities in income and wealth lead to inequality of opportunity.[44]   Hence, Giddens both defends meritocracy and equality of opportunity and yet at the same time also questions these concepts due to the inequalities that they create.

Such confusion on this issue arises out of the alternative concepts that Giddens uses as part of Third Way discourse and the policies which he advocates. In place of equality of opportunity and outcome, Giddens asks "what then should equality be taken to mean? The new politics defines equality as *inclusion* and inequality as *exclusion*."[45] Inclusion is taken to be the availability of essential features of modern citizenship including the availability of work or training and also of education.   Exclusion takes two forms.   The first is the involuntary exclusion of the poor who lack opportunities for training or work and also the voluntary exclusion of those at the top who withdraw from the rest of society.[46] This is an interesting formulation of egalitarian politics since a concern with social exclusion of the poor has been a consistent feature of New Labour policy since 1997. However, it still fails to resolve the issue of the nature of the Third Way commitment to equality. What could be said is that the discussion of the exclusion of the poor is framed very much in terms of the denial of opportunities.[47]   The policies advocated for the reduction of the voluntary exclusion of the rich also show the limits of the Third Way concern with inequalities of income at the top end of the income scale, since as will be shown below Giddens has rejected calls for higher direct taxation as advocated by some in favour of other policies.

Before looking at the policies advocated by Giddens for the narrowing of income and wealth inequalities, it is necessary to address one further theoretical issue, namely the Third Way conception of empowerment. Power can be defined roughly in one of two ways: as power *over* or as power *to*. The former is relational or positional since its use depends on its exercise over others. The latter concerns only the power of individuals to exercise their liberties. These concepts relate to equality since the former would require a trade-off as power (or resources) is taken away from one individual to increase the power (or resources) of others; it is relative. In the latter case the power or resources of an individual can be increased without limiting those of others. In *Modernity and Self-Identity*, Giddens distinguishes between 'emancipatory politics' and 'life politics'.[48] The former is concerned with the removal of barriers to individual politics: "I define emancipatory politics as a generic outlook concerned above all with liberating individuals and groups from constraints which adversely affect their life chances."[49] In contrast, life politics "does not primarily concern the conditions which liberate us in order to make choices: it is a politics of choice. While emancipatory politics is a politics of life chances, life politics is a politics of lifestyle."[50] The key values associated with emancipatory politics are justice, equality and participation. In contrast, life politics is concerned with self-actualisation. There is a clear implication for the nature of power here since within life politics "power is generative rather than hierarchical."[51] Power shifts from the power *over* definition to power *to*. In other words, within the life politics approach advocated by Giddens, a central argument of the traditional social democrats for the reduction of inequality in income and wealth is less important since empowerment does not concern the barriers to freedom so much as self-actualisation.[52] This is an original idea, but again one that could be questioned from a traditional social democratic perspective and I return to this below.

Turning to the Third Way approach over means, there is again a shift from the traditional social democratic perspective. Giddens rejects the call of the *Fabian Commission on Taxation and Citizenship* for a new higher rate of income tax of 50% for those earning over £100,000 per annum, saying that, "putting up the tax rate to 50% is token politics… It is not going to make any difference to overall inequality."[53] Giddens rejects this despite recognising the need for redistribution if equality of opportunity is not to lead to intergenerational inequalities.[54] The case against a new higher rate of income tax, according to Giddens is that it penalises individual effort and will not raise much revenue.[55] Indeed, Giddens uses the Laffer curve, the claim that higher tax rates reduce incentives and lead to falling tax revenue and what constituted a central part of the neo-liberal case for lower rates of direct taxation, to defend New Labour's decision not to raise income tax rates on higher earners.[56] In more general terms, Giddens argues that redistribution is a difficult strategy for five reasons. Firstly, it is not easy to decide who the rich are since wealth is relative and also more widely distributed than previously. Secondly, steeply progressive taxation acts as a disincentive and thus needs to be avoided. Thirdly, social democrats should be more supportive of tax cuts since they can increase economic efficiency and distribute wealth more widely. In addition, governments cannot simply take more in taxation they also need to justify both increases in taxation and how it will be spent. Finally, Giddens argues that the welfare state as currently constituted may reinforce or even increase current inequalities and so welfare reform may reduce inequalities more effectively than further redistribution.[57]

Giddens has been critical of traditional social democrats for, among other things, placing too much emphasis on direct taxation as the most effective means to reduce inequality. Instead, Giddens advocates a number of measures to reduce inequality, which he says will meet the traditional social democratic objective, including higher taxes on consumption, the fostering of greater corporate responsibility to avoid large pay settlements and share packages for company directors, efforts to open-up access to public schools and finally the increase in philanthropic activity.[58]   On the final point, Giddens draws on U.S. experience where tax cuts for the rich did not reduce the money available for welfare due to the increases in voluntary contributions to charities to compensate for reduced state spending.   Giddens sees increased emphasis on philanthropic endeavour as an alternative to unpopular increases in higher rates of direct taxation. This forms the basis for a 'new egalitarianism' advocated by Giddens and others sympathetic to the Third Way approach to redistribution and outlined in a new book on the subject.[59] Again, this raises philosophical issues for the relationship between the Third Way and traditional social democratic approaches to equality. By way of conclusion, the focus for the rest of this chapter will be an assessment of the claim made by Blair and Giddens that the Third Way offers 'traditional values' in a modern context.

Assessment

In order to answer the question - does the Third Way offer a revision of ends as well as means - it is necessary to examine the claims made by Giddens outlined above regarding the relationship between equality of outcome and equality of opportunity, the nature of empowerment and the nature and limits of taxation.

From a traditional social democratic perspective it is possible to claim that the Third Way fails to take account of four issues: the continuing importance of relative poverty, the existence of unjustified market outcomes, the relevance of welfare rights and the nature of power within a market economy. A possible reason why Giddens is unable in his account of the Third Way to find an adequate position in relation to equality is that he realises that inequalities in income and wealth have a substantial impact on equality of opportunity and yet at the same time seeks to be supportive of a modernised social democracy that seeks to play down the importance of inequalities of outcome. In fact, it could be argued that income inequality is an even more important issue now than it was when the post-war generation of social democrats argued the case for greater equality of outcome since income inequality has increased substantially since the mid-1970s. Levels of income inequality have remained broadly constant since New Labour came to power in 1997.[60] While, on the one hand, this shows the impact of redistribution under New Labour since income inequality would have increased without the fiscal stance adopted after 1997, it also shows that income inequality is only likely to be reduced with higher rates of direct taxation and particularly income tax. However, this policy is rejected explicitly by Giddens when he criticises the tax proposals of the *Fabian Commission on Taxation and Citizenship*. Such income inequality is shown to reduce equality of opportunity since educational attainment, career development and even life expectancy are all shown to correlate closely with income inequality. Since the factors collectively called 'social exclusion' are all related to poverty and inequality – higher crime rates, drug abuse, poor housing and so forth – it would seem that measures to achieve greater social inclusion are likely to have limited impact under current levels of inequality.

A second feature of social exclusion noted by Giddens is the voluntary exclusion of the rich. However, it would again be possible to argue that the most effective way to tackle this is again higher rates of direct taxation on top income earners. Indeed, it is possible here to argue that the Third

Way is revisionist not just in terms of means but also ends for two reasons. It will be remembered that the Third Way policy for tackling the social exclusion of the rich is not higher rates of direct taxation but the fostering of philanthropy. However, there are good grounds for social democrats to reject this, not just because it is far from clear that this policy will provide a stable source of income to fund welfare provision but also on grounds of ends. First, taxation was justified by post-war social democrats to rectify unfair market outcomes. It was argued that market outcomes were unfair as they are not wholly earned since they are the result of an arbitrary set of human characteristics that are not the 'responsibility' of individuals (genetic inheritance, family background, educational background and so forth). Taxation was justified since it offset this element of unearned or 'undeserved' income.[61] Hence, from the perspective of a concern with social justice, taxation is not just a means to raise higher income that could be replaced by philanthropy - if that was shown to be a more effective mechanism to pay for welfare provision - but an essential means for the realisation of more 'just' outcomes. A second ends-based justification for higher direct taxation is a 'rights-oriented' argument. This is the claim that there is a 'right' to welfare, a core argument made by social democrats. This was part of the critique of social democracy launched by Hayek (as detailed in the previous chapter). There could be no claim to a right to welfare since such a claim was resource dependent. Since resources for welfare are limited there could be no valid claim to such a right. Hence a distinction was drawn by neo-liberals between civil rights which are clearly enforceable and welfare rights which are not. The provision of welfare should be the responsibility not of the state, as there is no right to welfare, but of individual charity. While such provision should be encouraged it should not be enforced. This argument was countered by social democrats such as Raymond Plant[62] who argued that the enforcement of all rights are resource dependent and are thus limited to the level of resources available. This is the case for the enforcement both of civil rights and of welfare rights. Taxation is therefore part of the enforcement of a right to welfare provided through the state. The philanthropy of the wealthy, while it should be encouraged to supplement state provision, should not be seen as an alternative to taxation since this makes welfare provision a gift to be bestowed rather than a right to be enforced. There is therefore a risk of changing the nature of welfare in the Third Way from constituting a 'right' to merely being a 'gift'. This would appear to imply a revision of ends as well as means in relation to the social democratic conception of welfare.

A final issue arising from the Third Way conception of equality is the nature of empowerment. It will be recalled that by power, Giddens emphasised what he called 'generative' power, or what is frequently called power *to*. This is offered as an alternative conception of power to what Giddens calls 'hierarchical' power, or what is often called power *over*. The implication for this discussion is that we should be less concerned with inequality and more concerned with poverty – with absolutes rather than with relativities. Leaving aside both the issue of the extent to which poverty can be defined as an 'absolute' concept without reference to the average level of income present at any given point and the extent to which poverty can be reduced without reducing the absolute income level of top earners in the form of taxation, there is also an issue of the nature of power in a market economy. From the perspective of traditional social democracy, power is related to income and wealth inequalities since the power of individuals in the market place will be related directly to income levels.[63] An objective of the pursuit of greater income equality is to empower individuals in the market. Hence, it would seem that the reduction of substantive inequalities is a concern for social democrats if individuals from poorer backgrounds are to be 'empowered'. Social democrats therefore need to be concerned with power in its 'hierarchical' form.

In conclusion, the Third Way offers a distinctive contribution to modern social democracy in Britain and its influence can be seen most notably with the Prime Minister. However, once subjected to closer academic scrutiny it is seen to lack philosophical clarity. In terms of its treatment of equality at least, it would appear to be deficient as both an ethical and intellectual response to neo-liberalism and as a basis for a policy framework for the pursuit of traditional social democratic objectives such as greater income and wealth equality. The Third Way fails to identify the interrelationship, or at least is inconsistent on the relationship, of equality of outcome and equality of opportunity, so that these cannot be held to be two separate concepts. Moreover, the Third Way position on the relationship of ends and means is untenable since a change in the latter does not *necessarily* leave the former unaltered. As has hopefully been demonstrated in this chapter, the Third Way marks a change of ends in terms of issues such as the existence of welfare rights and the nature of empowerment. A more viable strategy for a modernised social democracy is one that will secure greater equality without undermining the confidence secured in New Labour's macroeconomic policy stance.

[1] I am grateful to Professor, Lord (Anthony) Giddens for agreeing to be interviewed for this chapter.

[2] T. Blair, *The Third Way: New Politics for a New Century* (Fabian Society, London, 1998), p.1.

[3] A. Giddens, *The Third Way: The Renewal of Social Democracy* (Polity, Cambridge, 1998), p.vii.

[4] When it was generally replaced by terms such as the 'new progressivism'. The definition of the Third Way emphasised in this chapter is that of a set of ideas which constitutes, or attempts to constitute, a modernised social democracy. For a broader discussion of the Third Way see A. Gamble, 'The Meaning of the Third Way' in D. Kavanagh and A. Seldon (eds.) *The Blair Effect 2001-2005* (Cambridge University Press, Cambridge, 2005), who describes the Third Way as an electoral strategy, new politics and as a new policy agenda, with different levels of success depending on the particular emphasis.

[5] See Giddens, *The Third Way*; *The Third Way and Its Critics* (Polity, Cambridge, 2000); 'Introduction' in Giddens (ed.) *The Global Third Way Debate* (Polity, Cambridge, 2001); and *Where Now for New Labour?* (Polity, Cambridge, 2002).

[6] See Giddens, *The Third Way*, pp.17-26.

[7] There is an extensive literature debating the Third Way, usefully summarised by Giddens in *The Third Way and Its Critics*. Since then the most comprehensive analysis of the Third Way is S. Hale, W. Leggett and L. Martell (eds.) *The Third Way and Beyond* (MUP, Manchester, 2004).

[8] In Giddens, *The Third Way and Its Critics*.

[9] See S. Ludlam and M. Smith (eds.) *New Labour in Government* (Palgrave, Basingstoke, 2001); S. Ludlam and M. Smith *Governing as New Labour* (Palgrave, Basingstoke, 2004); A. Seldon (ed.) *The Blair Effect* (Little, Brown and Company, London, 2001) and D. Kavanagh and A. Seldon (eds.) *The Blair Effect 2001-2005* (CUP, Cambridge, 2005) for comprehensive discussions of New Labour in power.

[10] This is not to deny the importance of other aspects of the Third Way such as the balance of rights and responsibilities, on which there is an extensive literature.

[11] D. Miliband (ed.) *Reinventing the Left* (Polity, Cambridge, 1994).

[12] A. Giddens, *Beyond Left and Right: The Future of Radical Politics* (Polity, Cambridge, 1994).

[13] Blair, *The Third Way* and Giddens, *The Third Way*.

[14] See Gamble, 'The Meaning of the Third Way'.

15 The starkest distinction between New Labour and Old Labour is made by P. Mandelson and R. Liddle in their, *The Blair Revolution: Can New Labour Deliver* (Faber and Faber, London, 1996).

16 See Giddens, *The Third Way*, pp.3-16.

17 Interview with Professor, Lord Giddens (London, 29 July 2005).

18 Giddens, 'Introduction' in Giddens (ed.) *The Global Third Way Debate*, p.1.

19 T. Blair and G. Schroder, *Europe: The Third Way – die Neue Mitte* (Labour Party and SPD, London, 1999).

20 For a discussion of European social democracy and the Third Way see the chapters by B. Clift in Ludlam and Smith (eds.) *New Labour in Government* and *Governing as New Labour*.

21 Giddens, *The Third Way and Its Critics*, pp.1-26.

22 S. Hall, 'The Great Moving Nowhere Show' *Marxism Today*, November/December 1998, pp.9-14.

23 Giddens, 'Introduction' in *The Global Third Way Debate*, p.3.

24 "I see the Third Way as a label you can use or not to refer to the world-wide revival of social democracy." Interview with Professor, Lord Giddens (London, 29 July 2005).

25 Giddens, *Where Now for New Labour?* pp.8-10.

26 As demonstrated by the opening quotations to this chapter.

27 Giddens, *The Third Way*, p.26. In a recent interview Giddens emphasised three changes in particular – globalisation, the growth of the service sector and a 'new individualism'. (Interview with Professor, Lord Giddens, London, 29 July 2005).

28 Giddens, *Beyond Left and Right*, pp.3-7.

29 Ibid., pp.12-20.

30 Giddens, *The Third Way*, pp.28-64.

31 See S. Hall and M. Jacques (eds.) *New Times: The Changing Face of Politics in the 1990s* (Lawrence and Wishart, London, 1989).

32 A point made by Hattersley himself (interview, London, 28 June 2005).

33 For example C. Hay *The Political Economy of New Labour: Labouring Under False Pretences* (Manchester University Press, Manchester, 1999).

34 Interview with Professor, Lord Giddens (London, 29 July 2005).

35 Blair, *The Third Way*, p.1.

36 Giddens, *The Third Way*, pp.17-20.

37 Giddens, *The Third Way and Its Critics*, pp.31-32.

38 Interview with Professor, Lord Giddens (London, 29 July 2005).

39 Blair, *The Third Way*, pp.3-4.

40 Hence Blair talks of "reaching deep into the values of the left," *The Third Way*, p.1.

[41] As demonstrated amply in his book *Equality* (Allen and Unwin, London, 1931).

[42] Giddens, *The Third Way and Its Critics*, p.86.

[43] Ibid., p.86.

[44] Ibid. p.89. The idea of meritocracy is rejected explicitly in *The Third Way*, pp.101-102.

[45] Giddens, *The Third Way*, p.102.

[46] Ibid., pp.102-111.

[47] An early expression of this argument is contained in R. Plant, 'Crosland, Equality and New Labour' in D. Leonard (ed.) *Crosland and New Labour* (Macmillan, London, 1999).

[48] A. Giddens, *Modernity and Self-Identity* (Polity, Cambridge, 1991) pp.210-217. I discuss these issues in 'Equality' in R. Plant, M. Beech and K. Hickson (eds.) *The Struggle for Labour's Soul: Understanding Labour's Political Thought since 1945* (Routledge, London, 2004).

[49] Giddens, Ibid., p.210.

[50] Ibid., p.214.

[51] Ibid., p.214.

[52] Interview with Professor, Lord Giddens (London, 29 July 2005).

[53] Interview with Professor, Lord Giddens (London, 29 July 2005). See also, Giddens, *Where Now for New Labour?* p.40 and Fabian Society, *Paying for Progress: A New Politics for Tax and Public Spending* (Fabian Society, London, 2000).

[54] See note 36 above.

[55] Giddens, *Where Now for New Labour?* pp.40-42.

[56] Giddens, *The Third Way and Its Critics*, p.97.

[57] Ibid., pp.96-99.

[58] Interview with Professor, Lord Giddens (London, 29 July 2005). Also, Giddens, *Where Now for New Labour?* pp.41-43.

[59] A. Giddens and P. Diamond (eds.) *The New Egalitarianism* (Polity, Cambridge, 2005). These issues were discussed in some detail in my interview with Professor, Lord Giddens (29 July 2005).

[60] See K. Stewart, 'Equality and Social Justice' in Kavanagh and Seldon *The Blair Effect 2001-2005*.

[61] See the discussions of Crosland and Hattersley in this volume.

[62] Discussed in depth in R. Plant, H. Lesser and P. Taylor-Gooby *Political Philosophy and Social Welfare: Essays on the Normative Basis of Welfare Provision* (Routledge, London, 1980).

[63] In this sense Giddens' definition of power is similar to David Owen's view that the market is like continuous referenda, a view rejected by social democrats on the then Labour right in the 1980s. See the previous two chapters in this volume.

13

GORDON BROWN

'The challenge for New Labour is, while remaining
true to our values and goals, to have the courage to
affirm that markets are a means of advancing the
public interest; to strengthen markets where they work
and to tackle market failures to enable markets to
work better; and instead of reverting to the left's old,
often knee-jerk, anti-market sentiment, to assert with
confidence that promoting the market economy helps
us achieve our goals of a stronger economy and a
fairer society.'[1]

In one sense including Gordon Brown in a book of essays
on the most influential Labour Party thinkers since the
1920s may appear slightly odd.[2] As a politician for over
twenty years he has not produced a definitive statement of
social democracy in the form of a book. The pieces that he
has authored have been short including his Crosland
Memorial Lecture that became 'Equality – Then and Now'[3]
in Dick Leonard's *Crosland and New Labour* was light on
political philosophy but spelt out New Labour's perspective
on the economic and social imperative of reducing
unemployment. Noteworthy as that may be, it is indicative
of a politician who has not given time to writing about his
beliefs in social democracy and perhaps his response would
be that he was too busy getting on with implementing his
political vision in government. Nevertheless, for a Labour
politician with an acknowledged intellectual pedigree and a

PhD in Scottish Labour history, Brown appears fairly un-philosophical. Compared to Tony Blair he seems a paragon of ideas but placed alongside the other subjects of this book he does not appear to warrant inclusion. Brown's contribution to Labour's thought namely his Fabian pamphlet *Fair is Efficient*, 'Equality – Then and Now', 'State and Market: Towards a Public Interest Test'[5] and a myriad of speeches on policy and campaign issues lack ideological depth. Why, therefore should the authors include him amongst Labour's most important thinkers? Several reasons exist for our logic. Firstly, it is undeniable that Brown with Blair has created an electorally successful social democratic grouping in the Labour Movement known as New Labour. Therefore, Brown's approach to social democracy and his authorship of the majority of New Labour's economic and social policy agenda make him a significantly influential Labour figure, so for this reason alone he warrants inclusion. Secondly, Blair's intellectual influence is represented in this volume by the sociologist Anthony Giddens suggesting that the authors believe that he is un-philosophical and not a student of Labour's intellectual history. Thus, by focussing on Brown and Giddens we are able to evaluate the two influential thinkers behind New Labour's modernised social democracy. Thirdly, it is argued that Brown's role in New Labour and his place in the wider Labour Movement has enabled him to act as a transmitter of New Labour ideas and thus promote this brand of modernised social democracy in the Labour Party and the trade union movement. It is contended that New Labour represents the new right-wing of the Labour Party (though far from being unified as the most notable differences are between the Brownite and Blairite factions) and Brown warrants inclusion on the basis that he has had a clear hand in developing policy commitments and perspectives for Labour's new right-wing.

Since the birth of New Labour an often-wondered philosophical question has been 'What type of equality do they believe in?' One way to attempt to answer this question is to examine the intellectual history, the policy commitments and delivery of the Chancellor and co-architect of New Labour. The reasons for such intense speculation over New Labour's commitment to equality are several. Firstly, the process of becoming New Labour meant a large degree of policy reform during the late 1980s and early 1990s to reposition the Labour Party in the centre ground of British politics. Secondly, part of that process meant appealing to crucial elements of the British electorate notably southern English, middle-class voters whose natural constituency had been the ideas and values espoused by the Conservative Party. Thirdly, New Labour courted the City of London and the business vote. Labour felt it needed to appeal to the business community to reassure the international markets (as well as the middle classes) that it was responsible enough to run the economy better than the Major Government. Fourth and finally, the impact of the phenomenon of globalisation has appeared to make the goals of social democratic governments more difficult due to the relative ease with which multinational corporations can relocate to more cost-effective nations with cheaper labour costs due to the absence of policies such as minimum wages, robust employment rights for individual workers and sufficient welfare provisions. Therefore, the question 'what type of equality does New Labour believe in?' is a complex one and is grounded in a specific economic and political context. This chapter seeks to find out what type of equality Brown believes in. Firstly, the chapter will chart Brown's political development and discuss some of the influences on his thought. Secondly, the chapter attempts to unpack the different conceptions of equality that are often prevalent in discussions of social democracy. Thirdly, the chapter highlights Brown's two main pronouncements relating to his principles for creating a just society whilst he has been Chancellor. They are 'equality of opportunity and fairness of outcome' and 'progressive universalism'. Fourth and finally, the chapter offers two theoretical notions of equality that appear to fit Brown's political approach. They are a commitment to a 'generous sufficiency' conception of equality and a commitment to a 'non-strict prioritarianism'.

Brown's Political Development

Much has been said about Brown's intellectual development by his various biographers.[6] It is certainly true to say that his time as an undergraduate reading history at Edinburgh University and then throughout his long postgraduate days as Rector of Edinburgh shaped his political outlook. In addition it is worthwhile highlighting that as a young lecturer, first at his *alma mata* and then at Glasgow College of Technology, his politics were more radical than they are today. It is accepted in the Labour Movement that the Scottish Labour Party is historically more leftwing than the national party and Brown occupied a centre-left position in Scottish Labour politics during the 1970s.[7] This would put him on the Labour left nationally, during that decade. In many obvious ways Brown's politics were essentially the politics of the New left with their focus on extra-parliamentary protest; widespread public ownership; workers' control of industry; and a commitment to a significant redistribution of wealth.[8] Like so many other New Labour politicians Brown's heritage is from the New left rather than its closer cousin, the Old right.[9] One more point should be noted in relation to positioning Brown in the 1970s namely he was never a member of the Campaign for Nuclear Disarmament (CND) and he was an advocate of Scottish devolution[10], which perhaps alludes to a pragmatic streak that one biographer of Brown - William Keegan - has recorded as an ubiquitous characteristic of Brown the man and the politician.[11] The issue of unilateral nuclear disarmament was the most divisive issue for Labour during the 1980s and one that affected its national prestige and which pigeon-holed politicians within entrenched factions. Therefore unlike most of the Old and New left of the Labour Party, Brown appeared to be politically pragmatic over the issue of unilateral nuclear disarmament. Likewise Brown's commitment to devolution was also tempered by pragmatism inasmuch as when he was appointed Chairman of the Scottish Labour Party's devolution committee he worked hard for a compromise, as Paul Routledge notes:

'In some senses he was the obvious choice: untainted by the old right-wing hostility to limited home rule, and capable of seeing a compromise that would suit a majority of Scots. His former political ally Robin Cook argued Labour could not oppose nationalism by creating some kind of middle way. Brown was convinced it could be done.'[12]

It is argued here that such political pragmatism would begin to assert itself and ultimately define his approach to Labour politics throughout his days as a backbench MP, up to and including his tenure as Chancellor in Blair's Labour Governments. The following quotation by Alf Young in conversation with Routledge makes this precise point:

'There is a very, very powerful thread of pragmatism in Gordon Brown's character. If you bring that up to the present day – what he did then and what he does now in terms of fiscal constraints he has adopted willingly to abolish Labour's tax and spend image and ensure victory – there is some kind of willingness to compromise in pursuit of a bigger objective that was already present in the 1970s.'[13]

It is conceivable that Brown's pragmatism and the political and economic context that developed New Labour can explain his attitude to the principle of equality.

Conceptions of Equality

It is apparent when discussing equality, particularly when discussing it in relation to social democratic ideas that three versions are often outlined. [14] They are equality of opportunity, greater equality of outcome (sometimes called 'democratic equality'[15]) and equality of outcome. Equality of opportunity is a principle which social liberals, conservatives (both neo-liberals and liberal conservatives) and social democrats openly support. It is a principle, which maintains that each individual is to have equal access to jobs and positions such as holding public office. It includes equal treatment regardless of gender, race, class or religion and desires a society based on merit. [16] Equality of opportunity forbids nepotism and any form of preferential treatment and privilege of individuals and it attempts to guarantee the same starting point for all individuals. It is equality as non-discrimination. [17] However, when studying contemporary political theory it is apparent that there is another form of equality of opportunity that is discussed at length in the literature. It attempts to neutralise differences in an individual's social circumstances such as their class, family background and culture. It is known as 'fair' equality of opportunity whereas the traditional reading of equality of opportunity is deemed to be 'procedural' equality of opportunity. Fair equality of opportunity attempts to ensure that an individual's social differences do not translate into differences in chances of success and from this point of view it has some similarities with the idea of greater equality of outcome.[18] The principle of greater equality of outcome is held by social democrats and to a lesser extent by social liberals. It extends the principle of equality of opportunity to include issues determined by one's background, education, talents or abilities by mitigating against misfortune, genetic endowment and social injustice.[19] It attempts to redistribute incomes and wealth from the better off to the worst off and in doing so, reduce material and social inequalities within society. Political parties who hold a commitment to greater equality of outcome do so on the basis that many inequalities, such as differences in genetic endowment are arbitrary and therefore unfair and also because as a community, they believe individuals have a responsibility to help the disadvantaged further than merely guaranteeing equality of opportunity in the procedural non-discriminating sense, by securing to a certain extent greater equality of outcome. The principle of equality of outcome (or complete equality of outcome) has been held by a small number of individuals and groups in the Labour Party such as George Bernard Shaw, the Marxist SDF and the Labour Marxists of the 1920s and 1930s. Marxist political economy asserts that with the ultimate collapse of capitalism, work will become a communal act for the benefit of the 'common good' and therefore, differences in wages and rewards will be irrelevant.

However, it is asserted that whilst the principles of equality of opportunity and strict equality of outcome are relatively clear, the principle of greater equality of outcome is open to various interpretations by different types of social democrats and this inevitably leads to significant confusion. It is partly for these reasons that the author prefers to follow the terminological distinction, but not all of the conclusions, set out by the political philosopher Derek Parfit in his article entitled 'Equality and Priority'[20] and therefore distinguish between the following positions concerning the principle of equality: a commitment to raising people up to a particular level where they have 'sufficient' resources to lead a satisfactory life; a commitment to always give priority to the worst off members in society; and a commitment to strict egalitarianism (in other words, the pursuit of abolishing all inequalities of income and wealth). These three positions can be respectively termed, the sufficiency conception of equality, the priority conception of equality, and the strict egalitarian conception of equality.

Brown's Two Views of a 'Just Society'

New Labour has espoused two ideas during its time in office, which claim to express its commitment to equality. These are 'equality of opportunity and fairness of outcome'[21] and 'progressive universalism'.[22] Both of these ideas have originated from the Treasury and this is sufficient evidence that Brown is interested in political ideas and in communicating them to the electorate. Nevertheless, the terms employed are not overtly ideological or synonymous with Labour's traditional rhetoric. Again, this demonstrates pragmatism and a deliberate moderation when attempting to outline his view of a just society. In Brown's speeches, there does not appear to be a clear definition of equality of opportunity and fairness of outcome. One possible interpretation implies both a commitment to the procedural form of equality of opportunity and a commitment to guaranteeing outcomes so they do not fall below a minimum level. A policy example of this idea could be the *Pensioner Credit*. It seems therefore that Brown is quite vague about the principle of equality. Akin to this debate surrounding the principle of equality is the issue of whether he favours an absolute, a relative or what is sometimes referred to as a rising absolute level of measuring poverty.[23] For example, Brown has used relative measurements in outlining his strategy for combating child poverty and subsequently announced figures showing a significant reduction in the absolute level of child poverty. New Labour's idea of 'progressive universalism' was most recently used by Brown in the 2003 Budget to describe the principle underpinning the new tax and benefit system. Progressive universalism, simply put, is the principle of providing nearly all citizens (apart from the wealthy) with some form of financial support, but focusing more financial support on those who are in greatest need, when they are in greatest need. Yet the debate surrounding Brown's commitment to equality is clouded further according to a conversation with the former Liberal Democrat Leader Paddy Ashdown, in the lead up to the 1997 General Election. Ashdown recounts in his memoirs that a letter from Brown stated:

'I have been trying to think of a single, central theme which expresses all our ideas and ties them all together. It would be wrong to call this an - *ism* - that sounds too ideological. I have decided that the central idea is 'equality of opportunity' – something you were talking about in your book *Citizens' Britain*. Like you, I have come to believe that we cannot engineer outcomes. What we must have is a Government that is prepared to intervene to provide equality of opportunity for all.'[24]

Therefore, Ashdown recounts in his memoirs that Brown was an advocate of equality of opportunity and implied that this principle was central to his view of contemporary social democracy for New Labour. This raises some possible questions. Did Brown change his mind between his meeting with Ashdown in 1997 before the General Election and during his time in office when he outlined the principles of equality of opportunity and fairness of outcome and later progressive universalism? Is his account of equality of opportunity and fairness of outcome merely equality of opportunity in its traditional, procedural format? It is argued that the answer to the first question is that Brown changed his view of equality of opportunity as the central principle of New Labour's social democracy and the evidence of this is that his budgets have been substantially redistributive. A further point pertinent to this discussion is that in 'Equality:

Then and Now' he says that Crosland's conception of democratic equality is

'...a concept that offers more than equality of opportunity but something other than equality of outcome...Today we argue for equality not just because of our belief in social justice but also because of our views of what is required for economic success...Democratic equality means we tackle unjustifiable inequalities, but it also, of course, presupposes a guaranteed minimum below which no one should fall.'[25]

It seems fairly clear that he is endorsing Crosland's conception of democratic equality (*pace* Rawls) and that he feels that his generation of Labour politicians need to link it to the argument that a fairer society with more chances for individuals and less inequalities is necessary for producing sustained economic success.[26] In addition, it does yet again make the task of gaining a clear and robust answer to the research question difficult as the apparent contradictions and ambiguities come to light at various times in his career and in various speeches and articles whilst in government.

In an interview with a senior Treasury civil servant it was stated that Brown places part of his emphasis on opportunity as the driver of social change, meaning that the Government focuses on providing individuals with opportunity throughout their lives so they can get good training and secure jobs: 'Gordon Brown would talk about multiple opportunities at each stage in life. The question we have to ask ourselves is, "Are we doing what we can for people at birth, nursery age, secondary school age, in adulthood and working age?"'[27] This response by implication suggests that the granting of opportunity throughout life can help to reduce the causes of poverty and therefore reduce inequality of income and wealth in society. Moreover, from the response above it seems that for Brown the primary principle is equality of opportunity and it has an enabling character in the form of equipping people with education and skills so they can get into the job market and also so they can get better paid jobs. The overarching view at the Treasury is that highly skilled and well educated individuals are more likely to maintain a good level of income and are better equipped to face the uncertainties of the global marketplace.

The second aspect that was revealed in the interview was an emphasis on payments to worst off societal groups specifically to guarantee fairer outcomes. These individuals and families are receiving more money each month to reduce poverty and inequality *per se* and the hope is that in doing so the prospects of the children from these poorest families are improved. Summarising his view the Treasury civil servant stated: 'We want to be judged by whether we deliver fairer outcomes. The dilemma for the progressive left is defining the fairness and justice of those outcomes. The best route is to tackle the causes of poverty and inequality.' [28] When it was suggested that aiming to guarantee fairer outcomes was not the same as reducing inequalities between individuals the Treasury civil servant replied: 'Are we satisfied with widening inequality? No. We want to see a narrowing of inequalities and we would like to see more equal outcomes. But what we are not willing to do, is to do that on a penal approach to success, not pulling down the average but raising the average.' [29] The interviewee was then asked to comment on the view put forward by Roy Hattersley that New Labour's conception of equality and by implication Brown's conception of equality is different to Crosland's and this marks a departure from the traditional social democratic perspective. The Treasury civil servant responded as follows:

'The difference between us and Crosland is that Crosland thought that economic growth was the driver of opportunity through the welfare state as a safety net. Objectives and

values have not changed. The economic process is
potentially a much more unequal one – therefore widening
wage inequality occurs...But do not pretend it is a
philosophical difference. It is the same value.'[30]

Brown: a Prioritarian at Heart

So amidst this ambiguity, how is it best to explain Brown's
conception of equality? It is argued here that Brown's
equality can be conceived in socialist terms through two
different components neither of which is the strict
egalitarian conception of equality. The first component is a
commitment to raising people up to a particular level
whereby they have 'enough' to lead a satisfactory life. One
can refer to this (as is noted above) as the sufficiency version
of equality. Of course, this is problematic because what is
meant by the term 'enough'? What is 'sufficient'? There is
no general understanding or consensus in British society
about the minimum level one must have met before one can
claim to lead a satisfactory life.[31] Nevertheless, the
sufficiency conception of equality is understood as providing
a sufficient level of income and services. Historically, this
has been the job of the welfare state through a variety of
welfare payments and entitlements. In one sense, this
conception of equality is greater equality up to a sufficient
level and then it permits individuals to earn incomes
unreservedly. The *National Minimum Wage* is an example of
the sufficiency conception of equality inasmuch as it
regulates that labour is paid at a sufficient minimum level.[32]
The second component to Brown's conception of equality is
a commitment to giving financial priority to the worst off
members in British society. This (as we have noted above)
can be referred to as the priority conception of equality. It is
perhaps worth pointing out that the priority conception of
equality can have two strands or can be interpreted in two

different ways. We can refer to them as strict and non-strict prioritarians. Strict prioritarians want to give priority to the worst off groups in society no matter how well off they are in absolute terms. For example, such members of the worst off groups could in fact (according to strict prioritarians) possess a relatively high level of disposable income, own their own homes, holiday abroad, possess a relatively high amount of savings and still would warrant financial priority given to them, because in relative terms they may still be one of the worst off groups in a given society.[33] Non-strict prioritarians also want to give priority to the worst off groups in society but they believe that giving priority becomes less important the better off the worst off groups become.[34] Thus, for example, if one of the two worst off groups in a society gradually became better off in absolute terms, non-strict prioritarians would gradually cease to give such a group priority status. Of course, in contemporary Britain the worst off groups have a long way to go before priority status should be withdrawn. An issue such as this rests on defining two questions. Firstly, who are the worst off groups in society? Secondly, at what level of resources does a government (which holds a commitment to the priority conception of equality) draw the line and cease to give such groups financial priority? In this chapter it is suggested that Brown holds a commitment to the non-strict priority conception of equality.

Examples of the non-strict priority conception of equality are the *Pensioner Credit, Working Tax Credit*, and *Child Tax Credit* programmes for the poorest pensioners and the poorest families with and without children. [35] Other examples of his commitment to the priority conception of equality include its £580 million investment in *Sure Start* for young children, nursery places for every four year old; £450 million in the Children's Fund for children's charities to spend; £5 billion investment in *The New Deal* for 18-25 year olds, *New Deal* for the over 25's; *New Deal Plus* for the over

50 year olds, *New Deal* for single mothers and for disabled people; also, *Action Teams* for jobs in the 2000 poorest areas; and the *Connexions* programme for 11-25 year olds who fail to gain educational attainment and skills training.

Conclusion

This chapter began with a defence of the inclusion of Brown in a volume on the Labour Party's most important thinkers since 1920. Although that justification is not the main purpose of the chapter the task was necessary because as is mentioned above Brown is not an established thinker in the sense that the other figures in this volume patently are. Nevertheless, Brown has been of enormous influence in the evolution and development of modernised social democratic politics in Britain since the early 1990s. In the Labour Movement, in the press and in the academy, social democrats have persistently raised equality and social justice as issues that Brown and New Labour should be concerned with. Hence the question put forth in this chapter, 'What type of equality does Brown believe in?' It was noted that his political development was akin to other leading Labour politicians who are now situated on the new right-wing of the Labour Party and are described as New Labour. Brown began his political days as a member of the New Left, far more radical than he is today. As an MP entering Parliament at the 1983 General Election Brown like Blair served his apprenticeship in national Labour politics with thirteen years in Opposition. This was sufficiently long enough for Brown's radical, New left socialism to be diluted and repackaged into the mainstream social democracy of New Labour. Brown's pragmatism has been noted and this attribute demonstrates his willingness to compromise to 'get things done'. It is the mark of a moderate who is too focused on implementing social justice to concern himself with ideological purity. It would be interesting to interview Brown and ask him what he thinks of the 'means and ends debate' recently raised by Raymond Plant[36] which asserts that in some situations changing one's means to implement an end can potentially involve one changing the end. In other words, the thesis suggests that by being non-ideological over means such as markets or taxation can potentially affect the ends - namely social justice and a reduction in inequalities. That said the danger with this thesis is that you assume that all means are ideological and have a causal relationship with a set of given ends. The truth lies somewhere in-between and the crucial point is that the voracity of the means and ends thesis is issue specific. In certain circumstances means affect ends in others they do not. In Brown's case by embracing markets as a means to create prosperity and deliver social justice some inequalities are created but they appear to be mitigated by a prioritarian approach to the tax and benefit system. Also where Brown is hesitant about the virtue of markets such as in health-care and education the merit of the means and ends debate is more obvious.

It has been asserted that Brown's pronouncements on the subject of equality are vague. In particular, the two views of a just society that he has enunciated whilst in office namely 'equality of opportunity and fairness of outcome' and 'progressive universalism' are ambiguous. In an interview with a senior Treasury civil servant the following two precepts were given regarding Brown's perspective on equality and his concomitant social and economic policy agenda: The first precept is an emphasis on equality of opportunity; through the provision of constant opportunities for individuals to gain education and skills training - thus increasing the chances to secure well paid jobs in a fiercely competitive and uncertain global marketplace. The second precept is an emphasis on redistribution to reduce poverty and income inequality. It has been argued in this chapter that it is more useful to explain Brown's commitment to equality as a commitment to a non-strict prioritarianism and a generous sufficiency conception of equality. Prioritarianism therefore should be the message that Brown in particular, and the Labour Party in general conveys to its supporters - both those who have remained active and those who have felt disillusioned with their cautious approach to reforming British society and their somewhat tainted record in office. Prioritarianism taps into the historic Labour themes of altruism, community responsibility and compassion, so from this point of view a pragmatic Brown may see its value. It is also a robust ideational concept that supports his approach for distributing tax credits and benefits. Thus, when connected to the communitarian framework of rights and responsibilities championed by New Labour prioritarianism allows Brown to maintain a commitment to a conception of equality (satisfying the left) and simultaneously encourages the virtues of work and prosperity. One possible disadvantage to this approach is its complexity. Non-strict prioritarianism is a difficult sell and so was 'neo-endogenous growth theory', so perhaps Brown's attempts to use 'progressive universalism' as his guiding political principle is more understandable yet equally unsuccessful in capturing people's imagination.

[1] G. Brown, 'State and Market: Towards a Public Interest Test' *Political Quarterly*, 2003, p.270.

[2] As well as substantial new research and argument in this chapter some parts have been taken from two chapters of my monograph see M. Beech, *The Political Philosophy of New Labour* (I.B. Tauris, London, 2005).

[3] G. Brown, 'Equality – Then and Now' in (ed.) D. Leonard, *Crosland and New Labour* (Palgrave Macmillan, London, 1999), pp.36-45.

[4] G. Brown, *Fair is Efficient* (Fabian Society Tract 563, London, 1994).

[5] G. Brown, 'State and Market: Towards a Public Interest Test'.

[6] See, P. Routledge, *Gordon Brown: The Biography* (Simon & Schuster, London, 1998), pp. 17-40 and W. Keegan, *The Prudence of Mr Gordon Brown* (Wiley, Chichester, 2003), pp.19-36.

[7] Routledge notes that Brown was not committed to either the trade union right or the left in the Scottish Labour Party. See P. Routledge, *Gordon Brown: The Biography*, pp.75, 79-80, 93-94.

[8] W. Keegan, *The Prudence of Mr Gordon Brown*, p.40.

[9] I have made this point before in my essay on the political ideas of New Labour. For a fuller account of the ideological trajectories of key New Labour politicians see M. Beech, 'New Labour' in (eds.) R.Plant, M. Beech and K. Hickson, *The Struggle for Labour's Soul* (Routledge, London, 2004), p.87.

[10] See, H. Drucker, and G. Brown, *The Politics of Nationalism and Devolution* (Longman, London, 1980).

[11] See, W. Keegan, *The Prudence of Mr Gordon Brown*, pp.32-35, 45-47.

[12] See, P. Routledge, *Gordon Brown: The Biography*, p.80.

[13] Ibid. p.80. Routledge interviewing Alf Young on Brown.

[14] See, R. Plant, 'Social democracy' in D. Marquand and A. Seldon, (eds.) *The Ideas That Shaped Post-War Britain* (Fontana, London, 1996).

[15] In 'Socialism Now' Crosland refers to his belief in equality as democratic equality and takes this from Rawls. See C.A.R. Crosland, *Socialism Now and Other Essays* (Jonathan Cape, London, 1974), p.15 and J. Rawls, *A Theory of Justice* (Harvard University Press, Cambridge, 1971).

[16] See, R. Plant, 'Democratic socialism and equality' in D. Lipsey and D. Leonard, (eds.) *The Socialist Agenda* (Jonathan Cape, London, 1981), pp.138-144.

[17] See, J. Rawls, *A Theory of Justice* (Oxford University Press, Oxford, Revised Edition, 1999), pp.73-78 and A. Flew, *The Politics of Procrustes* (Temple Smith, London, 1981), pp.45-58.

[18] See, J.Rawls, *A Theory of Justice*, pp.73-78.

[19] See, R. Plant: 'Democratic socialism and equality', pp.138-144.

[20] See, D. Parfit, 'Equality and Priority' in A. Mason, (ed.) *Ideals of Equality* (Blackwell, Oxford, 1998).

[21] See, G. Brown, 'Speech to the Child Poverty Action Group's Child Poverty Conference', London, 15th May 2000 and G. Brown, 'A Modern Agenda for Prosperity and Social Reform', Cass Business School, London, 3rd February 2003 and interview with Senior Treasury Civil Servant, HM Treasury, December 2002.

[22] See, G. Brown, *Budget 2003* (HMSO, London, 2003) ch.5, pp.1-3, J. Prescott, 'Speech at World Seminar on Sustainable Development, Johannesburg', 17th May 2002, p.4 and J. Carvel, 'Chancellor offers more cash help for parents' *The Guardian*, 6th December 2000.

[23] Once again senior New Labour figures appear to be sending out conflicting signals. Blair famously stated that the absolute level of poverty is what he considered important when questioned by Jeremy Paxman in an interview on the BBC's Newsnight programme 5th June 2001 and came close to advocating the neo-liberal trickle down theory.

[24] P. Ashdown, *The Ashdown Diaries: 1988-1997* (Penguin, London, 2001), p.406.

[25] G. Brown, 'Equality: Then and Now' in (ed.), D. Leonard, *Crosland and New Labour*, pp.40-44.

[26] In an interview with a senior Treasury civil servant I was told that the governing philosophy in Brown's office was Croslandite social democracy in a contemporary setting. Interview with senior civil servant at H.M. Treasury, London, December 2002.

[27] Ibid.

[28] Ibid.

[29] Ibid.

[30] Ibid.

[31] Although a benchmark which is often used is the European Union's measurement which suggests that individuals are living in poverty if they earn below half the average wage.

[32] Legislation and social programmes which endorse the priority conception of equality may well also endorse the sufficiency conception of equality and vice versa. The *National Minimum Wage,* the *Pensioner Credit,* and the *Working Tax Credit* are all appropriate examples of this.

[33] It is interesting to note the similarity between the strict prioritarians and the strict egalitarian conception of equality mentioned earlier. Both conceptions of equality are underpinned with the assumption that inequality is objectionable because it is bad in itself, yet they differ in their remit.

[34] Non-strict prioritarianism has more in common with sufficiency conceptions of equality. They each draw a line whereby the state ceases

to have either as much responsibility or any special responsibility towards groups who have surpassed a specific level of need. Non-strict prioritarians, like those who hold a sufficiency conception of equality regard inequality objectionable only when it is unjust and because these specific conceptions of equality draw a finite level of wealth, opportunities and financial need that once it is surpassed these groups are then deemed to have 'sufficient' resources and do not warrant further priority.

[35] For an examination of New Labour's social legislation see, P. Toynbee and D. Walker, *Did Things Really Get Better?* (Penguin, London, 2001), pp.10-44.

[36] See R. Plant, 'Ends, Means and Political Identity' in (eds.) R. Plant, M.Beech and K. Hickson, *The Struggle for Labour's Soul*, pp.105-119.

14

CONCLUSION

This book has attempted to provide a fresh perspective of the political thought of the Labour Party through an examination of twelve of its most important thinkers. Simultaneously, the book as a research project has sought to contribute to the existing body of knowledge and understanding of British socialism.

Our approach has not been comprehensive but selective, including only twelve individuals whose work - and by this we mean their most notable socialist publications - was published from the 1920s until the contemporary era. In the case of Tawney, Cole and Laski some of their work predates 1920 but their most penetrating socialist ideas fall in the chronological period from 1920 onwards. The 1920s as a decade is an especially fascinating period in the history of the Labour Party and in the evolution of an array of socialist ideas. It witnessed such notable events as the first Labour Government under Ramsay MacDonald, the General Strike, universal adult suffrage and the beginning of the Great Depression. In this decade the three 'Red Professors', Tawney, Cole and Laski established themselves nationally and internationally as socialist intellectuals, as has been stated in the respective chapters on them their importance and contribution to the development of ideas in the Labour Party cannot be underestimated.

Our methodological approach that guides the research perspective of this project is hermeneutical. Each chapter of this volume demonstrates a desire to interpret the main socialist works of each thinker in the hope of recovering the meaning of the authors' ideas and appreciating their intellectual contribution in their given historical setting. It is our contention that the hermeneutic school of thought provides the most rigorous approach to explaining ideas and values and promotes the understanding of the intellectual history of British socialism in its historical context. Akin to this methodology the authors are keen where appropriate to utilise primary sources such as elite interviews and have done so in the course of this study. In particular, we hope that the elite interviews with Roy Hattersley, Anthony Giddens and a senior Treasury civil servant close to Gordon Brown as well as correspondence with Stuart Holland, provides a closer seat of observation when evaluating the ideas of the aforementioned political thinkers.

Some scholars will no doubt question why the book is not longer and why more Labour Party thinkers are not assessed. This is understandable but books in their nature are finite and only a limited amount of space exists. Additionally, our purpose was not to provide a comprehensive survey of the Labour Party's political thought through the evaluation of every intellectual who has written on British socialism in its one-hundred and six year history. Our purpose was to suggest that since 1920 certain Labour thinkers have stood out above their peers in terms of the significance of their thought; in terms of their influence over others in a set period; and in several instances, in terms of the endurance of their socialist ideas. The authors are confident that all of the major intellectual branches of democratic socialism in the Labour Party since the 1920s are represented in the study although this was not deliberate and certain ideological traditions such as the Old right (revisionist right) do receive greater attention than others because of the quality of individual thinkers such as Crosland, Hattersley and arguably to a certain extent Owen.

This study has its limitations and the authors are aware of certain controversial issues that some scholars may deem to be shortcomings. For example, the authors acknowledge that thinkers like Crosland have been subject to extensive scholarship. In this case it would be negligent to omit such individuals from a study of Labour's most important thinkers on the grounds that their socialist thought has been subject to significant comment and analysis. It simply makes the task of assessing an overlooked or misunderstood aspect of Crosland's socialist thesis more challenging. Other limitations include the inherently subjective nature of the selection process of the twelve thinkers. However, our approach as students of Labour history and socialist thought was not to try and devise artificial intellectual themes which limits our selected thinkers because even if this could be done — and we believe that bar their association with the Labour Party it cannot be meaningfully achieved - it would be a limited exercise of questionable value. The nature of British socialism is complex and diverse as is the intellectual output of the twelve selected Labour thinkers. A final limitation that is recognised is that each essay should try and evaluate each thinker in a uniform way enabling a cogent conclusion to be drawn. The aforementioned comment stands as a defence once again — namely, that the diversity and complexity of each individual thinker makes such a strictly comparative approach overly-narrow and rather banal. It is hoped that this study is of interest to students of Labour history and socialist thought in its attempt to argue that certain socialist thinkers are more important and influential in their given period than others and that this study reveals something fresh about an aspect of the thought of each thinker. Moreover, in the case of Durbin, Crossman and Owen unfashionable thinkers are brought to the fore and this enables some of their socialist ideas to be evaluated more fully.

As there is no overarching argument presented in this book - because it is a volume of essays on Labour's most important thinkers since the 1920s — the task of drawing a straight-forward concomitant conclusion is difficult. That said there are several notable points that can be made which pertain to the study of British socialism and which pertain to the nature of contemporary social democracy in Britain. Firstly, the book demonstrates that the role of ideology or doctrine is essential in providing political direction for political parties such as the Labour Party. Thus, the role of thinkers and intellectuals is important and this book evinces this fact. However, an understanding of the Labour Party's most important thinkers since the 1920s does not provide the student of Labour history with a comprehensive knowledge of the Labour Party's history. In essence, Henry Drucker's point remains salient, namely the Labour Party is a party where both doctrine and ethos play their respective historic and contemporary roles.[1] The ethos of the Labour Party is part of the ethos of the Labour Movement and it can be compared to what John Saville termed 'Labourism' which refers to the Labour Party attempting to secure the interests of the working class via the trade unions.[2] The roles of ethos and of 'Labourism' have at times seemed remote to Labour intellectuals and they themselves are marginal figures to much of the working class membership of the Labour Party. Often, Labour intellectuals are not 'party men' but are instead concerned with elite forms of dialogue and political activism at the level of ideas. Therefore, to understand the Labour Party's most important thinkers since the 1920s is not to understand the Labour Party in its totality.

We can draw together some common themes from the individual chapters in the volume by looking at certain thinkers together. Perhaps Tawney, Cole and Laski the 'Red Professors' fit most easily together as they were writing during the 1920s and 1930s; were all professional academics; and can be evaluated collectively because their main works are critically acclaimed and have influenced succeeding generations of socialists in the Labour Party. Tawney, Cole and Laski were all important and influential but not equally enduring. The Guild socialist ideas of Cole and the Marxist socialism in Laski's final period did not influence the Attlee Government nor did post-war Labour thinkers endorse these variants of socialism. Tawney, on the other hand has been enduring because his ethical socialism was appealing to a broad range of Labour thinkers both religious and secular. His Christian socialist critique of laissez-faire capitalism, the culture of acquisitiveness and the desire for greater equality so individuals are more free and British society more fraternal has become established as a leading definition of British democratic socialism. Few notable Labour thinkers have endorsed his Christian beliefs but have accepted his normative justification for striving for a democratic socialist society. Thus, Tawney remains the most enduring Labour thinker in the pre-1945 period.

Durbin and Strachey were in many ways during the 1930s and 1940s very different Labour thinkers. Durbin was one of the first Labour intellectuals to accept Keynesian demand management as an economic doctrine that the Labour Party could use to transform Britain from a capitalist society in to a socialist society, providing it was coupled with widespread economic planning and nationalisation. Durbin was therefore less moderate than has been assumed but he was never influenced by Marxism and was one of its vociferous critics inside the Labour Party. Strachey by contrast was a Marxist in his early career but similarly to Durbin, extolled the need for planning and nationalisation. In time Strachey converted to democratic socialism and became convinced of the virtue of using Keynesianism as an economic doctrine. By the end of his career Strachey's democratic socialism was quite similar to that of Durbin and both can be understood as figures of the centre-left within the Labour Party.

By grouping Strachey, Crossman, Crosland and Holland together one is dealing with several different perspectives on democratic socialism in the post-1945 era. Strachey also made a contribution to post-1945 thought. Although he accommodated himself to Keynesianism he did continue to express concerns about the anti-democratic concentration of capitalist power and in so doing shared similar concerns with Crossman. Crossman's work belied his intellectual pedigree and is indicative of the Old left's preoccupation with foreign affairs. Nonetheless Crossman was only temporarily a Bevanite, finding Bevan too much of an individualist to lead the faction well. He was given jobs by Gaitskell and liked him personally. However, he remained critical of Revisionism, expressing his view of the anti-democratic nature of capitalism but he failed to produce a robust socialist thesis from his perspective. Crosland's *The Future of Socialism* rightly deserves its place as the focal expression of British social democracy in the post-war era. Holland's work in the 1970s provided much of the intellectual basis for the New left and was designed to critique Croslandite social democracy. This it did and it pre-empted later discussions of globalisation by highlighting the power and flexibility of global capital in the form of multinational corporations. Crossman's work did not endure and when placed alongside the work of Crosland and Holland appears insignificant. Holland's work provided the New left in the Labour Party with an alternative political economy and Crosland's thesis lived on through another generation of social democrats. Crosland rightly remains the most enduring Labour thinker in the post-1945 era.

Hattersley is a disciple of Crosland and his work influenced by Raymond Plant was a restatement of Croslandite social democracy in the face of a dominant neo-liberal ideology during the 1980s and in the face of the challenge of the Bennite New left. Hattersley's ideas endure in the Labour Party and the Labour Movement particularly in the campaigning think-tank Catalyst that he established in 1998. Owen like Hattersley is from the Old right of the Labour Party. Owen's work is mildly anti-statist or seen another way, decentralist and it is also notable in that he emphasised the socialist principle of community responsibility that New Labour similarly espouse. Both Hattersley and Owen are important thinkers who attempted to restate social democracy with contrasting emphases during the 1980s. Hattersley through the Labour Party and Owen through the SDP, but both fought a rearguard against the neo-liberalism of Thatcherism and the radical socialism of the Bennite New left. Owenite social democracy does not formally live on in a think-tank or in a political faction on the left but his role in the SDP had a bearing upon the emergence and outlooks of New Labour.

Giddens and Brown represent two views of the modernised social democracy of New Labour and their ideas and attitudes are in fact quite similar. Giddens' work though sociologically sound is philosophically light and fairly ahistorical in terms of understanding the political thought of the Labour Party. It is often said that Giddens is Blair's main intellectual influence though in recent years talk of the Third Way has diminished from 10 Downing Street and from Blair himself. Nevertheless Giddens' work has been influential and Blairites easily relate to his distinctions between the traditional left and the modernised left. Also, Progress a Blairite campaigning think-tank endorses many of the attitudes found in Giddens' modernised social democracy. Brown has yet to produce a definitive statement of social democracy and perhaps never will. However, his role in New Labour and the fact that he has never referred to, let alone endorsed the Third Way reveals that he has his own interpretation of New Labour's social democracy. It is important to state that Brown would not disagree with the majority of Giddens' conclusions, though like many academics he may question Giddens' position as a social democratic 'political theorist'. Both the work of Giddens and Brown draws attention to the constraints and challenges to social democrats in the era of globalisation through the growth in power of multinational corporations, finance markets, information technology, and increased global competition from China, India and the Eastern Europeans states and domestic changes such as class de-alignment, multiculturalism and rising standards of living. Overall both Giddens and Brown are important and currently influential thinkers in the Labour Party.

At this point it seems appropriate to comment a little on the future of Labour Party scholarship and research on British social democracy. In the era of New Labour Tony Blair and Gordon Brown have dominated the political landscape of what is best described as modernised social democracy since the mid-1990s. Although nothing is certain in politics it appears highly probable that Brown will succeed Blair as Leader of the Labour Party and thus as Prime Minister. The interesting issues pertaining to this transfer of power include its timing, whether Brown will succeed in winning the ensuing general election – probably in 2009 – and the nature of a Brown-led Labour Government. Of course Brown is as much the co-author of New Labour as is Blair and in terms of his domestic policy influence one could say that he has shaped the majority of New Labour's economic and social agenda making him the most powerful Chancellor of the Exchequer in the history of the Labour Party. It is therefore accurate to suggest that Labour under Brown will still be New Labour, as one cannot divorce Brown the co-architect of New Labour from the project itself. With this political context in mind some of the pertinent debates in forthcoming Labour Party scholarship will include assessing the role and limits of markets by social democratic governments, especially in the provision of public services such as education and healthcare. This, on a rhetorical level at least seemed to be a fault line between Blair and Brown during New Labour's second term and the use of private companies in the provision of such goods will continue to be an important issue for a Brown-led Labour Government. Another area of discussion concerns the

conception of equality held by leading contemporary social
democrats such as Brown and this will continue to be an
area of significant study as it is one of the yardsticks used by
scholars in assessing whether globalisation and the alleged
dominance of the neo-liberal paradigm has forced
governments of the centre-left to water-down or completely
abandon their more radical egalitarian aspirations.
Additionally, it could be argued that the attitude of Labour
Governments and their Leaders to the conception of
equality and the precise principles they espouse indicates
whether social democracy is still their political doctrine or
whether it has been replaced with a more modest
commitment to social reformism. Another area of
controversy that will warrant further academic inquiry is the
current constitutional settlement of devolved assemblies
within the United Kingdom. For social democrats this
poses a range of potential problems including guaranteeing
as far as possible equity amongst citizens in terms of the
provision of public services. With more bodies deciding the
nature, cost and supply of public services for certain groups
of citizens within specific areas of the United Kingdom such
as Scotland, Wales and Northern Ireland, Westminster is no
longer the epicentre of decision-making over all public
provision. Thus, the principle of a unified, equal citizenship
which guarantees certain public services for all citizens of
the UK is now fractured due to devolution. For social
democrats the benefit of decentralisation of decision-making
and greater democratisation is in tension with conceptions
of equal citizenship and equal access to high quality and free
public services for all citizens of the UK.

Therefore it is hoped that this volume has contributed to
the existing canon of scholarship on Labour history and
socialist thought and that through the selection and
evaluation of these twelve outstanding socialist figures,
students of the Labour Party will more fully understand the

ideas and values of these Labour thinkers in their historical context.

---

[1] H.M. Drucker, *Doctrine and Ethos in the Labour Party* (George Allen & Unwin, London, 1979), p. 2.

[2] J. Saville, 'The Ideology of Labourism' in R. Benewick, R.N. Berki and B. Parekh (eds.) *Knowledge and Belief in Politics: The Problem of Ideology* (Allen & Unwin, London, 1973), p.215.

BIBLIOGRAPHY

Interviews

Professor Lord Giddens, London, 29 July 2005
Lord Hattersley, London, 28 June 2005
Senior Treasury civil servant, London, December 2002

Archives

Crosland Papers, British Library of Political and Economic Science, London
Crossman Papers, Modern Records Centre, University of Warwick
Dictionary of Labour Biography Archive, University of Hull
Durbin Papers, British Library of Political and Economic Science, London
Hattersley Papers, University of Hull
Labour History Archive, Manchester
Laski Papers, University of Hull
Owen Papers, University of Liverpool
Tawney Papers, British Library of Political and Economic Science, London

Books and Articles

Abel-Smith, B. and Titmuss, K. (eds.), *The Philosophy of Welfare: Selected Writings of Richard Titmuss* (Allen and Unwin, London, 1987)
Acland, R., et.al. *Keeping Left* (New Statesman, London, 1950)

Arblaster, A. 'Liberal Values and Socialist Values' in R. Miliband and J. Saville (eds.) *Socialist Register* (Merlin, London, 1972)

Ashdown, P. *The Ashdown Diaries: 1988-1997*, (Penguin, London, 2001)

Attlee, C. *The Labour Party in Perspective* (Gollancz, London, 1937)

Bacon, R. and Eltis, W. *Britain's Economic Problem: Too Few Producers* (Macmillan, London, 1976)

Barker, B. (ed.) *Ramsay MacDonald's Political Writings* (Allen Lane, London, 1972)

Barratt Brown, M. 'The Insiders' *Universities and Left Review*, Winter, 1958

Barratt Brown, M. 'The Controllers' *Universities and Left Review*, 4, 1959

Barratt Brown, M. *From Labourism to Socialism: The Political Economy of Labour in the 1970s* (Spokesman, Nottingham, 1972)

Bebbington, D. *Evangelicalism in Modern Britain from the 1730s to the 1980s* (Unwin Hyman, London, 1989)

Beckerman, W. 'Labour's Plans for Industry' *New Statesman* (8 June 1973).

Beech, M. 'New Labour' in, R. Plant, M. Beech, and K. Hickson (eds.) *The Struggle for Labour's Soul* (Routledge, London, 2004)

Beech, M. 'Evan Durbin: Assessing a Patriotic Socialist' *Journal of Interdisciplinary Twentieth Century Studies*, vol.1, no. 2. 2006

Beech, M. *The Political Philosophy of New Labour* (IB Tauris, London, 2006)

Benn, A. *Arguments for Socialism* (Penguin, London, 1980)

Benn, A. *Arguments for Democracy* (Cape, London, 1981)

Benn, Tony, 'Foreword to 1981 Edition' *The Attack and Other Papers* (Spokesman, London, 1981)

Berle, A. and Means, G. *The Modern Corporation and Private Property* (Macmillan, New York, 1932)

Bernstein, E. *Preconditions of Socialism* (Cambridge University Press, Cambridge, 1993, edited by T. Jones)

Bevan, A., Brown, W.J., Strachey, J. and Young, A. *A National Policy, an account of the emergency programme advanced by Sir Oswald Mosley* (Macmillan, London, 1931)

Bevan, A. *In Place of Fear* (Heinemann, London, 1952)

Blair, A. *The Third Way* (Fabian Society, London, 1998)

Blair, A. and Schroder, G. *Europe: The Third Way – die Neue Mitte* (Labour Party and SPD, London, 1999)

Blunkett, D. and Crick, B. *The Labour Party's Aims and Values: An Unofficial Statement* (Spokesman Press, Nottingham, 1988)

Blunkett, D. *Politics and Progress* (Politicos, London, 2001)

Braddock, J. and Braddock, B. *The Braddocks* (Macdonald, London, 1963)

Bradley, I. *Breaking the Mould?: The Birth and Prospects of the Social Democratic Party* (Martin Robertson, Oxford, 1981)

Brittan, S. *The Economic Consequences of Democracy* (London, Temple Smith, 1977)

Brivati, B. *Hugh Gaitskell* (Richard Cohen Books, London, 1997)

Brooke, S. 'Revisionists and Fundamentalists: The Labour Party and Economic Policy during the Second World War', *The Historical Journal* 1, (March 1989), 157-175

Brooke, S. 'Problems of 'Socialist Planning': Evan Durbin and the Labour Government of 1945', *The Historical Journal* 3 (Sep. 1991), 687-702

Brooke, S. 'Evan Durbin: Reassessing a Labour "Revisionist"', *Twentieth Century British History* 1 (1996), 27-52

Brown, G. *Fair is Efficient*, Fabian Tract 563 (Fabian Society, London, 1994)

Brown, G. 'Equality - Then and Now' in Leonard, D. (ed.), *Crosland and New Labour* (Palgrave Macmillan, London, 1999)

Brown, G. 'State and Market: Towards a Public Interest Test', *Political Quarterly* vol. 74, 3, (Blackwell, Oxford, 2003)

Burnham, J. *The Managerial Revolution* (Putnam, London, 1942)

Canto, V.A., Joines, D.H. and Laffer, A.B. (eds.) *Foundations of Supply-side Economics: Theory and Evidence* (Academic, New York 1983)

Carpenter, N. *Guild Socialism* (D. Appleton, London, 1922)

Carter, M. *T.H. Green and the Development of Ethical Socialism* (Exeter, Imprint Academic, 2003)

Clegg, H. *A New Approach to Industrial Democracy* (Blackwell, Oxford, 1960)

Coates, K. and Topham, T. (eds.), *Readings and Witnesses for Workers' Control*, (Spokesman, London, 1968)

Coates, K. and Topham, T. *The New Unionism: The Case for Workers' Control* (Owen, London, 1972)

Cole, G.D.H. *The World of Labour* (G. Bell & Sons, London, 1913)

Cole, G.D.H. *Self-Government in Industry* (G. Bell & Sons, London, 1917)

Cole, G.D.H. *Chaos and Order in Industry* (F.A. Stokes, New York, 1920)

Cole, G.D.H. *Guild Socialism Re-Stated* (Leonard Parsons, London, 1920)

Cole, G.D.H. *Social Theory* (Methuen, London, 1920)

Cole, G.D.H. *The Next Ten Years in British Social and Economic Policy* (Macmillan, London, 1929)

Cole, G.D.H. *A History of the Labour Party From 1914* (Routledge and Kegan Paul, London, 1948)

Cole, M. *The Life of G.D.H. Cole* (Macmillan, London, 1971)

Cooney, R., Fielding, S. and Tiratsoo, N. (eds.) *The Wilson Government 1964-70* (Pinter, London, 1993)

Corina, J. 'Introduction to the 1972 Edition' in Cole, G.D.H. *Self-Government in Industry* (Hutchinson Educational, London, 1972)

Crewe, I. and King, A. *SDP: The Birth, Life and Death of the Social Democratic Party* (Oxford University Press, Oxford, 1995)

Crick, B. 'Socialist Literature in the Fifties' *Political Quarterly* (1960)

Crick, B. *Socialist Values and Time* (Fabian Society, London, 1984)

Crosland, C.A.R. 'The Transition from Capitalism' in

Crosland, C.A.R. *The Future of Socialism* (Cape, London, 1956)

Crosland, C.A.R. 'The Future of the Left' *Encounter*, March 1960

Crosland, C.A.R. *Can Labour Win?* Fabian Tract 324 (Fabian Society, London, 1960)

Crosland, C.A.R. 'Radical Reform and the Left' *Encounter*, October 1960

Crosland, C.A.R. (ed.) *The Conservative Enemy: A Programme of Radical Reform for the 1960s* (Cape, London, 1962)

Crosland, C.A.R. *Socialism Now and Other Essays* (Cape, London, 1974; edited by Dick Leonard)

Crosland, S. *Tony Crosland* (Cape, London, 1982)

Crossman, R.H.S., Foot, M. and Mikardo, I. *Keep Left* (New Statesman, London, 1947)

Crossman, R.H.S. (ed.) *The God that Failed: Six Studies in Communism* (Hamilton, London, 1950)

Crossman, R.H.S. *Socialist Values in a Changing Civilisation*, Fabian Tract 286 (Fabian Society, London, 1951)

Crossman, R.H.S. (ed.) *New Fabian Essays* (Turnstile, London, 1952)

Crossman, R.H.S. 'Towards a Philosophy of Socialism' in R.H.S. Crossman (ed.) *New Fabian Essays* (Turnstile, London, 1952)

Crossman, R.H.S. 'On Political Neuroses' *Encounter*, May 1954

Crossman, R.H.S. (ed.) *The Charm of Politics and Other Essays in Political Criticism* (Hamilton, London, 1958)

Crossman, R.H.S. 'The Spectre of Revisionism' *Encounter*, April 1960

Crossman, R.H.S. *Labour in the Affluent Society*, Fabian Tract 325 (Fabian Society, London, 1960)

Crossman, R.H.S. 'Introduction' to W. Bagehot, *The English Constitution* (Collins/Fontana, London, 1963)

Crossman, R.H.S. (ed.) *Planning for Freedom: Essays in Socialism* (Hamilton, London, 1965)

Crossman, R.H.S. *The Myths of Cabinet Government* (Harvard University Press, Cambridge, 1972)

Dalton, H. *Unbalanced Budgets* (Routledge, London, 1934)

Dalton, H. *Practical Socialism for Britain* (Routledge, London, 1935)

Dalyell, T. *Dick Crossman: A Portrait* (Weidenfeld and Nicolson, London, 1989)

Deane, H.A. *The Political Ideas of Harold J. Laski* (Columbia University Press, New York, 1954)

Dennis, N. and Halsey, A.H. *English Ethical Socialism* (Clarendon Press, Oxford, 1988)

Durbin, E. *New Jerusalems* (Routledge, London, 1985)

Durbin, E. *Purchasing Power and Trade Depression* (Jonathan Cape, London, 1933)

Durbin, E. 'Democracy and Socialism in Britain' *Political Quarterly*, 1935

Durbin, E. 'The Importance of Planning' in G. Catlin (ed.) *New Trends in Socialism* (Lovat Dickson & Thompson, London, 1935)

Durbin, E. 'The Social Significance of the Theory of Values' *Economic Journal*, 1935

Durbin, E. 'The Response of the Economist' in (ed.) T.H. Marshall, *The Ethical Factor in Economic Thought* (Ethical Union, London, 1936)

Durbin, E. *The Politics of Democratic Socialism* (Routledge, London, 1940)

Durbin, E. *The Economic Basis of Peace* (National Peace Council, London, 1942)

Durbin, E. *What Have We To Defend?* (George Routledge and Sons, London, 1942)

Durbin, E. 'Socialism: the British Way' in (ed.) D. Munro, *The Socialist Experiment carried out in Great Britain by the Labour Government of 1945* (Essential Books, London, 1948)

Drucker, H.M. *Doctrine and Ethos in the Labour Party* (George Allen & Unwin, London, 1979)

Drucker, H.M. and Brown, G. *The Politics of Nationalism and Devolution* (Longman, London, 1980)

Fabian Society, *Paying for Progress: A New Politics of Tax for Public Spending* (Fabian Society, London, 2000)

Fielding, S. *The Labour Party: Continuity and Change in the Making of 'New' Labour* (Palgrave, Basingstoke, 2003)

Figgis, J.N. *Churches in the Modern State* (Longmans, London, 1913)

Flew, A. *The Politics of Procrustes* (Temple Smith, London, 1981)

Foote, G. *The Labour Party's Political Thought: A History* (Palgrave, Basingstoke, 1997, 3rd edition)

Friedman, M. *Monetarist Economics* (Blackwell, Oxford, 1990)

Gaitskell, H. 'Public Ownership and Equality' *Socialist Commentary*, June 1955

Gaitskell, H. *Socialism and Nationalisation* (Fabian Society, London, 1956)

Gaitskell, H. 'An Appreciation' in R.H. Tawney, *The Radical Tradition* (ed) Hinden, R. (George Allen & Unwin, London, 1964)

Galbraith, J.K. *The Affluent Society* (Hamish Hamilton, London, 1958)

Gamble, A. *The Free Economy and the Strong State: the Politics of Thatcherism* (Macmillan, Basingstoke, 1986)

Gamble, A. 'The Meaning of the Third Way' in D. Kavanagh and A. Seldon (eds.) *The Blair Effect 2001-2005* (Cambridge University Press, Cambridge, 2005)

Garnett, M. 'The Centre' in Hickson, K. (ed.) *The Political Thought of the Conservative Party since 1945* (Palgrave, Basingstoke, 2005)

Garnett, M. and Hickson, K. *Conservative Thinkers* (Manchester University Press, Manchester, forthcoming)

Giddens, A. *Modernity and Self-Identity* (Polity, Cambridge, 1991)

Giddens, A. *Beyond Left and Right: The Future of Radical Politics* (Polity, Cambridge, 1994)

Giddens, A. *The Third Way: The Renewal of Social Democracy* (Polity, Cambridge, 1998)

Giddens, A. *The Third Way and Its Critics* (Polity, Cambridge, 2000)

Giddens, A. (ed.) *The Global Third Way Debate* (Polity, Cambridge, 2001)

Giddens, A. *Where Now for New Labour?* (Polity, Cambridge, 2002)

Giddens, A. and Diamond, P. (eds.) *The New Egalitarianism* (Polity, Cambridge, 2005)

Glyn, A. and Sutcliffe, B. *British Capitalism, Workers and the Profits Squeeze* (Penguin, Harmondsworth, 1972)

Gould, B. *Socialism and Freedom* (Macmillan, Basingstoke, 1985)

Gould, B. *A Future for Socialism* (Cape, London, 1989)

Hale, S., Leggett, W. and Martell, L. (eds.) *The Third Way and Beyond* (Manchester University Press, Manchester, 2004)

Hall, S. and Jacques, M. (eds.) *New Times: The Changing Face of Politics in the 1990s* (Lawrence and Wishart, London, 1989)

Hall, S. 'The Great Moving Nowhere Show' *Marxism Today*, November/December 1998

Harris, J. 'Labour's political and social thought', in D. Tanner, P. Thane and N. Tiratsoo (eds.) *Labour's First Century* (Cambridge University Press, Cambridge, 2000)

LABOUR'S THINKERS

Haseler, S. *The Gaitskellites: Revisionism in the British Labour Party 1951-64* (Macmillan, London, 1969)

Hattersley, R., Heffer, E., Kinnock, N. and Shore, P. *Labour's Choices* (Fabian Society, London, 1983)

Hattersley, R. *Choose Freedom: The Future for Democratic Socialism* (Michael Joseph, London, 1987)

Hattersley, R. 'Afterword' in K. Hoover and R. Plant, *Conservative Capitalism in Britain and the United States: A Critical Appraisal* (Routledge, London, 1989)

Hattersley, R. *Who Goes Home?* (Little, Brown and Company, London, 1995)

Hattersley, R. 'Tone of the times' *The Guardian*, 27 April, 1995

Hattersley, R. *Fifty Years On: A Prejudiced History of Post-war Britain* (Little, Brown and Company, London, 1997)

Hattersley, R. 'It's no longer my party' *The Observer*, 24 June, 2001

Hay, C. *The Political Economy of New Labour: Labouring Under False Pretences* (Manchester University Press, Manchester, 1999)

Hayek, F.A. *Prices and Production* (Routledge, London, 1931)

Hayek, F.A. *The Constitution of Liberty* (Routledge, London, 1960)

Hayek, F.A. *Law Legislation and Liberty: Volume II -The Mirage of Social Justice* (Routledge, London, 1976)

Hayek, F.A. 'Denationalisation of Money' *Hobart Paper* 70, (Institute of Economic Affairs, London, 1976)

Healey, D. 'Power Politics and the Labour Party' in Crossman, R.H.S. (ed.) *New Fabian Essays* (Turnstile, London, 1952)

Healey, D. *Neutralism* (Ampersand, London, 1955)

Healey, D. *The Time of My Life* (Penguin, London, 1990)

Heffernan, R. and Marqusee, M. *Defeat from the Jaws of Victory* (Verso, London, 1992)

Hickson, K. 'Equality' in R. Plant, M. Beech and K. Hickson (eds.) *The Struggle for Labour's Soul: Understanding Labour's Political Thought since 1945* (Routledge, London, 2004)

Hickson, K. *The IMF Crisis and British Politics* (IB Tauris, London, 2005)

Hickson, K. 'Revisionism Revisited: From Crosland to New Labour' *Imprints* vol. 8, no. 3 (2005)

Hill, D. 'Constitutional Reform' in R. Plant, M. Beech and K. Hickson (eds.), *The Struggle for Labour's Soul* (Routledge, London, 2004)

Hinden, R. 'The New Socialism' *Socialist Commentary* November 1956

Hirsch, F. *The Social Limits of Growth* (Routledge, London, 1977)

Holland, S. (ed.) *The State as Entrepreneur: the IRI State-holding Formula* (Weidenfeld and Nicolson, London, 1972)

Holland, S. *The Socialist Challenge* (Quartet, London, 1975)

Holland, S. (ed.) *Beyond Capitalist Planning* (Blackwell, Oxford, 1978)

Holland, S. 'An Alternative Economic Strategy' in M. Barratt Brown, K. Coates, K. Fleet and J. Hughes (eds.) *Full Employment: Priority* (Nottingham, Spokesman, 1978)

Holland, S. 'Capital, Labour and the State' in K. Coates (ed.) *What Went Wrong* (Spokesman, Nottingham, 1979)

Holland, S. *Uncommon Market* (Macmillan, Basingstoke, 1980)

Holland, S. 'Out of Crisis: International Economic Recovery' in J. Curran (ed.) *The Future of the Left* (Polity and New Socialist, Cambridge, 1984)

Holland, S. *The European Imperative: Economic and Social Cohesion in the 1990s* (Spokesman, Nottingham, 1993)

Holland, S. 'Ownership, Planning and Markets' in R. Plant, M. Beech and K. Hickson (eds.) *The Struggle for Labour's Soul: Understanding Labour's Political Thought since 1945* (Routledge, London, 2004)

Holloway, R. *Doubts and Loves: What is Left of Christianity* (Canongate Books, Edinburgh, 2002)

Holloway, R. *Godless Morality* (Canongate Books, Edinburgh, 2004)

Holtham, G. 'Ownership and Social Democracy' in A. Gamble and T. Wright (eds.) *The New Social Democracy* (Blackwell, Oxford, 1999)

Hoover, K. and Plant, R. *Conservative Capitalism in Britain and the United States: A Critical Appraisal* (Routledge, London, 1989)

Howard, A. (ed.) *The Crossman Diaries: Selections from Dairies of a Cabinet Minister, 1964-70* (Hamilton and Cape, London, 1979)

Howard, A. *Crossman: the Pursuit of Power* (Cape, London, 1990)

Howell, D. *British Social Democracy* (Croom Helm, London, 1976)

Hughes, C. and Wintour, P. *Labour Rebuilt* (Fourth Estate, London, 1990)

Jay, D. *The Socialist Case* (Faber, London, 1937)

Jay, D. *Socialism and the New Society* (Longmans, London, 1962)

Jefferys, K. *Anthony Crosland* (Cohen, London, 1999)

Jenkins, R. *The Pursuit of Progress* (Heinemann, London, 1953)

Jenkins, R. *What Happens Now* (Fontana, London, 1972)

Jenkins, R. 'Dimbleby Lecture: Home Thoughts From Abroad' in W. Kennet (ed.) *The Rebirth of Britain* (Weidenfeld & Nicolson, London, 1982)

Jenkins, R. *Partnership of Principle* (Secker and Warburg, London, 1985)

Jenkins, R. *A Life at the Centre* (Macmillan, London, 1991)

Jones, T. *Remaking the Labour Party: from Gaitskell to Blair* (Routledge, London, 1996)

Joseph, K. *Equality* (Murray, London, 1979)

Kavanagh, D. and Seldon, A. (eds.) *The Blair Effect 2001-2005* (CUP, Cambridge, 2005)

Keegan, W. *The Prudence of Mr Gordon Brown* (Wiley, Chichester, 2003)

Keynes, J.M. *The General Theory of Employment, Interest and Money* (Macmillan, London, 1936)

Kogan, D. and Kogan, M. *The Battle for the Labour Party* (Kogan Page, London, 1983)

Kramnick, I. and Sheerman, B. *Harold Laski: A Life on the Left* (Allen Lane, London, 1993)

Labour Party, *Industry and Society* (Labour Party, London, 1957)

Labour Party, *Statement of Democratic Socialist Aims and Values* (Labour Party, London, 1988)

Lamb, P. *Harold Laski: Problems of Democracy, the Sovereign State and International Society* (Palgrave Macmillan, Basingstoke, 2004)

Laski, H. *Studies in the Problem of Sovereignty* (Yale University Press, New Haven, 1917)

Laski, Harold, *Authority in the Modern State* (Yale University Press, New Haven, 1919)

Laski, H. *The Foundations of Sovereignty and Other Essays* (Harcourt Brace and Co., New York, 1921)

Laski, H. *A Grammar of Politics* (George Allen & Unwin, London, 1925)

Laski, H. *Communism* (Thornton Butterworth, London, 1927)

Laski, H. *Democracy in Crisis* (George Allen & Unwin, London, 1933)

Laski, H. *The Labour Party and the Constitution* (Socialist League, London, 1933)

Laski, H. *The State in Theory and Practice* (George Allen & Unwin, London, 1935)

Laski, H. *Parliamentary Government in England* (Viking, New York, 1938)

Laski, H. *Where Do We Go From Here?* (Penguin Books, London, 1940)

Laski, H. *Reflections on the Revolution of Our Times* (Viking Press, New York, 1943)

Laski, H. *Faith, Reason and Civilisation* (Viking, New York, 1944)

Laski, H. *The American Democracy* (Viking Press, New York, 1948)

Laski, H. *Trade Unions in the New Society* (Viking Press, New York, 1949)

Lee Sykes, P. *Losing From the Inside: The Cost of Conflict in the British Social Democratic Party* (Transaction Books, New Brunswick, 1988)

Lenin, V. *Imperialism: The Highest Stage of Capitalism* (Lawrence and Wishart, London, 1948)

Leonard, D. (ed.) *Crosland and New Labour* (Macmillan, Basingstoke, 1999)

Lipsey, D. and Leonard, D. (eds.) *The Socialist Agenda: Crosland's Legacy* (Cape, London, 1981)

Ludlam, S. and Smith, M. (eds.) *New Labour in Government* (Palgrave, Basingstoke, 2001)

Ludlam, S. and Smith, M. *Governing as New Labour* (Palgrave, Basingstoke, 2004)

Lukes, S. 'Socialism and Equality' in Lukes, S. (ed.) *Essays in Social Theory* (Macmillan, London, 1977)

Lutman, S. 'Orwell's Patriotism', *Journal of Contemporary History* 2, (April 1967), 149-158.

MacCallum, G. 'Negative and Positive Freedom' (1967) *Philosophical Review*

MacIntyre, A. 'A Mistake About Causality in Social Science' in P. Laslett and W. G. Runciman (eds.) *Philosophy, Politics and Society*, 2nd series (Blackwell, Oxford, 1972)

Mandelson, P. and Liddle, R. *The Blair Revolution* (Faber and Faber, London, 1996)

Marquand, D. (ed.) *John P. Mackintosh on Parliament and Social Democracy* (Longman, London, 1982)

Marquand, D. *The Unprincipled Society* (Cape, London, 1988)

Marquand, D. *The Progessive Dilemma: from Lloyd George to Blair* (2nd edition, Phoenix, London, 1999)

Marshall, T.H. *Citizenship and Social Class* (Cambridge University Press, Cambridge, 1950)

Marx, K. *The Communist Manifesto* (Peking Books, London, 1974)

McGrath, A. *Evangelicalism and the Future of Christianity* (Hodder and Stoughton, London, 1995)

Mead, L. *Beyond Entitlement: The Social Obligations of Citizenship* (Free Press, New York, 1986)

Miliband, D. (ed.) *Re-inventing the Left* (Polity, Cambridge, 1994)

Miliband, R. *Parliamentary Socialism* (Allen and Unwin, London, 1961)

Mitchell, A. *Competitive Socialism* (Unwin, London, 1989)

Morgan, J. (ed.) *The Backbench Diaries of Richard Crossman* (Hamilton and Cape, London, 1981)

Morgan, K. O. *Labour in Power 1945-51* (Oxford University Press, Oxford, 1984)

Murray, C. *Losing Ground: American Social Policy 1950-80* (Basic Books, New York, 1984)

Murray, R. *Multinational Companies and Nation States* (Spokesman, Nottingham, 1975)

Morris, W. *News From Nowhere* (Longmans, London, 1896)

Newman, M. *John Strachey* (Manchester University Press, Manchester, 1989)

Newman, M. *Harold Laski: A Political Biography* (Macmillan, Basingstoke, 1993)

Niskanen, W. *Bureaucracy and Representative Government* (Aldine and Atherton, Chicago and New York, 1971)

Orwell, G. *The Lion and the Unicorn* (Secker and Warburg, London, 1941)

Owen, D. 'Communism, Socialism, and Democracy', *The Washington Review of Strategic and International Studies* Vol.1, No.2, April 1978, pp.4-15.

Owen, D. *Face The Future* (Oxford University Press, Oxford, 1981)

Owen, D. 'Agenda for Competitiveness with Compassion' *Economic Affairs* 4 (1983)

Owen, D. *A Future that will Work: Competitiveness and Compassion* (Penguin Books, Harmondsworth, 1984)

Owen, D. *A United Kingdom*, (Penguin Books, Harmondsworth, 1986)

Owen, D. *Personally Speaking to Kenneth Harris* (Pan Books, London, 1987)

Owen, D. and Steel, D. *The Time Has Come: Partnership for Progress* (Weidenfeld and Nicholson, London, 1987)

Owen, D. *A Time To Declare* (Michael Joseph, London, 1991)

Parfit, D. 'Equality and Priority', in A. Mason (ed.) *Ideals of Equality* (Blackwell, Oxford, 1998.)

Plant, R., Lesser, H. and Taylor-Gooby, P. *Political Philosophy and Social Welfare: Essays on the Normative Basis of Welfare Provision* (Routledge, London, 1980)

Plant, R. 'Socialism and Equality' in D. Lipsey and D. Leonard (eds.) *The Socialist Agenda: Crosland's Legacy* (Cape, London, 1981)

Plant, R. *Equality, Markets and the State* (Fabian Society, London, 1984)

Plant, R. *Citizenship, Rights and Socialism* (Fabian Society, London, 1988)

Plant, R. 'Social democracy' in D. Marquand and A. Seldon (eds.) *The Ideas That Shaped Post-War Britain* (Fontana, London, 1996)

Plant, R. 'Crosland, Equality and New Labour' in D. Leonard (ed.) *Crosland and New Labour* (Macmillan, London, 1999)

Plant, R. 'Blair and Ideology' in A. Seldon (ed.) *The Blair Effect* (Little, Brown, London, 2001)

Plant, R., Beech, M. and Hickson, K. *The Struggle for Labour's Soul: Understanding Labour's Political Thought since 1945* (Routledge, London, 2004)

Plant, R. 'Ends, Means and Political Identity' in R. Plant, M. Beech and K. Hickson (eds.) *The Struggle for Labour's Soul: Understanding Labour's Political Thought* (Routledge, London, 2004)

Radice, G. *Revisionism: Labour's Path to Power* (Macmillan, Basingstoke, 1989)

Rawls, J. *A Theory of Justice* (Harvard, Cambridge, 1971)

Rawls, J. *A Theory of Justice* (Oxford University Press, Oxford, 1999)

Rodgers, W. *The Politics of Change* (Secker & Warburg, London, 1982)

Routledge, P. *Gordon Brown: The Biography* (Simon & Schuster, London, 1998)

Sabine, G. and Thorson, T. *A History of Political Theory* (Dryden Press, Illinois, 1973)

Sassoon, D. *One Hundred Years of Socialism: The West European Left in the Twentieth Century* (Fontana Press, London, 1997)

Saville, J. 'The Ideology of Labourism' in Benewick, R., Berki, R.N. and Parekh, B. (eds.) *Knowledge and Belief in Politics: The Problem of Ideology* (Allen & Unwin, London, 1973)

Shaw, G.B. *The Intelligent Woman's Guide to Socialism and Capitalism* (Constable, London, 1928)

Seldon, A. (ed.) *The Blair Effect* (Little, Brown and Company, London, 2001)

Smith, J. 'Reclaiming the Ground: R.H. Tawney Memorial Lecture 20th March 1993' in Bryant, C. (ed.), *Reclaiming the Ground* (Hodder and Stoughton, London, 1993)

Socialist Union, *Socialism: A New Statement of Principles* (Socialist Union, London, 1952)

Spong, J. S. *Born of a Woman: A Bishop Rethinks the Birth of Jesus* (Harper, San Francisco, 1992)

Spong, J. S. *Resurrection: Myth or Reality? A Bishop's Search of the Origin's of Christianity* (Harper, San Francisco, 1994)

Stewart, K. 'Equality and Social Justice' in D. Kavanagh and A. Seldon *The Blair Effect 2001-2005* (CUP, Cambridge, 2005)

Stott, J. *Evangelical Truth* (Inter-Varsity Press, Leicester, 1999)

Strachey, J. *Revolution by Reason* (Leonard Parsons, London, 1925)

Strachey, J. *The Coming Struggle for Power* (Gollancz, London, 1932)

Strachey, J. *The Menace of Fascism* (Gollancz, London, 1933)

Strachey, J. *The Nature of Capitalist Crisis* (Gollancz, London, 1935)

Strachey, J. *The Theory and Practice of Socialism* (Gollancz, London, 1936)

Strachey, J. *What are we to do?* (Gollancz, London, 1938)

Strachey, J. *A Programme for Progress* (Gollancz, London, 1940)

Strachey, J. *The Just Society: a reaffirmation of faith in socialism* (Labour Party, London, 1951)

Strachey, J. 'Tasks and Achievements of British Labour' in Crossman, R.H.S. (ed.) *New Fabian Essays* (Turnstile, London, 1952)

Strachey, J. 'The Objects of Further Socialisation' *Political Quarterly*, January-March 1953

Strachey, J. 'The New Revisionist' *New Statesman and Nation*, October 6, 1956

Strachey, J. *Contemporary Capitalism* (Gollancz, London, 1956)

Strachey, J. *The End of Empire* (Gollancz, London, 1959)

Strachey, J. *The Strangled Cry* (Bodley Head, London, 1962)

Strachey, J. *On the Prevention of War* (Macmillan, Basingstoke, 1962)

Tawney, R. H. *Acquisitive Society* (Bell, London, 1921)

Tawney, R.H. *Equality* (Allen and Unwin, London, 1931)

Taylor, M. 'Patriotism, History and the Left in Twentieth-century Britain', *The Historical Journal* 4 (1990), 971-987.

Terrill, R. *R.H. Tawney and His Times* (Andre Deutsch, London, 1973)

Thomas, H. *John Strachey* (Methuen, London, 1973)

Thompson, N. *John Strachey: An Intellectual Biography* (Macmillan, Basingstoke, 1993)

Thompson, N. *The Political Economy of the Labour Party* (UCL, London, 1996)

Thompson, N. 'The Centre' in Plant, R., Beech, M. and Hickson, K. *The Struggle for Labour's Soul: Understanding Labour's Political Thought since 1945* (Routledge, London, 2004)

Tomlinson, J. *The Unequal Struggle? British Socialism and the Capitalist Enterprise* (Methuen, London, 1982)

Toynbee, P. and Walker, D. *Did Things Really Get Better?* (Penguin, London, 2001)

Wickham-Jones, M. *Economic Strategy and the Labour Party: Politics and Policy-making, 1970-83* (Macmillan, London, 1996)

Williams, J.R., Titmuss, R. M. and Fisher, F.J. *R.H. Tawney: A Portrait by Several Hands* (Shenval Press, London, 1960)

Williams, S. *Politics is for People* (Jonathan Cape, London, 1981)

Winter, J. 'R.H. Tawney's Early Political Thought', *Past and Present* May 1970 pp.71-96

Winter, J. and Joslin, D. (eds.) *R.H. Tawney's Commonplace Book* (Cambridge University Press, Cambridge, 1972)

Wright, A. *G.D.H. Cole and Socialist Democracy* (Clarendon Press, Oxford, 1979)

Wright, A. *R.H. Tawney* (Manchester University Press, Manchester, 1987)

Wright, A. 'New Labour, Old Crosland?' in D. Leonard (ed.) *Crosland and New Labour* (Macmillan, Basingstoke, 1999)

Young, M. *The Rise of the Meritocracy* (Thames and Hudson, London, 1958)

Zenter, P. *Social Democracy In Britain: Must Labour Lose?* (Hohn Martin Publishing, London, 1982)

INDEX

1917 Club 78-79
1963 Club 196
1976 IMF Crisis 178, 229
2003 Budget 272

A Fresh start for Britain 199
A Future that will Work 195
A Grammar of Politics 64, 70
A History of Socialist Thought 52
A Key to Communism 68
A Life at the Centre 202
A National Policy 102
A Programme for Progress 105
A United Kingdom 195, 211
Action Teams 278
Adam Smith Institute 221
Alternative Economic Strategy (AES) 124, 173, 178-182, 184-185, 190, 230
Amalgamated Engineering Union (AEU) 49
America 39, 58, 60, 71-72, 106
Ancient Greeks 27
Anglican Church 23-25, 31
Anti-collectivism 38, 41, 45, 50
Anti-Socialist Union 41
Arblaster, Anthony 4, 203
Ascension 25
Ashdown, Paddy 273
Attlee Government 13, 71-72, 80, 82, 100, 107, 109, 111-112, 114, 122, 126-127, 129, 133, 135, 138, 145-148, 156-157, 160, 231, 288
Attlee, Clement 51, 65, 66, 93, 130, 137
Austria 53

Authority in the Modern State 60

Bacon, Richard 222
Bad Godesberg 204
Bagehot, Walter 135-136
Baldwin, Stanley 71
Balliol College 33
Balogh, Thomas 134
Bank of England 48
Baptist 96
Barratt Brown, Michael 10
Battle of the Somme 20, 22
Baxter, Richard 31
Beales, Lance 65
Beloff, Max 72
Benn, Tony 9, 21 49-50, 179, 230
Bennites 49-50, 289-290
Berle, Adolf 147
Bernstein, Eduard 2, 21, 145
Bevan, Aneurin 9, 81, 102, 112, 129-130, 132, 138
Bevanites 289
Bevin, Ernest 67
Beyond Left and Right 246, 249
Bible 23, 25
Birmingham proposals 101
Blair, Tony 10, 14, 165, 211, 213, 237-238, 244-247, 249, 251-252, 257, 266, 269, 290-291
Blairites 213, 266, 290
Blunkett, David 11, 235
Bolshevism 64
Braddock, Bessie 123
Bradley, Ian 196, 200
Brandeis, Louis 58

Braunthal, Julius 52
Breaking the Mould? 196
Bretton Woods 175
Britain 1-2, 22, 30, 32, 39, 46-
    47, 49, 52, 58, 63, 67-69, 72-
    73, 77, 79, 80, 82, 84-90, 93,
    95-96, 100, 102-104, 108, 115,
    117, 122-123, 126, 133, 135-
    136, 138, 144-145, 147-148,
    152-155, 159, 161-162, 164,
    172, 176-177, 181, 184-185,
    187-190, 197, 203-204, 209,
    244-248, 261, 267, 276-277,
    280, 285-289
British Army 20, 22-23, 60
British Empire 89, 94
British Left 94, 201, 214
British Union of Fascists 68
Brivati, Brian 78
Brown, George 186
Brown, Gordon 2, 4, 7-8, 14,
    191, 265-269, 272-274, 276-
    280, 284-285, 290-292
Brownites 266
Burnham, James 147

Callaghan Government 196
Callaghan, Jim 186, 202, 230
Calvary 34
Calvin, John 24
Cambridge Economic Policy
    Group 185
Campaign for Democratic
    Socialism (CDS) 196-197
Campaign for Nuclear
    Disarmament (CND) 268
Canada 60
Capitalism 2-3, 28-31, 41, 47,
    52, 62-63, 65-69, 72, 79, 81,
    91, 93, 100-101, 103-112,
    115-116, 126-128, 133, 145-
    146, 148, 150, 152-153, 158,
    161, 172, 177, 181-182, 184-

186, 189, 204, 248, 271, 288-
    289
Catalyst 166
Centre 19, 80, 83, 108, 123,
    131-132, 138
Centre for Policy Studies 204,
    221
Centre-left (in the Labour Party)
    80-81, 83, 288
Chamberlain Government 94
Chaos and Order in Industry 38
Charity Organisation Society
    (COS) 24
Child Tax Credit 277
China 291
Choose Freedom 220, 232, 234-
    236, 238
Christ 25-26, 33
Christianity 18, 21-28, 30-32, 96
Christianity and the Social Order 26,
    29
Christian socialism 19, 21-23,
    26, 28, 64, 69, 150, 288
Christianity 288
Churches in the Modern State 60
City of London 267
Citizen's Britain 273
Clarke, Kenneth 205
Clause IV 131-133, 138, 237,
    246
Clegg, Hugh 183
Clegg Report 159
Coates, Ken 10, 49
Cold War 72
Cole, G.D.H. 2, 4, 7-9, 12, 38-
    42, 44-48, 50-53, 59-61, 65-
    66, 72, 78, 137, 207, 284,
    287-288
Cole, Margaret 40, 65-66
Collectivism 40-42, 50, 52-53,
    64, 70, 207
Colonies 89
Common Market 197

Communism 19, 23, 29, 52, 58, 64-65, 67-69, 83-84, 89, 91, 93, 100, 102-104, 127-128
Communism 71
Communist Party of Great Britain 33, 45-46, 52, 92, 104-105, 178
Communitarianism 21, 164, 211, 280
Community 3-4, 21-22, 72, 162-165, 205, 208, 210-211, 213, 235, 252, 280, 290
Confederate of Socialist Parties 190
Connexions 278
Conservatism 156, 205, 247
Conservative Party 4, 60, 72, 80, 115, 121, 130, 148-149, 165, 197, 201-202, 205, 208, 212, 219, 221-223, 232, 267, 270
Contemporary Capitalism 101, 109-110, 112, 114, 116
Cook, Robin 269
Council for Social Democracy 199
Crewe, Ivor 200, 209, 214, 231
Crick, Bernard 10, 71, 151-153, 198, 235
Cripps, Francis 185
Cripps, Stafford 9, 58, 65-66
Crosland and New Labour 265
Crosland, Anthony 2-4, 6-8, 11, 13-14, 20-21, 101, 109, 111-117, 122, 128, 134, 139, 144-160, 173, 175-178, 182, 185190, 196-198, 204, 219, 229-230, 233, 245, 252, 274-275, 285-286, 288-289
Crossman, Richard 2, 7-9, 13, 81, 101, 112, 117, 121, 123-138, 145-146, 286, 288-289
Cunningham, Jack 236

Daily Herald 91
Dalton, Hugh 10, 67, 78, 82-83, 158
Davenport, Nicholas 78
Deane, Herbert 59-60, 63, 68
Decentralisation 42, 45, 49-52, 61, 71, 163, 203, 206-208, 211-213, 289, 292
Delors, Jaques 190
Dell, Edmund 229
Democracy 27, 32-33, 43, 49, 63, 67, 70-71, 78-79, 84, 87-88, 90-92, 96, 165, 172, 207-208, 250
Democracy in Crisis 66
Democratic equality 152
Democratic socialism 5, 12, 14, 18, 21, 26, 28, 32-33, 39-40, 46, 49-50, 52, 64, 66, 72, 77-80, 83-84, 92-93, 95-96, 211, 213, 220, 233, 239, 245, 288
Democratisation 138
Department of Economic Affairs 187
Devolution 163
Difference principle 154
Downing Street 290
Durbin, Evan 2, 7-8, 11-12, 21, 63, 77-96, 147, 286, 288
Drucker, Henry 287

Eastern Europe 291
Edinburgh University 268
Edwardian liberalism 60
Edwards, Jonathan 24
Eltis, Walter 222
Encounter 7, 132
Ends 3-5, 13-14, 20, 26, 29, 32, 41, 64, 113-114, 128, 149-150, 156, 159, 164, 186, 249, 253, 257, 259-261, 279
Engels, Friedrich 103

England 27, 51, 62, 88, 91, 94-95, 163
Equality 12, 20, 29
Equality 3-5, 13-14, 20, 33, 70, 114, 116, 128, 133, 144, 150-151, 154-156, 164-165, 187, 198, 205, 207-208, 213, 224-226, 229-233, 238, 245, 253, 255, 257-258, 260-261, 266-270, 272-274, 276-279, 292
Equality of opportunity 3-4, 144, 151-154, 166, 231, 234, 238, 252-254, 256-258, 261, 270-271, 273-274, 279
Equality of opportunity and fairness of outcome 267-268, 272-273, 279
Equality of outcome 152, 257, 270-271, 274
Equality and Priority 271
Equality: Then and Now 265-266, 273-274
Erhard, Ludwig 204
Euro-dollar market 175
Europe 31, 68, 84, 248
Europe: The Third Way 247
European Commission 172
European Community 197
European Economic Community (EEC) 181, 184, 190, 197, 229, 231-232
European social democracy 245
Evangelicalism 23-24

Fabian Society 8-9, 12, 19, 40-42, 44, 51-52, 59, 62, 64-65, 82, 100, 125, 150, 207
Fabian Commission on Taxation and Citizenship 238, 256, 258
Face the Future 195-196, 198-199, 205-207, 211
Fair is Efficient 266
Faith, Reason and Civilisation 63

Falklands War 200, 209
Fascism 63, 68, 84, 86, 89, 92-93, 102, 104, 106
Fellowship 40, 52, 72, 199, 208
Figgis, J.N. 60
Foot, Michael 9, 70-71, 210
Foote, Geoffrey 44, 80-81, 124
France 49, 183-184, 190
Frankfurter, Felix 58
Fraternity 70, 150-151, 207-208
Freedom (See Liberty)
Free-market 107, 111, 148, 180, 202-204, 209-210, 222, 246-247
Friedman, Milton 222

Gaitskell, Hugh 20, 78, 81-83, 123-124, 130-133, 137-138, 149, 162, 195, 289
Gaitskellites 19, 105, 108, 123-124, 131, 197, 213
Galbraith, J.K. 134-135
Gang of Four 196, 205, 209-210, 213
Gang of Three 198
General Strike 47, 65, 284
German Fascism 63
German Marxists 91
Germany 53, 67, 80, 84, 86-88, 95, 204
Giddens, Anthony 2, 4-5, 7-8, 14, 165, 239, 244-258, 260, 266, 285, 290-291
Glasgow College of Technology 268
Globalisation 164, 175, 189, 206, 249-251, 267, 289, 290, 292
Godley, Wynne 185
Great Depression 68
Greater equality of outcome 112, 154, 156, 199, 220, 232-233, 237, 270, 288

Green, T.H. 33
Guild Congress 43
Guild socialism 12, 19, 38-40,
    42-48, 50-51, 53, 59, 61-62
Guild Socialism Re-stated 38

Hall, Stuart 247, 250
Harvard University 60
Haseler, Stephen 162
Hattersley, Roy 2, 4-8, 10, 14,
    21, 210, 219-220, 226, 229-
    239, 245, 249-250, 252, 275,
    285, 289-290
Hayek, Friedrich Von 107, 111,
    221-222, 224-225, 227-228,
    234, 259
Healey, Denis 10, 124, 200, 202,
    210, 229-230
Heath Government 229
Heffernan, Richard 236
Hermenuetics 6-7, 284-285
High-Tory 89
Hill, Dilys 51
Hinden, Rita 162
Hirsch, Fred 227
Hitler, Adolf 68, 94, 105-106
Hobson, J. A. 12, 47, 80-81
Holland, Stuart 2, 7-8, 13, 117,
    124, 145, 160, 162, 172-178,
    181-191, 230, 285, 288-289
Holloway, Richard 25
Holmes, Oliver Wendell 58
Holtham, Gerald 166-167
House of Commons 77, 85,
    132, 136, 172, 201
House of Lords 136
Howard, Anthony 124, 130
Howe, Geoffrey 221
Howell, David 151-153

*Imperialism: The Highest Stage of
    Capitalism* 90

In Place of Fear 9, 112
Independent Labour Party (ILP)
    12, 64-65, 150
India 89-90, 291,
Individualism 30, 32, 39, 70,
    147, 246, 250, 252
Industrial Democracy 10, 115-
    116, 126, 129, 136, 158, 180,
    183-184
Industrial Unionism 46-47, 52
Industry and Society 160
Institute for Economic Affairs
    (IEA) 221
Institute of Workers' Control
    (IWC) 49
International Monetary Fund
    (IMF) 116, 230
Ireland 60
Italy 183
Italian IRI 177

Jay, Douglas 11, 21, 81-82, 106,
    108, 128, 131, 147, 149, 158
Jenkins, Roy 11, 162, 177, 198-
    199, 202-203, 209
Jones, Jack 49
Joseph, Keith 204, 209, 221,
    227
Joslin, David 22

Keep Calm Group 108
Keep Left 126, 129-130, 138
Keeping Left 126, 129
Keegan, William 268
Keith Joseph Memorial Lecture 204
Keynes, J.M. 47, 80, 106-109,
    127, 174
Keynesianism 80-83, 100l, 106-
    107, 116, 127-128, 146, 173-
    175, 178, 181-182, 200, 209,
    222, 230, 288-289
King, Anthony 200, 209, 214,
    231

Kinnock, Neil 210, 214, 231, 234-237
Kogan, David 198
Kogan, Maurice 198
Korea 129
Kramnick, Isaac 62, 64, 66-67, 70

Labour in the Affluent Society 134
Labour left 5, 8, 12-13, 19, 47, 59, 64-65, 67, 81, 101, 126-129, 156, 159, 173, 177-179, 214, 230, 268
Labour Marxism 20, 78, 82-83, 93, 123, 271
Labour Movement 38, 40, 45-47, 49, 51, 54, 72, 78, 105, 109, 208, 214, 266, 268, 278, 287, 289
Labour Party 1-3, 5-11, 13-14, 18-22, 28-29, 38-39, 44-50, 52-53, 58-59, 65, 67, 71-72, 77-78, 80-81, 83-84, 94, 102-104, 106, 108-109, 114, 121-127, 131-135, 137-138, 146, 148-149, 156-158, 160, 163, 172-174, 176-178, 182, 190-191, 196-198, 200, 202, 205, 208-214, 219-220, 226, 229-237, 245, 246, 251, 265-267, 269, 272, 274, 278, 280, 284-291, 293
Labour Party Conference 130, 236
Labour Party Constitution 131, 149, 237
Labour Representation Committee (LRC) 9
Labour right 6, 10, 12, 83, 105, 126, 149, 156, 176-177, 198-199, 208, 219, 229, 231-232, 235-236, 250, 269

Labour's Programme 1973 177, 179, 182
Labourism 39, 52, 287
Laffer, Arthur 222, 256
Laissez-faire capitalism 19, 29, 31, 33, 39, 41, 72, 81, 111, 180, 288
Lancashire 20
Lansbury, George 64
Lamb, Peter 68-69
Laski, Frida 59-60, 62, 72
Laski, Harold 2, 7-8, 12, 38, 58-72, 284, 287-288
Lee-Sykes, Patricia 200, 202
Lenin, Vladimir 58, 66, 91, 103
Leninist 68
Leonard, Dick 265
Lever, Harold 230
Liberals 4, 39, 198, 201-202
Liberal Christians 25
Liberal Party 60, 134, 196, 199-201, 208-210, 232
Liberalism 65
Libertarianism 39, 50, 58, 60-64, 70, 163-164, 206
Libertarian socialism 12, 40, 52
Liberty (Freedom) 3-4, 14, 33, 39, 41-43, 52, 59-61, 68, 84, 93, 137, 155-156, 163-165, 199, 204, 206-208, 210, 212, 219-221, 223, 225-227, 233, 235, 238
Liddle, Roger 203, 205, 211-212
Liverpool 123
Liverpool City Council 123
London 33, 51
London School of Economics (LSE) 62, 93
Luther, Martin 24

MacCallum, Gerald 226
MacDonald Government 103

MacDonald, Ramsay 9, 58, 60, 62, 65, 68, 82, 102, 284
Mackintosh, John 10, 163
Maclennan, Robert 201
MacPherson, C.B. 71
Major Government 267
Major, John 195, 201, 214
Manchester 23, 28
Mandelson, Peter 203, 205, 211-212
Marquand, David 10, 124, 201
Marqusee Michael 236
Marshall, T.H. 10
Marx, Karl 2, 90-91, 103-104, 106, 109-111, 114, 145-146, 178
Marxism 2, 9, 12, 19-20, 44-45, 52, 61-64, 67-71, 78-79, 83, 90-92, 100, 103-108, 110, 114, 125, 127-129, 139, 145-146, 150, 158, 177-178, 271, 288
Marxist socialism 12, 44, 52, 59, 63, 66-70, 72
Maxton, James 64
McGill University 60
Means 3-5, 13-14, 29, 41, 64, 113-114, 128, 149, 156, 159, 164, 186, 244-245, 249, 253, 256-257, 259-261, 279
Means, Gardiner 147
Mellor, William 40
Menon, Krishna 71
Meso-economy 172-174, 178, 182-183, 185-186
Mikardo, Ian 9
Miliband, David 246
Miliband, Ralph 71
Militant Tendency 237
Modernity and Self-Identity 255
Monarchy 94
Monetarism 209, 222
Mont Perelin Society 221
Montreal 60

Morris, William 39-40, 150, 207
Morrison, Herbert 10, 67, 82, 126, 136, 156
Moscow 77, 85
Mosley, Oswald 12, 68, 100-102
Muller-Armack, Alfred 204
Munich Agreement 94
Murray, Robin 189
Mussolini, Benito 68

Nation 68
National Executive Committee (NEC) 177, 197, 236
National Guilds Congress 53
National Guilds League 40-41
National Health Service (NHS) 205
National Minimum Wage 276
Nationalisation 5, 41-42, 46, 63-64, 79, 82-83, 102, 104, 107, 109, 133, 146, 159-160, 183, 187-188, 207, 288
Nazism 67, 77, 80, 84-85, 90, 94-95, 105
Negative freedom 3, 207, 223, 225-226
Neo-endogenous growth theory 280
Neo-liberalism 195-197, 201-204, 214, 220-223, 225-228, 234, 239, 248, 252, 256, 259, 261, 270, 289-290, 292
Neo-Marxism 70, 110, 116
Neo-revisionism 162-164
Newman, Michael 60, 64-65
News From Nowhere 39
New Deal (USA) 106
New Deal 277
New Deal Plus 277
New Fabian Essays 108, 128, 135, 146, 148, 162

New Labour 5-6, 14, 19, 21, 51,
150, 163-166, 191, 195-196,
199, 205, 211-213, 219-220,
229, 234, 236-239, 244, 246-
247, 250, 254, 256, 258, 261,
265-269, 272-273, 275-278,
280, 290-291
New Left 12, 19, 21, 38, 48-50,
124, 77, 197-198, 268-269,
278
New Left Review 10
New Party 100
New Right 10, 14, 115, 190,
209, 211, 220-221, 233-236,
245-246
New right-wing of the Labour
Party 266, 278
New Testament 32
Nineteenth century 109, 111,
207
Non-conformists 31, 128, 134
Non-strict prioritarianism 268,
277, 280
Northern Ireland 51, 292

Old Labour 246
Old Left 19, 124, 269, 289
Old Right 19-21, 195, 197, 268,
285, 289
One-member one-vote 232
Opportunity 212
Orwell, George 92, 94-95
Owen, David 2, 4, 6, 8, 11-12,
14, 38, 50, 195, 198, 200-212,
214, 231, 285-286, 289-290
Oxford University 22, 33, 40,
59, 71, 145

Packenham, Frank 94
Parfit, Derek 271
*Parliamentary Government in
England* 68

Parliamentary Labour Party
(PLP) 108, 129-130, 162, 210
Patriotism 12, 77, 83-96, 106
Pensioner Credit 272, 277
Penty, Arthur 40
Philosophical Idealism 33
Planning for Freedom 81, 125
Plant, Raymond 10, 151-152,
226, 228, 238-239, 259, 279,
289
Pluralism 58, 61, 63-64, 223,
225, 228
Policy Review 235-236, 251
Positive freedom 3, 207, 223-
226, 229, 233, 239
Powell, Enoch 221
Prentice, Reg 229
Progress 290
Progressive universalism 268,
272-273, 279-280
Protestant Christianity 23-25,
30, 127
Public ownership 5, 10, 13, 20-
21, 104, 107-108, 113-117,
126, 131, 145, 149-150, 156,
158-160, 163, 166-167, 172-
173, 178-179, 182-189, 200,
268
*Purchasing Power and Trade
Depression* 80
Puritans 30-31

Rawls, John 3, 152, 205, 227,
274
Red Professors 38, 62, 284, 287
Reformation 23
Re-inventing the Left 246
Reisman, David 110
Religion and the Rise of Capitalism
30
Resurrection 25
Revisionism 10-11, 13, 123, 125,
127-128, 134, 138-139, 149,

173, 178, 185, 197, 213, 249,
289
Revisionists 5, 13, 80, 83, 100-
101, 105, 108, 110, 112, 114-
116, 122, 128-130, 132-133,
138, 145-146, 149-150, 158-
159, 162, 166, 172-173, 177-
179, 186, 196, 213, 246, 251,
259, 285
Revolution by Reason 101
R.H. *Tawney* 22
R.H. *Tawney and His Times* 22
R.H. *Tawney's Commonplace Book*
22-23, 33
Rodgers, William 198, 230
Roosevelt, Franklin 106
Routledge, Paul 269
Russian Revolution 64

Sabine, George 91
Sassoon, Donald 78
Saville, John 71, 287
Scanlon, Hugh 49
Schleiermacher, Friedrich 25
Schroder, Gerhard 247
Scotland 51, 163, 292
Scottish Labour Party 268-269
Scripture 30-31, 33
SDP-Liberal Alliance 199, 201,
209
Seamen's Strike 49
Secularism 22
Self-Government in Industry 38, 42,
53
Shaw, George Bernard 152, 271
Sheerman, Barry 62, 64, 67, 70
Sheffield 231
Shore, Peter 178
Skidelsky, Robert 204
Smith, John 21, 210, 236
Snowden, Philip 9, 82, 102
Social Contract 180

Social democracy 1-5, 8, 11, 14-
15, 21, 50, 69, 102-104, 145,
150, 162, 164-165, 177, 185,
190, 195-198, 201, 203, 206-
207, 209-214, 220, 223-225,
227, 229, 231, 233, 235, 239,
244-246, 248-252, 255-261,
265-266, 270, 273, 275, 278,
287, 289-292
Social Democracy in Britain 210
Social democrat 2, 4, 149, 161,
164, 195, 200, 203, 205, 208-
210, 221, 223, 226-228, 230,
238, 244-246, 249-250, 252,
259, 261, 276, 271, 278, 290
Social Democratic Federation
(SDF) 9, 271
Social Democratic Party (SDP)
6, 10, 14, 38, 50, 195-196,
198-199, 202-203, 205-206,
208, 210-213, 231, 290
Social justice 22, 78, 91-92,
127-128, 153, 210, 221, 223-
229, 244, 259, 278-279
Social liberal 223, 270
Social market 204, 209
Social Theory 38
Socialisation 41, 42, 47, 53, 66,
79
Socialism 2, 5, 9-10, 12-13, 18-
21, 26-28, 33, 40, 43, 45, 47-
49, 53, 58, 60, 62-64, 66-67,
70-71, 73, 77-78, 87-88, 93-
96, 101-102, 105, 107-109,
112, 115, 117, 121-123, 125-
126, 128, 135-139, 145-146,
149-150, 156, 158-162, 164,
173, 178-179, 181-182, 184,
189, 219, 234, 251, 284-287,
289
Socialism in the New Society 11
Socialism Now and Other Essays
144, 152, 162, 186, 188

Socialist 22, 32, 79, 81-82, 100, 113-114, 144, 172, 186, 188, 199, 202, 207, 232, 235, 276, 290
Socialist Commentary 162
Socialist League 65-66
Socialist Union 162-163
Socialist Values and Time 198
Society for Socialist Inquiry and Propaganda (SSIP) 65
Solidarity Campaign 231
SPD (Sozialdemokratische Partei Deutschlands) 204
Spong, John Selby 25
Soviet Union 63, 65, 67, 71-72, 77-78, 80, 83, 85, 103, 105, 133
St. Martin-in-the-Fields 20
Stalin, Josef 84, 103, 105
Stalinist 68
State and Market: Towards a Public Interest Test 266
Statement of Democratic Socialist Aims and Values 232, 235-237
Steel, David 199, 201, 210
Strachey, John 2, 7-8, 11-13, 66, 82, 91, 93, 100-105, 107-116, 122, 135, 138-139, 145, 148, 162, 288
Strict prioritarianism 277
Studies in the Problem of Sovereignty 60
Sufficiency conception of equality 268, 272, 276, 280
Suffrage movement 59-60
Sure Start 277
Sweden 152
Syndicalism 44-46, 50, 60-61

Tawney, R.H. 2-4, 6-9, 11-12, 18-33, 38, 65, 69, 233, 252, 284, 287-288
Temple, William 28, 33

Terrill, Ross 22, 24-25, 28
Thatcher Governments 221, 231
Thatcher, Margaret 166, 202-203, 209-210, 214, 221
Thatcherism 165, 246-248 250, 296
The Acquisitive Society 12, 19-20, 29-30
The Attack and Other Papers 21
The Coming Struggle for Power 102
The Conservative Enemy 144, 149
The English Constitution 135
The European Imperative 190
The Financial Times 221
The Foundations of Sovereignty and Other Essays 60
The Future of Socialism 11, 109, 112-113, 116, 144, 146, 148, 158, 162-163
The Gaitskellites 162
The General Theory 47, 108, 127
The Global Third Way Debate 248
The God that Failed 127
The Guardian 198
The Just Society 108
The Labour Party and the Constitution 66
The Lion and the Unicorn 95
The Menace of Fascism 102
The Myths of Cabinet Government 135
The Nature of Capitalist Crisis 103
The Next Ten Years 47
The Politics of Democratic Socialism 11, 78, 83-85, 87, 95
The Progressive Dilemma 124
The Socialist Case 11, 108
The Socialist Challenge 13, 172-173, 177-178, 182, 184
The Spectre of Revisionism 134
The State as Entrepreneur 177
The Struggle for Labour's Soul 124

The Theory and Practice of Socialism 93, 103
The Third Way 246-248, 250, 253
The Third Way and Its Critics 247-248
The Times 221
The Time Has Come 195, 210-211
The Uncommon Market 184
The World of Labour 38, 43
Third Way 4-5, 14, 165, 239, 244-261, 290
Thirty-Nine Articles 24
Thomas, J.H 65
Thompson, Noel 80, 101, 109, 112, 115
Thorson, Thomas 91
Titmuss, Richard 10
Tories 66, 71, 94, 134, 202
Tots and Quots 78
Toynbee Hall 22, 24, 33
Trade unions 9, 40, 43-44, 46-47, 49, 71, 102, 104, 116, 136-137, 147, 158-159, 180, 183, 200, 204, 209, 211, 213, 222, 232, 234, 266, 287
Transport and General Workers' Union (TGWU) 49
Trickle-down theory 224, 227-228
Trudeau, Pierre 71
Treasury 137, 187, 272, 274-275
Tribune 8

Under-consumptionist 12, 47, 80-81
Unilateral nuclear disarmament 130, 269
Union flag 86, 94
United Kingdom 51, 103, 292
University of Nottingham 49

Upper-Clyde Shipbuilders 49
United States of America (USA) 63, 116, 126, 129, 152-153, 159, 191, 257
Utley, T.E. 115

Virgin Birth 25
Voltaire 70

Wales 51, 163, 292
War Cabinet Secretariat 93
Weber, Max 135
Webb, Beatrice 9, 58
Webb, Sidney 9, 58, 131
Wesley, John 24
Western Europe 91
Westminster 51, 292
What Are We To Do? 104
What Have We To Defend? 63, 83, 87-89, 94-96
What Went Wrong 177
Where Do We Go From Here? 63
Where Now for New Labour 249
Whitefield, George 24
Wickham-Jones, Mark 178-179
Williams, Philip 145
Williams, Shirley 209, 230-231
Wilson Government 122, 148, 176, 185-186, 188, 197
Wilson, Harold 131-132, 138, 176, 186
Winter, Jay 22
Wise, E.F. 65
Workers' control 12, 38, 41, 45, 47-48, 50-53, 172, 207, 268
Workers' Educational Association (WEA) 20, 22, 33, 47, 58, 93
Working-class 20, 41, 46, 53, 59, 70, 91, 103-106, 127, 150, 164, 181, 232-233, 287
Working Tax Credit 277

World War One 20, 22, 53, 60, 91

World War Two 38, 45, 63, 71, 84, 100, 145

Wright, Anthony 22, 24, 47, 49, 62

XYZ Club 78

Young, Alf 269
Young, Michael 10, 153

Zenter, Peter 210
Zwingli, Ulrich 24